# COOKING AND GARDENING WITH DIANNE

By Dianne Cage

Additional copies of *Cooking and Gardening with Dianne* may be obtained at the cost of $17.95 plus $3.00 postage and handling, each book. Louisiana residents add $1.55 sales tax, each book.

Send to:

Dianne K. Cage
119 Glenmar
Monroe, Louisiana  71201

ISBN 0-9654648-0-6

First Printing      November, 1996      5,000 Copies
Second Printing     February, 1997      10,000 Copies

Printed in the USA by

WIMMER
The Wimmer Companies, Inc.
Memphis

# COOKING AND GARDENING
# WITH
# DIANNE

This is a collection of some of my recipes, some of my Mother's, Grandmother's, and friends. I hope you enjoy!

On good health, diet, and fitness, build a healthy eating plan and use common sense – Don't deny it, you know what is good for you and you know what is bad for you! The key is moderation. Enjoy all; just do not over indulge. When you can cut back on the fat, do so. Substitute low fat; some are pretty good and you really cannot tell the difference.

Exercise, Exercise, Exercise! Take vitamins; stay active, physically, and mentally, read; stay involved with life and your higher power. Smile; be happy and be kind to all! Join the Roy Rogers Riders Club – this is one of mine and Mike Cage's favorite clubs. Here are the rules:

1.      Be neat and clean.
2.      Be courteous and polite.
3.      Always obey your parents.
4.      Protect the weak and help them.
5.      Be brave but never take chances.
6.      Study hard and learn all you can.
7.      Be kind to the animals and care for them.
8.      Eat all your food and never waste any.
9.      Love God and go to Sunday school regularly.
10.     Always respect our flag and our country.

Enjoy and God Bless,


Dianne

*To my children*

*George and Satchie Snellings*

*The man in my life, Mike Cage*
*and his children*
*Laura, Mike, Liz and Sara*

*Our pets - Rolex and Zack*

# Contents

# TABLE OF CONTENTS

## "PATH FINDER"

# ACKNOWLEDGEMENTS:

Cover Consultant
"French Women Know"
Cathi French


Photographer
Kevin Hawkins


Watercolors and Drawings
Lori Young


*A Special Thanks to*

• Martha Upshaw
and
• Suzanne Wolff

Spirit Helpers:
Love Potions &
War Medicines

Never Ever, But Forever
Don't
Forget
Beer

Beer is for any occasion or celebration
when you are serving spirits.

It is a good friend!
**Men love beer
and we sure want to take care of our men!**

# BLOODY MARY

1⅓   **cups vodka**
1⅓   **cups tomato juice**
1⅓   **cups V–8 Juice**
1     **cup Worcestershire**
12    **drops Tabasco – to
      your taste**
1     **teaspoon salt
      (optional –
      Worcestershire has
      lots of salt)
      Juice of 2 large
      lemons or limes
      Black pepper – to
      taste**
4     **stalks celery – finely
      chopped in food
      processor**

Mix all ingredients. Serve cold over ice.

Garnish with a celery or carrot stick, a pickled green bean or a hot cherry pepper.

# PEACH ROYAL                    ∨

Serves 6.

| | |
|---|---|
| 6 | ounces fresh or frozen peaches |
| 1 | ounce peach brandy |
| 6 | ounces vodka |
| 6 | ounces frozen pink lemonade concentrate |
| | Ice cubes |

In blender, combine peaches, vodka, lemonade concentrate and peach brandy. Add ice cubes and blend until slushy. Serve in crystal goblets.

So good when our fresh Louisiana peaches are in season! Garnish with a Nasturtium. You mean you did not plant your Nasturtiums last February? I'm surprised!

# CHAMPAGNE PUNCH

| | |
|---|---|
| 1 | cup sugar |
| 2 | bottles chilled sauterne |
| 6 | lemons |
| 6 | oranges |
| 2 | cups chilled brandy |
| 1 | block of ice made of 1 quart of water |
| 3 | bottles chilled champagne |
| 3 | more chilled bottles of champagne |

Stir the sugar and sauterne until the sugar is dissolved. Slice lemons and oranges and add to the sauterne mixture. Add the brandy, block of ice and 3 bottles of champagne. Just before serving, add the other 3 bottles of chilled champagne. At this time, you may also add a large ginger ale, if desired.

# SUNDAY MORNING MILK PUNCH

*For every glass of milk:*

1½  **jiggers of whiskey –
      Old Crow is good**
1    **full teaspoon sugar**
2    **drops of vanilla**

Stir together. Serve over plenty of ice. Top with fresh grated nutmeg.

Perfect for your Sunday morning parties and brunches!

**W. C. Fields "I never drink anything stronger than gin before breakfast!"**

# BILL RILEY'S FAMOUS GIN FIZZ— THE VERY BEST

      **Blender**
1    **hand full of ice**
1    **good ounce of gin**
1    **egg white**
1    **ounce half & half**
1    **ounce bar syrup
      (simple syrup)**
½    **ounce fresh lemon
      and lime juice**
2    **or 3 dashes orange
      flower water**

Blend away the first 6 ingredients (5 – 10 seconds) until good and frothy. Have glasses ready that have been packed in ice or chilled. Pour a little orange flower water in – swirl – pour out. Hit the blender 1 or 2 seconds. Pour mixture in the chilled aromatic glass.... Enjoy! These are served just in the morning for an elegant brunch and for a small group.

# BRANDY ALEXANDER

*For dessert, sip Brandy Alexander, a creamy blend of vanilla ice cream, brandy, and crème dé cacao.*

Yield: 2 servings.

2 **cups vanilla ice cream**
3 **to 4 Tablespoons brandy**
3 **to 4 Tablespoons white crème dé cacao**
**Garnish: White chocolate shavings**

Combine first 3 ingredients in container of an electric blender; process until smooth. Spoon into glasses. Garnish, if desired. Serve immediately.

A wafer roll is nice to serve with this...find them in your grocery gourmet cookie section!

# SANGRÍA

*Sangría crossed the Atlantic with the Spanish to Mexico. Fruity and refreshing. The perfect beginning for a Mexican "Fiesta".*

Makes 18 cups.

6 **oranges, sliced**
3 **lemons, sliced**
1 **lime, sliced**
1 **cup sugar**
½ **pint brandy**
1 **gallon dry red wine**

Arrange the lemons, limes, and oranges in the bottom of a very large pitcher or crock. Sprinkle sugar over fruit. More sugar may be added, if needed. Add the brandy and allow to sit at least 1 hour. Add wine, stir well, and allow to set 30 minutes. Serve over ice in stemmed glass.

# SIMPLE SYRUP OR BAR SYRUP

Yields two cups.

1  **cup water**
1  **cup sugar**

Boil until sugar is dissolved. Keeps indefinitely in the refrigerator. Use for mixing drinks or in a punch base.

# PLANTATION MINT JULEP

*"Hol ma magnolia, honey, while I take a sip o' this here bourbon"*

Makes one drink.

1  **9–ounce old fashioned glass**
6  **mint leaves**
2  **Tablespoons powdered sugar**
1  **ounce bourbon**
1  **ounce Southern Comfort**
1  **ounce simple syrup**
1  **cup crushed ice**
1  **sprig fresh mint**

Place mint leaves in the bottom of old fashioned glass along with powdered sugar. Add bourbon, Southern Comfort, syrup and crushed ice. Using an iced tea spoon, blend all ingredients well into the mint–sugar mixture. Garnish with fresh mint sprig and serve with a straw. This cocktail should be stirred long enough for frost to form on the outside of the glass. It's said that the early planters would only drink mint juleps from silver tumblers.

# COTTON COUNTRY'S ALMOND PUNCH

1   large can frozen
      orange juice
1   small can frozen
      lemon juice
1   large can pineapple
      juice
1   large can apricot
      nectar
½   cup sugar
½   to ¾ small bottle of
      almond extract

Dilute frozen juices accord-ing to directions. Mix all together and chill.

**This, my all–time favorite punch for any occasion.**

# HEART HEALTHY BANANA SHAKE

2   cups milk – can use
      skimmed
2   large ripe bananas –
      chunked
¼   cup honey
½   juice of a lemon
½   cup ice cubes

Combine all ingredients in blender. Whirl until thick and foamy (not too long). Serve in a pretty wine glass or silver cup with a sprig of mint.

# EGG NOG – THE GENERAL'S

1   **dozen eggs –**
    **separated**
1   **Tablespoon sugar to**
    **each egg**
12  **ounces whiskey**
    **(100 proof)**
½   **pint rum (Myers)**
1   **pint whipping cream**

Whip yellow of eggs about 10 minutes with sugar until sugar dissolves – mixture turns a creamy white.

Add: one ounce of 100 proof whiskey to each egg (whiskey cooks eggs – hmmm, wonder what it does to your brain) – anyway....

Add: ½ pint, or a little more, of Myers Rum for flavor.

Fix to set over night on a cold porch. Next day, whip the whites of eggs and one pint whipping cream. Fold in with egg mixture. Serve in a big silver punch bowl. Sprinkle with nutmeg.

It is nice to have small dollops of the egg whites floating.

General George Trousdale's Egg Nog as told by Garfield Washington. Garfield said you can substitute a carton of eggnog for the whipping cream!

For quick and easy, don't forget the commercial brand Egg Nog. I like the one you whip and I jazz it up with whiskey, rum, and nutmeg. Serve from a big

*(Continued on next page)*

*(Egg Nog – The General's, continued)*

punch bowl in your silver cups. Decorate base of bowl with fresh holly and juniper branches. So pretty for your Christmas party! Wonderful with the miniature fruit cakes and toasted pecans. Old–time South!

# RUM PUNCH

Serves 4.

3 ounces pineapple juice
3 ounces orange juice
3 ounces lime juice
8 dashes Angostura bitters
6 ounces rum
2 ounces simple syrup

Combine ingredients and shake well with ice. Serve in tall glasses.

# IRISH COFFEE

2 cubes sugar
2 jiggers good hot coffee
2 jiggers Irish Whiskey
Dab of whipping cream

Put sugar in bottom of cup, add hot coffee, then the whisky. Add whipping cream. Do not stir. Love to serve this at my winter dinner parties!

# CAFE BRULOT

Yield: 10 to 12 servings.

1   **small stick cinnamon**
12  **cubes sugar**
6   **to 8 cloves**
1   **cup warm brandy or Bookers Bourbon (126 proof) really works well**
    **Peel of 1 small orange**
1   **quart hot strong coffee**

Place cinnamon stick, cloves, orange peel, and sugar in brulot bowl or chafing dish. Place brandy in ladle and ignite. Pour into bowl or chafing dish and ladle contents while burning. Keep this up for a few minutes. Then pour in strong hot coffee gradually, ladling the mixture until flame fades. Serve at once. Dramatic presentation at your dinner table.

# ICED COFFEE

Easy and so good! Especially in hot weather – especially refreshing. Ice cubes dilute the full flavor of coffee brewed in the usual way, so brew it double strength, cool, and pour over lots of ice in a tall glass. I serve the cream and sugar along with the iced coffee.

# TRICKS TO MAKE ICED TEA MORE APPEALING

Frost the rims of the glasses by dipping them in lemon or orange juice, then in granulated sugar. For glamour and faster dissolving, pass a pitcher of simple syrup instead of sugar (equal parts of sugar and water, boiled 5 minutes). Always, but always, garnish with lemon and fresh mint .

# LELA'S MINT TEA

10 **tea bags**
2 **quarts boiling water**
2 **cups sugar – boiled down with 2 cups water (simple syrup)**
1 **large can frozen concentrated orange juice**
½ **cup lemon juice**

Steep tea for 10 minutes. Remove bags; add simple syrup, orange juice and lemon.

My Grandmother always served this for lunch — Wonderful! Good for a morning party, too. Garnish with a fresh sprig of mint!

## BAPTIST COUGH SYRUP

1    teaspoon paregoric
½    cup sugar
2    Tablespoons whiskey
     Juice of 1 lemon

Combine ingredients. If mixture is too thick, add more whiskey.

Daddy always kept this in the tool shed! <u>I wonder why</u>?

## PUD'S OLD TIMEY COUGH SYRUP

1    fifth whiskey
1    extra large
     peppermint stick –
     crushed

Pour whiskey over crushed peppermint in a large jar.

2 Tablespoons as needed for cough. If cough persists – try another tablespoon or two!!

Secret Society

# ANGELINOS

*"Angels on Horseback"*

| | |
|---|---|
| 24 | **raw fresh oysters** |
| 12 | **strips bacon, cut in half** |
| | **Salt, pepper, paprika, to taste** |
| | **Chopped parsley** |
| | **Lemon wedges to garnish** |

Partially cook bacon. Wrap each bacon slice around a raw oyster and secure with a toothpick. Sprinkle with salt, pepper, paprika and broil until bacon is crisp. Garnish with parsley and lemon and serve hot on toothpicks garnished with lemon wedges. You can bake in a 350 degree oven or over hot coals. Place oysters on a piece of foil about 15 minutes or until bacon is lightly done.

# CRABMEAT ELEGANTA

*(For a big party)*

| | |
|---|---|
| 5 | **to 8 pounds fresh lump crabmeat (whatever the pocket book will stand)** |
| 1 | **pound butter, melted** |
| 3 | **bunches green onions, tops & bottoms, finely chopped** |
| 1 | **large bunch parsley, finely chopped** |
| 2 | **to 3 lemons, juiced and the zest** |
| | **Salt & pepper to taste** |

Very carefully, drain the crabmeat. You do not want to break up lumps. In a large pot, sauté onions and parsley in melted butter for about 5 minutes. Gently fold in crabmeat and lemon. Add salt and pepper. Serve in a chafing dish with party toast. You get the full flavor of the crabmeat. The other ingredients just enhance this delicate gift of the sea.

# CAPONATA OR EGGPLANT CAVIAR OR RATATOUILLE

Serves 10.

1½  pounds eggplant
½   cup olive oil
1   28–ounce can
      tomatoes,
      undrained
3   cups onion, sliced
2   cups green bell
      pepper, chopped
2   medium cloves
      garlic, minced
½   cup fresh parsley,
      chopped
½   cup black olives,
      halved
⅓   cup red wine vinegar
2   Tablespoons sugar
2   Tablespoons capers,
      drained
2   Tablespoons tomato
      paste
2   teaspoons dried basil
1   teaspoon salt
½   teaspoon black
      pepper
½   cup pine nuts

Preheat oven to 350 degrees. Peel eggplant and cut into 1–inch cubes. Heat oil in a large, heavy pan. Sauté over medium heat. Add eggplant, tomatoes, onion, green pepper and garlic. Cook until eggplant is tender, 20 to 30 minutes. Add remaining ingredients, except pine nuts. Simmer 15 minutes. Meanwhile, toast pine nuts in oven until golden, about 8 minutes. Sprinkle with pine nuts just before serving. Serve at room temperature with Pita Triangles or toast points. Really good over pasta too.

## MARINATED CRAB CLAWS

2   pounds fresh crab
    claws
1   cup olive oil
4   Tablespoons
    Balsamic vinegar
1   teaspoon Oregano
    Juice of 1 large
    lemon and the zest
3   or 4 cloves garlic,
    minced
1   cup finely chopped
    fresh parsley
¼   cup finely chopped
    cilantro (optional)
3   teaspoons salt
½   teaspoon sugar
2   Tablespoons cracked
    black pepper
½   cup Dijon mustard
2   Tablespoons
    Worcestershire
    Sauce
    Red Tip lettuce

On a big shallow platter, arrange Red Tip lettuce. Place crab claws around. Mix all ingredients. Check seasonings and pour over crab claws just to coat. Cover and refrigerate. You will probably have some dressing left over. It keeps well in refrigerator and is wonderful on your salads.

## MARINATED SHRIMP

*Use the same sauce as for Marinated Crab Claws.*

3   pounds cooked,
    peeled shrimp
2   large sweet onions,
    cut in rings
2   small jars of large
    capers
4   or 5 crumbled bay
    leaves

Layer shrimp, onions, capers, and bay leaves. Cover with marinade and refrigerate at least 8 hours. Stir several times before serving. This is nice to serve in a big pretty glass bowl with ice under to keep it good and cold.

# HOT HOLIDAY CHEESE-N-SHRIMP

1   can Cream of Mushroom Soup
2   rolls garlic cheese
1   pound small shrimp, boiled and peeled
1   large can mushrooms, drained
1   Tablespoon Worcestershire Sauce
1   teaspoon lemon juice and the zest
    Red pepper to taste

Melt soup and cheese in double boiler over low heat. Add shrimp, mushrooms, Worcestershire Sauce, lemon juice and red pepper. Serve hot in a chafing dish, with large Fritos. You will not have any left! You could use two pounds of crawfish tails instead of the shrimp!

# LEHIGH VALLEY SHRIMP MOLD

1   can tomato soup
1   8-ounce package cream cheese
2   envelopes unflavored gelatin, dissolved in a small amount of water
2   pounds shrimp, cooked, peeled, deveined, and diced
1   cup diced celery
1   medium onion, diced
    Salt and pepper
    Dash of Tabasco
1   cup mayonnaise
2   Tablespoons horseradish, drained

Heat soup and add cream cheese and stir until cheese is melted. The mixture will be lumpy. Add dissolved gelatin. Stir in the remaining ingredients. Pour into a well greased mold. This recipe will fill a 1 quart mold with a small amount left over. Refrigerate until the mold is set. Unmold by running a sharp knife around the edge of the mold and invert on a large platter. This is a nice party salad. At Christmas it could be molded into a star, tree or ring and decorated with leaves. Serve with Ritz Crackers.

# PARTY PÂTÉ

*This is so easy and good and pretty on the table.*

| | |
|---|---|
| 1 | **14½–ounce can consommé** |
| 1 | **package unflavored gelatin** |
| ½ | **cup finely chopped onion** |
| 1 | **Tablespoon Tabasco** |
| ½ | **cup sherry** |
| 1 | **8–ounce package cream cheese, softened** |
| 1 | **8–ounce package Braunschweiger** |
| 1 | **teaspoon cracked black pepper** |
| | **Fresh parsley** |

Heat ½ cup consommé in a sauce pan. Add gelatin and stir until dissolved. In another saucepan, heat remaining consommé with onion, Tabasco and sherry. Add to dissolved mixture. Pour one–half of mixture into a greased 1–quart mold. Chill to set. Combine the cream cheese and Braunschweiger in food processor and blend well. Add remaining consommé mixture and mix well. Pour on top of set mold. Refrigerate. Garnish with parsley and serve with Toast Points.

# NORTHWEST SMOKED SALMON PÂTÉ

| | |
|---|---|
| 6 | **ounces smoked salmon** |
| 3 | **ounces softened cream cheese** |
| 1 | **Tablespoon plus 2 teaspoons cream style horseradish** |
| 1 | **Tablespoon lemon juice** |
| 2 | **Tablespoons minced onion (optional)** |
| 2 | **Tablespoons capers** |
| ¾ | **to 1 cup chopped nuts (I prefer pecans)** |
| | **Parsley, chopped** |

Drain off the excess oil of the smoked salmon. In a food processor, grind the salmon until fine. Transfer the salmon into a mixing bowl. With a mixer on medium speed, add the next four (4) ingredients in the order listed. Fold in capers. With your hands, shape the pâté into a ball then roll in chopped nuts, and sprinkle with parsley.

# HOT CLAM DIP

2    **large packages light cream cheese**
2    **cans minced clams, drained a little**
2    **Tablespoons Worcestershire Sauce or to taste**
2    **teaspoons lemon juice or to taste**
5    **or 6 green onions chopped finely, tops included**
    **Parsley, chopped finely**
    **Red pepper to taste**

Have cream cheese at room temperature. Combine all ingredients in a double boiler and cook until cheese is melted. This dip is served in a chafing dish with Melba rounds or other crackers. It is better if made ahead so the seasonings can blend. Very rich and good! Perfect for your holiday parties!

# PICKLED TUNA

2    **cans solid white tuna, drained**
1    **large onion, sliced paper thin**
1    **Tablespoon cracked black pepper**
½    **cup chopped parsley**
1    **large lemon, sliced thin**
1    **jar capers with juice**
3    **Tablespoons wine vinegar**
½    **to ¾ cup sour cream**

Break drained tuna into large pieces. Mix lightly with onions and lemon rings. Add capers, caper juice, vinegar and sour cream. Toss lightly and refrigerate. This may be prepared a couple of days ahead of time. It is better if refrigerated at least overnight but is not necessary. Serve with crackers. So pretty in a big crystal bowl.

# A CHAFING DISH OF SEAFOOD

*You will love this one! Quick and easy! So good!*

Serves 75–80.

2    cans cream of
      mushroom soup
1    can cream of shrimp
      soup
2    8-ounce package
      cream cheese
3    cans small shrimp,
      drained and rinsed
2    cans water
      chestnuts, sliced
1    pound lump
      crabmeat
3    8-ounce cans
      mushrooms,
      drained
1    teaspoon Tabasco
2    teaspoons dry
      mustard
2    teaspoons curry
      powder
4    Tablespoons
      Worcestershire
      Salt and cayenne to
      taste

Heat soups; stir in cheese until melted. Add remaining ingredients. Serve hot in a chafing dish with Melba rounds. Better made a day ahead – flavors can mingle. This is also wonderful served over rice or pasta for lunch. Serve with a good crispy salad and hot French bread with lots of sweet butter!

# OYSTERS ROCKEFELLER CASSEROLE

*This is a good one and it freezes well. Jack Tom Jackson makes the best Rockefeller and this comes pretty close!*

3   sticks butter
1   teaspoon thyme
1⅔ cups chopped green onions
1   cup chopped celery
1   large clove garlic, pressed
1   Tablespoon Worcestershire sauce
1   teaspoon anchovy paste
1½ cups seasoned bread crumbs
4   pints oysters, drained, reserving ½ cup liquid
¾  cup chopped fresh parsley
½  cup grated Parmesan cheese
2   Tablespoons Pernod (Anise liqueur or Herbsaint)
3   10–ounce packages frozen chopped spinach, cooked and drained
½  teaspoon salt
¼  teaspoon black pepper
¼  teaspoon cayenne pepper

Preheat oven to 375 degrees. In a large skillet, melt butter; add thyme, onions, celery, and garlic. Sauté 5 minutes; add Worcestershire sauce, anchovy paste, and bread crumbs. Stir 5 minutes until bread crumbs are toasted. Fold in oysters, liquid, parsley, cheese, and Pernod. Cook until oysters curl, about 3 minutes. Add spinach. Season with salt, black pepper, and cayenne. Place in a 3–quart casserole and bake 20 to 25 minutes. May be served in individual ramekins as an appetizer.

# LEMON MUSHROOMS

*A delicious, rich sauce for broiled fish or wonderful for cocktail party served in a Chafing dish with toast points.*

2   sticks butter
1   cup flour
6   large cans mushrooms, drained, reserve juice
3   cans beef bouillon
6   lemons, juiced and the zest
1   cup parsley, finely chopped
1   bunch green onions, chopped
    Black pepper and red pepper and salt
    Kitchen Bouquet

In a heavy pot, melt butter add flour and make a golden brown roux – do not burn. Add mushrooms and slowly add bouillon, lemon juice, and zest to taste. Add parsley, green onions, pepper, and Kitchen Bouquet (for a pretty brown color). Mix well and simmer for about 20 minutes. Check seasonings. If too thick, thin with a little of the mushroom juice. If too thin, thicken with corn starch. You can half this recipe or double easily!

# FIESTA CHILI DIP

*You can use canned chili – real easy. Good!*

Serves 50.

2 pounds ground chuck
2 large onions, chopped
4 cloves garlic, mashed
1 Tablespoon sugar
1 small bottle chili powder
2 Tablespoons cumin powder
6 or 8 chili pequins
1 Tablespoon salt or to taste
1 Tablespoon black pepper
2 large cans tomato sauce
4 cups hot water
2 cans Austex hot tamales
2 pounds grated sharp cheese
2 bunches green onions, chopped

Put meat and next eight ingredients in a large heavy iron or aluminum pot. Stir until the meat is no longer pink. Add tomato sauce and hot water. Cover the pot and simmer for about three hours. Cool and place in the refrigerator overnight. The next day remove the grease from the top; reheat, add hot tamales, sliced, and cook until disintegrated. Add cheese, reserving 2 cups, and stir until the cheese has melted. Put chili in two oblong flat baking dishes. Sprinkle the remaining cheese on the top and melt the cheese in the oven. Remove from the oven and sprinkle the chopped green onions on top. This freezes well, but do so before adding cheese and onion topping. Serve with Tostadas!

# HUMMUS

3   cans chickpeas (or ¾
      cup dried
      chickpeas, cooked
      according to
      directions) NOTE:
      also called
      garbanzos.
      Juice of 2 lemons, or
      to taste
¾   cup Tahini sesame
      paste
      Pita pocket bread
      Fresh parsley,
        chopped for garnish

Drain chickpeas, saving some of the liquid. Put chickpeas in food processor. Add 2 or 3 cloves of garlic, crushed. While processing, work in sesame paste and add lemon juice a little bit at a time. If it gets too thick, add liquid from chickpeas. Don't add too much lemon juice. Check seasonings and add salt to taste. Mixture should be firm, but thin enough to spread. To serve, put in a shallow bowl, make an indention in the center and fill with Extra Virgin Olive Oil. Garnish with lots of chopped fresh parsley. Serve with warm triangles of pita bread. NOTE: Tahini sesame paste is available at most health food stores and gourmet food stores.

# TARAMASALATA

1   (8–ounce) jar Tarama (a salty fish roe in oil; available in specialty food stores)
6   slices of bread, crust removed
½   cup water
1   cup olive oil
4   green onions, tops and bottoms, chopped
½   cup fresh lemon juice
    Black pepper, freshly ground
2   Tablespoons parsley

Make in cuisinart, mixer, or blender. Beat Tarama with lemon juice until smooth. Soak bread in the water, beat or whirl then gradually add olive oil, beating constantly. Continue beating until Tarama is light colored and soft in consistency. Add onions, parsley, beating well. Add pepper to taste. Keeps well 3 or 4 days covered, in the refrigerator. Serve chilled with warm pita or toast points or unsalted crackers. A Johnny Johnson favorite!

# BABA GHANOUJ

| | |
|---|---|
| 1 | or 2 eggplant, about 1¼ pounds |
| ¼ | cup sesame paste available in specialty food shops |
| 1 | Tablespoon finely minced garlic |
| 3 | Tablespoons lemon juice |
| 1 | Tablespoon water |
| ¼ | cup finely chopped parsley |
| ¼ | cup pine nuts |

Preheat the oven to 400 degrees. Place the eggplant on foil in the oven and bake for about 1 hour. Let cool. Scrape out the flesh and discard the skins. Put the sesame paste in a bowl and add the garlic. Stir rapidly while adding the lemon juice and water. Add the eggplant and parsley. Spoon the mixture into a serving bowl. Put the pine nuts in a skillet and cook, shaking the skillet and stirring the nuts until nicely browned. Garnish the Baba Ghanouj with the pine nuts. Serve with unsalted bread or wedges of sliced pita bread.

# BACON WRAPPED DATES

Makes approximately 3 dozen.

| | |
|---|---|
| 1 | 8-ounce package pitted dates |
| | Bacon |

Wrap each date in one third of a strip of bacon and skewer with tooth pick. Bake until bacon is crisp at 350 degrees, 15 to 18 minutes. Drain on paper towels. Serve hot.

# HOGSHEAD CHEESE – "SOUSE"

*If you are from the South, you cannot have a Christmas party without this! Very European!*

*Marvelous! Modern method of hogshead cheese.*

### I. First Cooking:
½   fresh hog jowl, 6 pigs feet, tails & ears, but best of all is a hogs head!
3   to 4 pound pork roast, Boston butt – if you do not use the head
1   onion, chopped
1   stalk celery
2   bay leaves
2   pods garlic
    Thyme, salt, pepper and red pepper to taste

### II. Second Cooking:
1   onion, chopped
4   green onions, chopped
2   stalks celery, chopped
2   or 3 pods garlic
4   Tablespoons Worcestershire sauce
1   Tablespoon lemon juice
    Red pepper to taste
    Black pepper
1   package gelatin, dissolved in ¼ cup cold water, optional

Boil first seven ingredients with the four seasonings. Let cook until meat falls off bones. Bone and cut off fat and discard. Strain cooled liquid and let grease rise to top. Skim grease. Put meat back into liquid with seasonings for second cooking. Let cook down until not much liquor is left, and it all looks like one mess. In small batches – in processor, bump 2 or 3 times – you do not want it pureed – just finely chopped. The very last – add 1 cup chopped green olives with pimentos, 1 cup finely chopped green onions, 2 or 3 finely chopped red and green peppers, so good and pretty. Add dissolved gelatin into hot liquid if you want to be sure it jells, but it is usually not necessary. Pour into ungreased pans and let set in refrigerator until firm. Serve on saltine crackers, with a small dash of pepper sauce and lemon wedges. If you use a hog's head, be sure and remove eyes and ear drums after cooking.

## CAVIAR PIE

6    eggs
2    Tablespoons
       mayonnaise
1    Tablespoon cracked
       black pepper
2    Tablespoons finely
       chopped parsley
3    4-ounce jars black
       Caviar, well drained
       in a colander
     Juice of ½ lemon, a
       little of the zest if
       you like
1    cup finely chopped
       green onions, tops
       and bottom
2    cups sour cream, stir
       it up good
     Minced parsley
     Paprika

Hard boil then rice the eggs; mix with mayonnaise, pepper and parsley. Butter a 9 or 10 inch cake stand (be sure there is a small rim) or round dish. Make a crust using the eggs. Refrigerate 4 hours. Drain caviar in colander; season with lemon juice and carefully fold in green onions; drain well. Spread Caviar mixture on egg crust. Ice the top with sour cream. Decorate the edges with minced parsley and sprinkle with paprika. To serve, slice into small wedges; place on individual plates and serve with either toast points, Melba rounds, or Triscuits as a first course. Pretty and wonderful for your big cocktail parties.

## TEX MEX DIP

*This is Satchie's recipe and it is the best and the prettiest!*

| | |
|---|---|
| 2 | cans Bean Dip |
| 3 | avocados |
| 2 | Tablespoons lemon juice |
| 1 | cup sour cream |
| ½ | cup mayonnaise |
| 1 | package Taco seasoning mix |
| 1 | large bunch green onions with tops |
| 3 | medium, cored, seeded and chopped tomatoes |
| 1 | 7 ounce can chopped black olives |
| | Lettuce and jalapeños (optional) |
| 8 | ounces shredded sharp cheese |
| | Tortilla Chips |

Spread Bean Dip on serving platter. Mash avocados and add lemon juice. Spread over bean dip.

Combine the sour cream, mayonnaise, and Taco seasoning mix and spread on the Bean Dip mixture.

Next layer: Chop a large bunch of green onions (with tops) and sprinkle on top. Add chopped tomatoes, black olives, and lettuce and jalapeños, if desired...

Top with shredded cheese. Serve with Tortilla Chips.

## HOT ROTEL DIP

*(Makes huge amount, can easily be halved)*

| | |
|---|---|
| 2 | pounds <u>Mexican</u> Velveeta (Hot or Mild) |
| 2 | cans Rotel Tomatoes (drained – save juice) |
| 1 | pound sausage (crumbled, cooked, and drained) |

Save the juice from the Rotel Tomatoes in case the dip gets too thick, and add a little as needed. Melt the cheese; add Rotel and mix together. Add cooked sausage. Mix well over low heat. Always use WHITE Tortilla chips (Restaurant Style) with this dip.

# FIESTA CORN DIP

*Easy, good and keeps well*

2   cans corn, drained
1   cup sour cream
1   cup mayonnaise
1   small can chopped
     green chilies
3   green onions,
     chopped
2   or 3 jalapeño
     peppers, chopped
½   cup red bell pepper
     or pimentos,
     chopped–adds a
     pretty color
4   ounces shredded
     Cheddar cheese
4   ounces shredded
     Monterey Jack
     cheese
     Red pepper to taste

Mix together. Season to taste. Chill and serve with Frito Scoops. This keeps well for several days in refrigerator.

# CURRIED CAULIFLOWER

2   cups mayonnaise
1   teaspoon salt
2   teaspoons curry
     powder
1   teaspoon garlic
     powder
1   Tablespoon grated
     onion
1   medium head
     cauliflower

Steam whole cauliflower until fork–tender (about 20 minutes). Cool thoroughly. Thoroughly mix together first five ingredients. Frost cooled cauliflower with mayonnaise mixture, covering completely. Cover frosted cauliflower and refrigerate for 24 hours. Serve with crackers as you would a cheese ball.

## BACON–CHEESE RYES

*My childrens' favorite!*

3   cups grated sharp
    cheese
1   small can sliced ripe
    olives
1   cup finely chopped
    green onions (tops
    and bottoms)
½   cup chopped
    jalapeño peppers
1   cup Hellmann's
    mayonnaise
1   cup crumbled bacon
1   package Rye rounds

Combine all ingredients. Spread on one loaf Pepperidge Party Rye. Bake at 300 degrees for 15 to 20 minutes. Can be made ahead and refrigerated or frozen, uncooked. These freeze well! Freeze on cookie sheets, then stack in zip lock bags.

## APACHE CHEESE BREAD

1   9–inch Apache* loaf
    of bread
16  ounces sharp
    Cheddar cheese,
    grated
1   8–ounce package
    cream cheese,
    softened
1   8–ounce carton sour
    cream
½   cup minced green
    onions
1   teaspoon
    Worcestershire
    sauce
2   4½–ounce cans green
    chilies, chopped
1   cup chopped ham

Cut the top off the bread, reserving top, and scoop out the inside. Combine remaining ingredients and mix well. This will be a very stiff mixture. Fill the bread with the cheese mixture, replace the top and place on a cookie sheet. Bake in a 350 degree oven for 1 hour and 10 minutes. Serve with tortilla chips or tear and dip with the bread.

*Any hard round loaf of bread may be used.

# NUT GLAZED BRIE

½   cup packed brown
sugar
¼   cup almonds,
slivered
1   teaspoon whiskey or
brandy
1   14 ounce round of
Brie (5-inch
diameter)

In a small mixing bowl, stir sugar, nuts and whiskey. Cover and chill up to 1 week. To serve, run cheese in 500 degree oven for 5 minutes or until cheese is slightly softened. Sprinkle sugar mix over top. Bake 2 or 3 minutes more or until sugar is melted.

# ADRIENNE'S DELIGHT

*Great for an afternoon Sherry Party!*

Serves 35.

12   ounces Philadelphia
cream cheese
1   stick butter
½   cup sour cream
½   cup sugar
1   envelope plain
gelatin
¼   cup cold water
½   cup white raisins
1   cup slivered
almonds, toasted
Grated rinds of two
lemons
Saltine crackers

Let cream cheese, butter, and sour cream come to room temperature. Cream well and add sugar. Soften envelope of gelatin in ¼ cup cold water. Dissolve over hot water. Add to cream cheese mixture. Then add raisins, slivered almonds, and lemon rind. Put in a one–quart mold in refrigerator. When firm, unmold and serve with Saltine crackers. This can be used at cocktail parties or as a dessert. Do not substitute for Saltine crackers. You can also freeze this after unmolding. When ready to use, just thaw.

# CURRIED CHEESE PÂTÉ

2    **8–ounce packages light cream cheese, softened**
2    **cups grated sharp Cheddar cheese, room temperature**
6    **Tablespoons sherry**
2    **Tablespoons Worcestershire sauce**
2    **teaspoons curry**
½    **teaspoon salt**
½    **teaspoon red pepper**

**Topping:**
1    **8–ounce jar Chutney, chop small**
½    **cup chopped peanuts**
½    **cup chopped green onions (tops and all)**
½    **cup grated coconut**

Cream cheeses with sherry, Worcestershire, curry, salt and pepper. Pour and mold on a big pretty plate or cheese board. Cover with plastic wrap and chill 4 hours. (Can make 2 or 3 days ahead or freeze. If frozen, defrost at room temperature before garnishing with condiments). Garnish in layers with Chutney, peanuts, onions, coconut. Serve with thin ginger snaps or Saltine crackers.

# STRAWBERRY CHEESE RING

*A Satchie and Sara Special!*
*Easy — Pretty — and delicious!*

1    **pound sharp Cheddar Cheese - grated**
1    **cup pecans, chopped**
¾    **cup Kraft Mayonnaise**
3    **or 4 green onions, finely chopped**
½    **teaspoon red pepper**
1    **cup strawberry preserves (a green hot pepper jelly is a pretty substitute)**

Combine and pat mixture into a ring mold. Chill. After unmolding, fill center with preserves; garnish with fresh parsley and serve with Ritz crackers.

## ITALIAN ARTICHOKE BALLS

| | |
|---|---|
| 1 | 6–ounce jar marinated artichoke hearts, drained and finely chopped |
| 1 | 14–ounce can artichoke hearts, packed in water, drained and finely chopped |
| 2 | eggs |
| 2 | cloves garlic, crushed |
| 1 | Tablespoon Worcestershire sauce |
| ½ | teaspoon Tabasco |
| ½ | teaspoon cracked red pepper |
| 1½ | cups Italian–seasoned bread crumbs |
| 1 | cup grated Romano cheese |

In a large bowl, beat eggs with reserved marinade; blend in garlic, Worcestershire, Tabasco and pepper. Add artichokes and bread crumbs. Form in small balls and roll in cheese. Refrigerate. Bake at 325 degrees for 15 to 20 minutes.

## CHUTNEY SAUSAGE BALLS

*Can be made ahead; freezes well.*

| | |
|---|---|
| 1 | pound ground hot sausage |
| 1 | pound ground mild sausage |
| ½ | cup dry sherry |
| 1 | cup sour cream |
| 1 | 8–ounce jar chutney, finely chopped |
| 1 | teaspoon curry powder |

In a bowl, blend sausages. Roll into 1–inch balls. In a heavy skillet, cook until brown. With a slotted spoon, remove balls. Pour off grease, reserving crusty bits in pan. Reduce heat and add sherry, sour cream, and chutney, stirring constantly. Add balls and cook until hot. Transfer to a chafing dish and serve with toothpicks.

# LIGHT CREAM CHEESE GLAZED HAM PÂTÉ

*This is Kaydell Jackson's recipe and she is the mother of Tommy and Julie, my God Children and Mike Cage's most devoted supporter while he was in Saudi Arabia "Desert Storm '91".*

| | |
|---|---|
| 1 | **3 pound canned ham, ground** |
| 1 | **10–ounce jar sweet pickle or India relish** |
| 4 | **eggs, hard boiled and finely chopped** |
| 1 | **cup mayonnaise** |
| 2 | **Tablespoons onion, grated** |
| 1½ | **teaspoons black pepper** |
| 1 | **teaspoon ginger** |

**Glaze:**

| | |
|---|---|
| 1 | **8–ounce package softened spreadable cream cheese** |
| 1 | **Tablespoon milk** |

Mix pâté ingredients well and pour and form in ham can.

Beat glaze ingredients until spreading consistency. Unmold ham on platter. Glaze with cream. Garnish with parsley, fresh rosemary and serve with Ritz crackers.

# CARROT SANDWICH SPREAD OR DIP

| | |
|---|---|
| 1 | **cup chopped carrots** |
| 1 | **cup chopped pecans** |
| 1 | **cup Miracle Whip** |
| ½ | **teaspoon red pepper** |

Mix together and let set 2 or 3 hours. This will make enough for one loaf of Pepperidge Farm or Earth Grain thin bread or spread on plain crackers.

## TEATIME SPINACH SANDWICHES

| | |
|---|---|
| 2 | packages frozen chopped spinach |
| 1 | can finely chopped water chestnuts |
| 1 | cup sour cream (light) |
| 1 | lemon juiced and the zest |
| ½ | cup mayonnaise (light) |
| ½ | cup minced parsley |
| 1½ | teaspoons salt |
| 1 | teaspoon red pepper |
| ¼ | teaspoon nutmeg |

Thaw spinach; place in a colander and press out excess water. Mix with remaining ingredients. Check seasonings. Cover and refrigerate at least 24 hours. Bring to room temperature before spreading on buttered bread. This can be used as a dip for fresh vegetables.

## COCKTAIL REUBEN SANDWICHES

*A Crowd Pleaser!*

| | |
|---|---|
| ½ | cup mayonnaise |
| 1 | Tablespoon chili sauce |
| | About 3 Tablespoons butter or margarine, softened |
| 12 | slices rye bread |
| 6 | slices Swiss cheese |
| 2 | (4–ounce) packages thinly sliced corned beef |
| 1 | (16–ounce) can sauerkraut, well drained |

Combine mayonnaise and chili sauce, stirring well. Spread butter on one side of each slice of bread; spread the other side with mayonnaise mixture. Arrange cheese, corned beef, and sauerkraut on mayonnaise side of 6 bread slices. Top with remaining bread, buttered side out. Each sandwich, slice in 3 or 4 long strips. Place sandwiches on a cookie sheet, and broil. Pass or layer in a chafing dish for cocktail parties.

# CHEESE STRAWS

| | |
|---|---|
| 1 | pound of flour |
| 1 | pound New York State sharp Cheddar cheese |
| 3 | sticks butter |
| 1 | teaspoon salt |
| 1 | Tablespoon red pepper |

Sift flour. Grate cheese. Cream butter and cheese and beat until fluffy. Work in flour, salt and pepper. Work through your cookie press. Bake at 325 degrees for 20 minutes or until done. Take the same pastry and cut 1½ inch long. Wrap pecan half or almond and bake at 325 degrees until done.

# TOASTED PECANS

*a Southern Treat!*

| | |
|---|---|
| 12 | cups pecan halves |
| 1 | stick butter |
| | Salt |
| | Red pepper |

In a 250 degree oven, in a large pan, toast pecans about 30 minutes. Add butter and coat well. Sprinkle generously with salt and pepper. Bake 30 more minutes, stirring often and adding more salt and pepper each time. You want them a nice crispy, toasted brown. Be careful and do not burn them. It is hard to over salt them.

# MARINADE OF ARTICHOKES, MUSHROOMS, BLACK OLIVES AND CAPERS

*"Baby, it is all yours!"*

3  large boxes fresh mushrooms

3  large cans whole artichoke hearts, maybe cut in two if too large

2  large cans <u>pitted</u> clossel back olives

1  small jar big capers

1  2½ ounce bottle Pick–a–Pepper sauce

¼  cup hot water

½  cup sugar

½  cup olive oil

½  cup tarragon vinegar

1  Tablespoon garlic, chopped

1  teaspoon salt

1  Tablespoon cracked black pepper

1  Tablespoon curry powder

2  Tablespoons Worcestershire

2  Tablespoons lemon juice

1  cup Catalina French dressing

Drain artichokes, olives and capers. Wash and stem mushrooms. Mix marinade well and pour over artichoke mixture. Marinate at least 12 hours to be really good. Serve in a big platter on a bed of fresh red tip lettuce. So pretty and wonderful!

Native Soups
&
Gumbos

# ROUX

1    **cup cooking oil**
1    **cup flour**

A roux is needed for many Cajun and French dishes such as gumbo, sauce piquante, stew and gravies. A roux is a mixture of oil and flour browned slowly to desired color (dark chocolate color for gumbos, stews and a peanut butter color for étouffés or gravies). Pour oil into a heavy pot, keeping heat low to medium. Stir in flour. Stir and stir and stir. Keep stirring almost constantly to prevent burning. If you notice some black specks in your roux, just throw it out and start over. The specks give it a bitter and burned taste. When the right color is obtained, add chopped onions, stirring well. Cool mixture. Master making this and have fun!

# OIL–FREE ROUX

**Flour**

Place about one inch of flour in a black iron pot or baking pan. Place in a 400 degree oven, stirring occasionally with a wooden spoon, until the desired darkness is obtained. Add dry roux to sautéed vegetables and stock, then add shrimp crab, chicken, etc.

# HOMEMADE CHICKEN, BEEF OR FISH STOCK

*A must for all soups, gumbos, sauces and gravies! Freezes well!*

2    pounds chicken necks, back bones, or a turkey carcass, or; beef bones – soup bones, or; fish bones, shrimp, shells and 1 cut up lemon
2    large yellow onions, chopped
2    carrots, chopped
1    stalk celery, chopped
3    bay leaves
2    Tablespoons salt
1    Tablespoon pepper
1    teaspoon thyme

In a large stock pot, cover all ingredients with water. Bring to a boil, reduce heat and simmer about 2 hours. Skim off any foam that comes to the top. Cool. Strain. Cover stock and refrigerate overnight. Skim any congealed fat from stock before using.

# SHRIMP FRANK

*This is divine!*

Serves 8.

3    cans mushroom soup
2    soup cans milk
4    green onions and tops, chopped
¼    cup finely chopped celery
     Small bud garlic, pressed
     Worcestershire sauce
     Tabasco
1    small can button mushrooms
1½   pounds raw peeled shrimp
3    Tablespoons dry sherry
     Salt and pepper

Stir mushroom soup and milk until smooth on low fire; add finely chopped green onions, celery, and pressed garlic. Season with Worcestershire sauce and Tabasco. Add 1 can small button mushrooms and 1½ pounds raw shrimp. When shrimp are done, add sherry. Season to taste with salt and pepper. Crabmeat may be used instead of shrimp.

# GUMBOS

Gumbo is an original creation and a cherished possession in South Louisiana kitchens. It may be made with filé or with okra as a thickening agent. Filé is the powdered sassafras leaf; it used to be made by the Choctaw Indians. Their word for sassafras is Kombo, from which we get our word – "Gumbo". Filé is never put in until just a minute before serving, whereas okra is cooked with the gumbo. Filé is added AFTER the gumbo is removed from the heat. Gumbo is a wonderful means of using leftovers; bits of ham or a ham bone, turkey, duck or chicken carcass, sausage, seafoods or bacon. (When using a carcass or a ham bone, boil the bones and use this stock in the gumbo.) The thickness of the gumbo depends on the amount of water. Gumbo is best served over mounds of hot rice in a large flat soup bowl.

## FILÉ GUMBO

(Seasoning Mix:
(To be done ahead):

4    bay leaves
4    teaspoons salt
1    teaspoon white
     pepper
1    teaspoon black
     pepper
1    teaspoon cayenne
     pepper (or less)
1    teaspoon thyme
     leaves
½    teaspoon oregano
     leaves
1    teaspoon filé

(To be done ahead):
4    cups chopped onions
3    cups chopped green
     pepper
2    cups chopped celery

To Serve 20

In a large cast iron Dutch oven, heat oil until smoking; add flour and whisk continuously over high heat until dark red–brown (do not burn). Add ½ vegetables, continue whisking (or wooden spoon) about 1 minute. Add remaining vegetables and seasoning mix; continue stirring constantly to prevent burning, reduce heat a little and stir approximately 5 minutes. Remove from heat. In a large stock pot, bring stock to boil. Add roux; spoonful

(Continued on next page)

*(Filé Gumbo, continued)*

1 cup chopped green
    onion
2 Tablespoons minced
    garlic
1½ cups vegetable oil
1½ cups flour
12 cups (more or less)
    seafood or chicken
    stock
    Peeled medium
    shrimp
    Crabmeat (claw)
    Crabs
    Okra (frozen or
    fresh), chopped

at a time, stirring after each addition. Bring to low boil. Add seafood or other meats in the order in which each degree of doneness is desired.

1. Sausage, duck or chicken – first simmer 20 – 25 minutes stirring occasionally.
2. Crabs – until meat comes from cavities.
3. Okra – takes 10 – 15 minutes.
4. Crab meat – 5 minutes before finished cooking.
5. Shrimp and oysters last – have at a boil, cover, remove from heat and let stand until shrimp is pink and oysters curl.

Serve over hot rice.

*If oil foam forms, this may be skimmed off. Allow to cool, place in refrigerator or freezer containers. Flavors improve if refrigerated at least 24 hours.

# CHICKEN, OKRA & SAUSAGE GUMBO

Turkey carcass
Water to cover
Celery, chopped
Bay leaves
Onion, chopped
Bell pepper, chopped
Garlic, chopped
1  cup oil
½  cup flour
1  cup chopped celery
1  cup onion
1  cup bell pepper
2  pods garlic, chopped
½  cup parsley, chopped
1  large can tomatoes
Salt & pepper
Cayenne
Worcestershire sauce
Chicken
Okra
A good andouille or
   smoked sausage
Cooked rice

The day before, in a large 8 to 10 quart pot, cover a turkey carcass – a smoked turkey carcass is wonderful or a small hen – with water. Add bay leaves, onions, celery, bell pepper and garlic. Simmer 6 to 7 hours. Add salt & pepper to taste. Strain, reserving meat pieces and vegetables. Chill stock and remove fat. Now you have a wonderful stock.

In a large pot, add 1 cup oil and ½ cup flour. Make a light roux. Add 1 cup chopped celery, 1 cup onion, 1 cup bell pepper, 2 pods garlic, and parsley. Sauté about 5 minutes; add tomatoes, salt and pepper, Cayenne, and Worcestershire sauce. Add chicken, okra and sausage. Slowly add hot stock, until desired thickness. Check seasonings.

This is a nice light gumbo. Serve with a lot of hot fluffy Louisiana rice, a cold green salad, hot French bread with creamy rich butter, and a good cold glass of Chardonnay.

# OYSTER AND ARTICHOKE SOUP

*Can be made ahead.*

4    artichokes
1    stick butter
½    cup finely chopped
       green onions
1    outer rib celery, with
       leaves, finely
       chopped
1    medium carrot,
       scraped and
       chopped
1    Tablespoon finely
       chopped fresh
       parsley
2    cloves garlic, pressed
½    teaspoon thyme
1    bay leaf
3    Tablespoons flour
1    quart chicken stock,
       warmed
¼    teaspoon anise seeds
¼    teaspoon cayenne
       pepper
1    teaspoon salt
1    teaspoon
       Worcestershire
       sauce
1    quart oysters and
       their liquid
½    cup vermouth
¼    cup dry white wine
¼    cup half and half
       cream
1    teaspoon lemon juice
       Grated rind of one
       lemon

Cook artichokes. Scrape leaves, chop hearts, and reserve. In a 4–quart heavy pot, melt butter; sauté onions, celery, carrots, parsley, garlic, thyme, and bay leaf until celery and carrot are tender. Add scrapings and hearts; stir well. Slowly stir in flour, but do not brown. Slowly stir in stock. Add anise, cayenne, salt, and Worcestershire sauce. Simmer 15 minutes. Drain oysters, reserving liquid. Chop oysters and add with liquid to artichoke mixture. Cook over low heat 10 minutes. Add vermouth, white wine, half and half, lemon juice, and lemon rind. Remove bay leaf. Blend until smooth. Heat. This is better made the day before.

# TURTLE SOUP

*A Great Delicacy*

*Chef Hans' Turtle soup is the very best and he is sweet enough to share the secrets of this soup's success. We used to have sea turtles. They are now an endangered species. We now use Loggerheads from our own Louisiana bayous, which there are many. This soup is a dark red, thick and rich stew type.*

**For Roux:**
1½  **sticks butter**
¾   **cup flour**
¼   **cup bacon drippings**

**For Meats:**
*1   **pound turtle meat**
*1   **pound ground chuck**
*1   **box frozen chopped spinach**
1    **cup celery, chopped**
1½  **cups onion, chopped**
4    **pods garlic, chopped**
½   **cup parsley, chopped**
1    **15–ounce can tomato puree or sauce**
3    **bay leaves**
1    **teaspoon oregano**
½   **teaspoon thyme**
2    **quarts beef stock**
     **Salt and pepper**
     **Paprika – lots for the pretty red color**
     **Chef Hans' Blackened Fish Seasoning**
     **Lemon pepper**

**Day 1:**
Make your beef stock (remove fat). Chop vegetables. Grind meat. Cover and refrigerate.

**Day 2:**
Put soup together.

It is more fun this way and not such an ordeal: Well worth the time.

Melt butter in a heavy skillet. Add flour, stirring well, over medium heat until the roux is a light brown. Set aside. In a large pot, add bacon drippings and brown the turtle-beef-spinach (ground) mixture. Cook over high heat. Add vegetables and seasonings and cook until transparent. Add tomato puree; lower heat and simmer for 10 minutes. Add hot stock slowly and simmer for 30 minutes. Add roux and cook over low

*(Continued on next page)*

*(Turtle Soup, continued)*

1    **Tablespoon Allspice –
      be careful, not too
      much**
1    **lemon, juiced and
      the zest**
1    **cup sherry, dry**
4    **hard boiled eggs,
      finely chopped**
½    **cup fresh chopped
      parsley**

heat, stirring well. Check seasonings! Add lemon juice, zest, sherry, chopped eggs, and parsley. This is best made the day before serving, as flavors mingle! Serve at the table. Add 1 teaspoon sherry per bowl. Garnish with chopped eggs and minced parsley and a thin slice of lemon.

*While partially frozen, have your butcher grind all three together on the Chili grind size.

**If turtle bones are available, add them to the beef bones in making the stock for extra flavor. A good beef stock is very important in the success of this soup!

# TORTILLA SOUP

*The Mansion on Turtle Creek*

Yield: 6 to 8 servings.

| | |
|---|---|
| 3 | **Tablespoons corn oil** |
| 1 | **cup onions (pureed)** |
| 2 | **cups fresh tomatoes (pureed)** |
| 1 | **Tablespoon cumin pepper** |
| 1 | **teaspoon chili powder** |
| 1 | **bay leaf** |
| 1 | **Tablespoon tomato paste** |
| 4 | **cloves garlic (finely chopped)** |
| 2 | **quarts chicken stock** |
| 2 | **corn tortillas, cut in strips** |
| | **Salt and pepper to taste** |

**Garnishes:**

| | |
|---|---|
| 1 | **breast of chicken** |
| 1 | **avocado (peeled and cubed)** |
| 3 | **ounces Cheddar cheese** |
| 3 | **corn tortillas (cut into thin strips and fried)** |

In a soup pot, heat the corn oil and sauté the tortillas with garlic. Add onions, fresh tomatoes pureed and bring to a boil. Add cumin, tomato paste, bay leaf, chili powder and chicken stock. Bring to a boil again. Add salt and cayenne pepper to taste and cook for one and a half hours. Stir through a fine strainer and remove all large particles.

Place the soup in a warm bowl and add the desired garnishes.

# GINGERED SWEET POTATO SOUP

4   to 5 cups, cubed,
    sweet potatoes
¼   cup sugar
2   stalks celery,
    chopped
1   onion, chopped
2   cloves garlic,
    chopped
3   Tablespoons ginger,
    minced
1   stick butter
2   Tablespoons curry
    powder
2   teaspoons salt or
    more
1   teaspoon red pepper
½   teaspoon cumin
¼   teaspoon cinnamon
¼   cup lemon juice and
    zest
2   cups chicken stock –
    well seasoned
1   pint half and half
    Sour cream or yogurt
    Parsley, chopped

In a soup pot, <u>barely</u> cover sweet potatoes. Add sugar and cook until tender. Do <u>Not</u> Drain! Set aside. Sauté in butter, celery, onion, garlic and ginger until soft. Add sweet potatoes and mix well. Add seasonings and lemon. Cook slowly about 5 minutes. In food processor, puree. Return to pot and add half and half and stock. Stir well. Simmer. Check seasonings. Serve in warm bowls with a dollop of sour cream or yogurt and chopped parsley. Note: This is best when made the day before serving.

## VEGETABLE SOUP

Serves 10.

2  pounds heavy beef brisket or soup bone
1  large onion, chopped
2  teaspoons salt
2  ribs celery, chopped
3  quarts water
1  can tomatoes
3  carrots, chopped
2  ribs celery, chopped
½  onion, chopped
½  potato, chopped
6  sprigs parsley, minced
   Pepper to taste (optional)
   Spaghetti or macaroni (optional)

In a four–quart covered pot, boil meat with salt, 2 whole ribs celery, and whole onion, very slowly for three hours or longer. Take soup meat from pot and remove meat from bone, chopping to bite size and discarding bone and fat. Return meat to liquid. Add tomatoes and other vegetables, cooking until vegetables are well done. A small amount of spaghetti or macaroni may be broken into soup during the last 20 minutes of cooking. Serve with Boo's Cornbread.

## CHEESY CREAM OF BROCCOLI SOUP

1  medium onion, chopped
3  Tablespoons margarine or butter
3  cans cream of mushroom soup
3  soup cans milk
1  roll jalapeño cheese
2  packages frozen chopped broccoli
   Salt and pepper to taste

Sauté onion in margarine or butter. Add cream of mushroom soup, milk, jalapeño cheese, and broccoli. Add salt and pepper to taste; simmer about 30 minutes. That's it! So good to be so easy.

# WHITE BEAN AND LAMB SOUP

2      Tablespoons olive oil
1      cup chopped celery
1      cup chopped onion
2      teaspoons minced
         garlic
2      teaspoons dried sage
6      cups chicken stock
         or broth
2      cups water
1      pound lamb shanks
1      pound dried navy
         beans
2      teaspoons fresh
         lemon juice
         Salt and freshly
         ground pepper
3      large plum tomatoes,
         pulp and seeds
         removed, cut into
         ¼–inch dice
¼     cup fresh basil
         leaves, cut into fine
         julienne

Heat oil in a 4–quart pot. When hot, add celery, onion, garlic and sage. Cook until the onion is softened, about 5 minutes. Add stock or broth and water. Bring to a boil. Add lamb and beans. Bring to a boil again. Simmer, covered, 2 hours, stirring occasionally.

Use a slotted spoon to remove the lamb. When cool enough to handle, remove meat from bone. Dice meat into ⅓–inch cubes. Puree 2 cups beans with 1 cup soup liquid until smooth. Return meat and pureed mixture to pot. Stir well to combine. Add lemon juice and season to taste. To serve, garnish with tomato and basil.

# FIESTA CORN SOUP

Serves 6.

3   Tablespoons butter
1   cup onion, chopped
3   medium cloves
    garlic, minced
2   17–ounce cans
    creamed corned
1   17–ounce can corn
    kernels
1   cup chicken stock
2   cups whole milk
1   4–ounce can green
    chilies, diced
1½  teaspoons ground
    cumin
2   teaspoons salt
1   teaspoon ground
    pepper
1   teaspoon Tabasco
    sauce
2   cups chicken breast,
    cooked and cubed
1½  cups Monterey Jack
    cheese, shredded

Garnishes:
    Black olives, sour
    cream, salsa, diced
    avocado, crumbled
    tortilla chips

In a large, heavy pot, melt butter and sauté onion over medium heat until translucent, about 6 minutes. Add garlic and cook 2 minutes longer. Do not allow onion and garlic to brown. Puree creamed corn, corn kernels, and chicken stock in a blender or food processor. The mixture should not be completely smooth, but should still have some texture. Add corn mixture to pot, and simmer gently over medium heat for 10 minutes. Stir in milk, green chilies, cumin, pepper and Tabasco. Add chicken and shredded cheese; stir until cheese melts. Ladle into soup bowls. Serve immediately with your choice of garnishes. Individual soup bowls may be lined with a warm tortilla before ladling in the soup. Place colorful garnishes in bowls to pass at the table.

Herbal Gatherings
Tossing &
Mixtures

# SLAW, A GARNISH OF FIREWORKS

1    **small head cabbage, shredded**
1    **small head purple cabbage, shredded**
3    **bunches green onions (tops and bottoms), finely chopped**
1    **large bell pepper, chopped**
8    **carrots, chopped, finely**
1    **large jar chopped pimento**
½    **cup chopped parsley**

**Dressing**:
½    **teaspoon celery seed**
1    **cup sugar**
2    **teaspoons salt**
1    **teaspoon dry mustard**
1    **cup white vinegar**
1    **cup salad oil**

In a large bowl, combine the first 7 ingredients. Get as much moisture out as possible (I pat mine with a paper towel).

Combine dressing ingredients except oil. Bring to a roaring boil. Stir in oil and bring to a boil again. Pour over cabbage mixture, cover and refrigerate overnight. This keeps well. Serve ice cold. Good with your fried fish or as a side condiment with a good 'ole hamburger. O Yes!

# FRIED OYSTER SALAD

*For very special friends!*

|   | |
|---|---|
| | A mix of 2 or 3 lettuces |
| 1 | Arugula |
| | Fried oysters or okra, 3 or 4 per salad |
| | Seasoned fish fry |
| | Peanut oil for frying |
| | Tartar Sauce |
| | French Dressing |
| | Nasturtiums and lemon slices for garnish |
| 1 | to 2 cups fresh corn kernels |

This is really easy if you plan ahead. Have French dressing and tartar sauce made several days ahead. Tear salad greens in bite size pieces. Cover and refrigerate. You always want your salad greens as dry as possible and ice cold. Fry oysters just before serving, keeping warm. Toss salad greens in a small amount of French dressing. To serve, place a generous amount of salad on each plate. Top with 2 or 3 fried oysters with a dollop of tartar sauce. Garnish with Nasturtiums and lemon slices.

# TUNA SALAD

|   | |
|---|---|
| 2 | 6–ounce cans tuna (1 in vegetable oil for the flavor, and 1 in spring water), drained |
| 3 | or 4 hard–boiled eggs, chopped |
| 1½ | cups celery, chopped |
| 1 | cup pickles, chopped |
| 1 | Tablespoon lemon juice |
| 1 | cup light mayonnaise |
| | Cracked black pepper |

Mix all ingredients and enjoy. For a pretty tuna mold, take one package plain gelatin and soften in cold water. Dissolve over hot water. Mix in salad. Pour in a lightly greased fish mold. Chill until firm. Unmold on red tip lettuce. Decorate with stuffed olives and pimentos. Serve with Ritz crackers.

# SUMMER SEAFOOD SALAD

*Make this only in the season of freshness!*
*"A Cocodrie, Louisiana Special"*

4   cloves garlic
2   pounds boiled shrimp
4   fresh tomatoes
2   cups Italian Olive Mix
    (I like the one from
    Central Grocery in
    New Orleans)
1   cup fresh Parmesan
    cheese, grated
1   pound lump crabmeat
1   large lemon, juiced
    and the zest
2   or 3 types of lettuce –
    Iceberg, Romaine,
    Boston, etc.
    Radicchio is good
    too.
1   or 2 Avocados –
    optional, but good
    Salt and pepper

In a large wooden salad bowl, crush garlic. Add shrimp, tomatoes and olive mix. Toss with cheese – save a little for garnishing. Add crabmeat, gently, trying not to break, lemon juice and zest. Chill! When ready to serve, break up lettuce and toss gently with salad mix. Salt and pepper to taste. Top with extra cheese. Serve with warm toasted saltine crackers and a chilled glass of Pouilly Fuisse. What a delightful, light summer brunch.

# CHICKEN SALAD SUPREME

2½  cups diced cold
      chicken (for
      sandwiches, shred
      the chicken)
1     cup celery, chopped
      fine
1     cup sliced white
      grapes (omit for
      Chicken Salad
      sandwiches)
½    cup shredded
      browned almonds,
      chopped (optional)
1½  cups minced parsley
1     teaspoon salt
1     cup mayonnaise
      (homemade is
      better)
¼    cup lemon juice –
      you know I love the
      zest!

Mold (use the same eight
ingredients, plus):
1½  Tablespoons gelatin
4     Tablespoons water
½    cup chicken stock

Combine and serve in let-
tuce cups garnished with
fresh tomato wedges.

This same mixture can be
made into a mold that is
delicious. Mix the chicken,
celery, grapes, almonds,
parsley, and salt. Soak
gelatin in the cold water
and dissolve in hot chicken
stock. When cool, add mayonnaise. Stir until thick
and fold in the chicken mixture. Pack in individual
molds or a large ring. Serve
garnished with deviled
eggs, fresh tomato wedges
or fresh fruit.

# COUSCOUS CHICKEN SALAD

*The first time I had Couscous was in Morocco at the La Momounia Hotel (Winston Churchill's favorite retreat) in Marrakech. Sean Connery was staying there filming "The Man Who Would Be King". Every morning he was in the beautiful lobby drinking coffee and reading the paper, he would smile or wink at me. I still get a little warm when I think about it.*

*Couscous is a coarse grind semolina made from coarsely ground wheat and is popular on the eastern and southern shores of the Mediterranean. This is one of my favorites! Try it – you will like it!*

**Salad:**
6   **chicken breast halves, skinned**
4   **cups chicken stock**
2   **cups couscous**
1   **tomato, chopped**
3   **green onions, thinly sliced**
1   **15–ounce can garbanzo beans, drained**
½   **cup red bell pepper, diced**
½   **cup dried currant**
1   **cup parsley, minced**

Place chicken and stock in a large skillet. Simmer gently until chicken is cooked through, about 15 to 20 minutes. Remove chicken from stock. Strain stock and return to skillet. Bring stock to a boil and slowly stir in couscous. Mix thoroughly with a fork, cover and remove from heat. Let stand until stock is absorbed, about 15 minutes. Fluff couscous with a fork and spread on a baking sheet to cool. Transfer to a large bowl. Remove chicken from bone and cut into bite–sized pieces. Add to bowl with couscous. Mix in tomato, green onion, garbanzo beans, red pepper, currants and parsley.

*(Continued on next page)*

*(Couscous Chicken Salad, continued)*

**Dressing:**

½    **cup lemon juice,
       freshly squeezed**
6    **Tablespoons olive oil**
1    **medium clove garlic,
       minced**
¼    **teaspoon cumin**
¼    **teaspoon curry
       powder**
¼    **teaspoon Tabasco
       sauce**
     **Salt and freshly
       ground pepper**
½    **cup pine nuts
       toasted**

For Dressing: blend lemon juice, oil, garlic, cumin, curry powder and Tabasco in a small bowl. Season with salt and pepper to taste. Add dressing to couscous mixture and toss well. Refrigerate at least 1 hour, or up to 1 day. Sprinkle with pine nuts before serving.

# ENGLISH PEA SALAD

2    **cans LeSueur peas,
       drained**
2    **large ribs celery,
       finely chopped**
¾    **cup sharp cheddar
       cheese, cubed**
1    **bunch green onions,
       chopped (tops and
       bottoms)**
½    **teaspoon cracked
       black pepper**
¼    **teaspoon garlic salt**
1    **teaspoon salt**
½    **teaspoon red pepper**
1    **teaspoon mustard**
1    **cup tartar sauce**

Toss all ingredients. Marinate overnight.

# SALATA

*(With Taratoor Dressing)*

1   cucumber, peeled,
      seeds removed and
      diced
2   tomatoes, peeled,
      seeded and diced
3   to 4 scallions,
      trimmed and
      thickly sliced
1   green pepper, cored,
      seeded and diced
      **Taratoor dressing
      (see below)**
      **Parsley sprigs (for
      garnish)**

**Taratoor Dressing:**
2   to 3 cloves of garlic,
      crushed
½   cup tahina (sesame
      paste)
      **Juice of 2 lemons
      and the zest**
¼   to ⅓ cup water
½   teaspoon ground
      cumin
      **Salt and red pepper**

Sprinkle the cucumber lightly with salt; let stand 30 minutes to draw out juices, then rinse and dry on paper towels. Mix the cucumber, tomato, scallion and green pepper, toss with the Taratoor Dressing and pile on a platter. Garnish with parsley sprigs just before serving.

Beat garlic into tahina; then gradually beat in lemon juice and enough cold water to make a smooth creamy dressing. Add cumin and salt to taste. You think you are in Istanbul! I like this best when the tomatoes are really fresh.

# CALYPSO BLACK BEAN AND CORN SALAD

1  15–ounce can black beans, drained and rinsed
1  11–ounce can Shoe Peg corn, drained
½  cup chopped parsley
½  cup chopped cilantro
1  medium tomato, finely chopped
1  small bell pepper, chopped fine (red & yellow are pretty)
1  avocado, finely chopped
   Juice of 1 lemon and zest
   Olive oil
   Salt and pepper – lots!
   Cumin and chili powder – just a bit!

Wrap beans, corn, parsley, cilantro, tomato and bell pepper in a paper towel and gently blot to get as dry as possible.

Mix all. Check seasonings – it is a poor cook who does not taste! This is better prepared the day before because the flavors mingle. Serve on a big pretty lettuce leaf. So good as a side dish, especially good with enchiladas.

# SHRIMP SALAD – MARIE LOUISE

5    **pounds small shrimp**
1    **large bunch of
     celery, chopped**
2    **bunches green
     onions, chopped
     (tops and bottoms)**
1    **cup parsley, chopped**
2    **Tablespoons capers,
     (optional)**
     **Lots of <u>Homemade
     Mayonnaise</u>**
     **Cracked black pepper**
     **Lemon juice and zest
     to taste**
     **Red pepper to taste**

Boil shrimp in a salty, seasoned water with bay leaves, lemon and crab boil. (Do not over cook them – takes just a few minutes – about 8 to 10). In a large bowl, layer shrimp, celery, onions, and parsley. Just before serving, toss with your homemade mayonnaise. Check seasoning and adjust with more lemon, salt, and pepper.

My children's Grandmother, Marie Louise Snellings, who was a famous hostess (a Renaissance woman), served this salad for an appetizer for big cocktail parties. It was always a hit. The secret is the homemade mayonnaise.

# MEXICAN SALAD

Serves about 20 people.

10  sliced ripe avocados,
    dipped in lemon
    juice
1   package cherry
    tomatoes
2   cans kidney beans,
    rinsed and drained

Dressing:
2   cartons sour cream
1   small bottle
    Wishbone Italian
    dressing
    Garlic salt
3   Tablespoons chili
    powder
    Salt and pepper to
    taste
2   or 3 heads lettuce
1   large package
    crushed Fritos

Marinate avocados, cherry tomatoes, halved, and kidney beans in sour cream and Wishbone dressing and seasonings for several hours or overnight. Just before serving, add lettuce in bite size pieces and Fritos. Delicious. Perfect to serve with Hot Tamales, Tostadas, cold beer or a Margarita...Olé.

# TABOULEH

*Cracked wheat and parsley salad.*

1    cup cracked wheat
     (bulger)
1½  cups parsley,
     chopped
3    large tomatoes,
     peeled, seeded, and
     chopped coarsely
1    medium cucumber,
     peeled, seeded and
     cut into small
     chunks
½   cup green onions –
     minced with tops
2    Tablespoons fresh
     mint leaves,
     minced
     Romaine lettuce

Vinaigrette:
½   cup extra virgin olive
     oil
¼   cup fresh lemon
     juice
1    teaspoon salt, or to
     taste
1    teaspoon pepper

Cover the wheat with cold water. Let stand 30 minutes. Drain and press out as much water as possible. Place wheat, parsley, tomato, cucumber, onions, and mint in a glass or plastic bowl. For the dressing, whisk together the Vinaigrette ingredients. Pour over the wheat mixture, and toss well. Cover and refrigerate at least one hour. Serve on a bed of Romaine lettuce leaves or cut a tomato in eighths; don't cut through the base – fan it out. Serve with a generous scoop of Tabouleh. Garnish with lemon slices and parsley.

Note: For a softer texture, cover cracked wheat with boiling water. Let stand 1 or 2 hours. The secret of this recipe is to get as much moisture out of your wheat and patting dry (with a paper towel) your other vegetables as dry as possible.

*(Continued on next page)*

*(Tabouleh, continued)*

Cracked wheat is also known as bulger and is a very popular grain in North Africa and the Middle East. This is cool and refreshing in the summer and wonderful with our home grown tomatoes and contains lots of fiber – and pretty to serve.

# LAYERED PARTY SALAD

1  large head lettuce
1  bag fresh spinach
4  hard–boiled eggs, chopped
1  12 ounce package bacon, fried, drained, and chopped, or 1 jar Bacon Bits
1  bunch green onions, chopped
½  pound fresh mushrooms, sliced
1  package frozen peas, uncooked
1  package Hidden Valley Green Goddess Salad Dressing Mix
1  cup mayonnaise
1  cup sour cream

Break lettuce and spinach into very large container (or Tupperware with top). Layer the rest of ingredients in order given. Mix salad dressing mix with mayonnaise and sour cream and "ice" the top of the salad. Cover and refrigerate overnight. Toss just before serving.

# BROCCOLI SALAD

Yield: 8 servings.
Makes about 2¾ cups dressing.

2    **large bunches fresh
      broccoli**
1    **cup sliced, stuffed
      green olives**
8    **green onions,
      chopped (including
      tops)**
5    **hard–boiled eggs,
      chopped**
1    **pound bacon, fried
      and crumbled
      Grated Cheddar
      cheese, optional
      Chopped purple
      onion, optional**

**Dressing:**
1    **cup mayonnaise**
¾    **cup grated Parmesan
      cheese**
1    **8–ounce bottle
      Italian dressing**
2    **Tablespoons finely
      chopped ripe
      olives, optional**

Clean broccoli and cut flowerettes into bite–size pieces. If the broccoli is fresh, you can cut up part of the stems. Drain well in colander. To prepare salad, combine salad ingredients and toss with dressing. Cover and refrigerate, stirring occasionally. This will keep for 3 days.

Combine dressing ingredients and mix well. Chill.

Crisp and cool.

# SWEET AND NUTTY BROCCOLI SALAD

**Bunch broccoli–**
  **chop flowerettes**
½ **red onion, chopped**
  **(or use green**
  **onions)**
½ **cup sunflower seeds**
½ **cup raisins**
½ **cup nuts, chopped**
1 **cup celery, chopped**
½ **pound bacon, fried**
  **crisp (break into**
  **pieces and add just**
  **before serving)**

<u>**Dressing**</u>:
1 **cup Mayonnaise –**
  **Light**
¼ **cup sugar**
¼ **cup vinegar**

Toss together the broccoli, onion, sunflower seeds, raisins, nuts, celery and bacon.

Mix dressing ingredients well and pour over salad and serve.

# PASTA SALAD

*A Favorite!*

1 **package vermicelli**
1 **bunch celery**
1 **large can pimentos**
4 **jalapeño peppers, or**
  **to taste**
1 **medium onion,**
  **grated**
1 **small bell pepper,**
  **optional**
2 **to 3 cups Kraft**
  **Miracle Whip**
  **Salt and pepper to**
  **taste**

Cook spaghetti according to directions. Drain and cool. Finely chop celery, pimentos and peppers. Grate onion. Add cooled spaghetti, mix and add salad dressing, salt and pepper. Keep in refrigerator covered for 24 hours. It is good when kept 4 or 5 days. Popular before pasta was so popular!

## ASPARAGUS MOLD

1   can of all green
    asparagus
1   cup hot liquid
1   tablespoon gelatin,
    dissolved in ¼ cup
    cold water
½   cup mayonnaise
½   cup cream, whipped
1   teaspoon salt
2   Tablespoons lemon
    juice
1   cup almonds – lightly
    toasted

Heat the liquid from the can of asparagus and pour over the dissolved gelatin. When partially set, fold in mayonnaise, whipped cream, salt, and lemon juice. Add asparagus and almonds, cut in small pieces. Pour into a mold and congeal. Serve with mayonnaise whipped with a little lemon juice. This is one of my favorites. Helen Corbitt said, "The first time this was served to me, was at the Governor's mansion in Baton Rouge and I wished I could have asked for more".

# RUSSIAN BEET SALAD

*Do not over look this one! Really outstanding!*

Serves 8 to 10.

2 No. 303 cans sliced beets
2 envelopes gelatin
½ cup cold water
½ cup sugar
1½ teaspoons salt
½ cup vinegar
1½ cups celery, minced
1½ cups green onions, minced
2 teaspoons horseradish
½ cup India Relish

Drain beets and bring liquid to a boil. Soften gelatin in cold water and add to hot liquid. Add sugar and salt; stir all to dissolve. Blend in vinegar. Set aside to cool to room temperature. Chop beets, celery and onion. Blend in horseradish and India Relish. Combine with gelatin mixture. Pour into a 6 to 8 cup mold. Refrigerate until firm. Wonderful and beautiful to serve!

# COPPER PENNIES

Serves 10 to 12.

| | |
|---|---|
| 2 | **pounds carrots, sliced crosswise** |
| 1 | **small onion, chopped finely** |
| 1 | **medium bell pepper, chopped finely** |
| 3 | **ribs celery, chopped finely** |
| 1 | **cup tomato soup, undiluted** |
| 1 | **cup sugar** |
| ¼ | **cup oil** |
| ¾ | **cup Apple Cider vinegar** |
| 1 | **Tablespoon dry mustard** |
| 1 | **Tablespoon Lea & Perrins** |
| | **Lettuce** |

Cook sliced carrots in salted water until fork tender. Add chopped onion, bell pepper and celery to the drained carrots. Set aside. Mix and bring to a boil soup, sugar, oil, vinegar, mustard and Lea & Perrins. Pour this hot mixture over the above vegetables. Refrigerate overnight. Serve on lettuce.

# WINDSOR COURT SALAD

## Salad:

1   head Romaine
     lettuce
2   bunches watercress
2   hard–boiled eggs —
     whites and yolks
     separated
6   radishes
2   ounces Roquefort
     cheese
2   large tomatoes
4   slices cooked bacon
1   large avocado

## Dressing:

1   raw egg yolk
1   teaspoon Dijon
     prepared mustard
1   Shallot
3   cups vegetable oil
1   cup red wine vinegar
     Salt and pepper to
     taste

Chop/grate all of the salad ingredients fine, and lay out in rows, each ingredient side by side to make a colorful presentation. (Present at table, and then toss with Windsor Court Salad Dressing; serve.)

For dressing, beat together lightly the egg yolk and the Dijon mustard, and begin to gradually add in the vegetable oil in a thin stream, beating quickly to form an emulsion. Alternately add in the wine vinegar with the oil, until both completely added. Then season mixture with salt and pepper, chopped shallot and chopped watercress. What can I say!

# CAESAR SALAD

*This is my son, George's. He makes the best!*

| | |
|---|---|
| 2 | heads Romaine lettuce, chilled and torn into bite size pieces |
| 1½ | cups croutons, toasted in olive oil |
| 2 | cloves garlic |
| 1 | teaspoon dry mustard |
| 1 | teaspoon black pepper |
| 1 | teaspoon salt |
| 1 | lemon, juiced |
| 1 | small tin of anchovies |
| 1 | teaspoon capers |
| ½ | cup olive oil |
| ¼ | cup Tarragon vinegar |
| 1 | Tablespoon Dijon mustard |
| 2 | eggs, coddle, 4 minutes |
| ½ | cup freshly grated Parmesan cheese |

In a big wooden salad bowl, crush garlic, add mustard, pepper, salt, lemon juice and anchovies. Smash and mix well. Add capers. Add ice cold lettuce. Whisk together oil, vinegar and mustard. Pour over and mix. Leaves should be marinated not swimming in dressing. Break the 2 coddled eggs and toss. Add cheese and Croutons, lightly tossing. Serve.

# THE BEST GREEN SALAD

2    or 3 lettuces –
        Iceberg, Romaine,
        Red Tip
1    Arugula, optional,
        but pretty and good

Garnish:
1    cup parsley, coarsely
        chopped
1    bunch green onions,
        chopped
2    cups celery, chopped
1    small purple onion,
        thinly sliced
1    cup bell pepper,
        chopped
     Fresh mushrooms
     Avocado
     Tomatoes
     Homemade
        Mayonnaise
     Homemade French
        Dressing
     Tony's or Cavender's
     Cracked black pepper

Wash, drain and chill lettuce and Arugula. In a large wooden salad bowl toss the garnish and add a generous amount of mayonnaise. Cover and chill until ready to serve. Add lettuces and about ½ cup French dressing. Mix well with garnish. Sprinkle a little Tony's or Cavender's. This is always a winner. The secret is marinating the garnish and the blend of the French dressing and mayonnaise.

# THE SECOND BEST GREEN SALAD

3   lettuces – Iceberg, Romaine and Red Tip (washed and torn in bite size pieces)
1   small red cabbage, coarsely shredded
1   block Romano cheese, grated
1   small blue cheese, crumbled
    Good Seasonings Italian dressing
    Cavender's Greek Seasoning

Wash, wrap in pillow slip and refrigerate lettuces and cabbage. When ready to serve, in a big wooden bowl, toss lettuces, cheeses (more Romano than blue cheese) and dressing. Check seasonings. Sprinkle with Cavender's. This is wonderful and easy for a big crowd.

# CONFETTI SPINACH SALAD

2   bunches fresh spinach leaves, washed, stemmed, dried well, and chilled
10  slices bacon, fried and crumbled
1   red onion, thinly sliced
1½  cups mandarin oranges
1   8–ounce package mushrooms, sliced

Wash all ingredients and refrigerate. Toss salad ingredients. Add dressing and mix lightly.

Dressing:
½   cup cider vinegar
¼   cup sugar
1   teaspoon dry mustard
1½  teaspoons salt
⅔   cup oil

# TROPICAL SPINACH SALAD

1½  pounds spinach,
      washed and
      steamed
¼   cup lightly toasted
      almonds, chopped
      or penion nuts
¾   cup chopped dates or
      raisins
1    large cold banana,
      sliced and
      sprinkled with
      lemon juice
1    Bermuda onion,
      sliced very thin or
      green onions,
      chopped

Curry Dressing:
¾   cup olive oil
3½ Tablespoons wine
      vinegar
1    clove, crushed
1    teaspoon curry
⅛   teaspoon pepper
1    Tablespoon salt

Have spinach very dry and ice cold. Toss with nuts, dates, bananas and onions. Add dressing. Serve. Good with fried quail or a grilled steak. Different and delicious!

# POTATO SALAD

| | |
|---|---|
| 4 | to 6 large potatoes |
| 4 | boiled eggs |
| | Salt and pepper |
| 1 | cup dill pickles, chopped |
| 2 | cups celery, chopped |
| ½ | cup parsley, minced |
| ½ | cup sliced olives with pimentos |
| 4 | slices bacon, cooked until crisp |

Dressing:

| | |
|---|---|
| 1 | cup mayonnaise |
| ½ | cup mustard |
| 3 | Tablespoons sugar |
| 1 | teaspoon salt |
| 1 | teaspoon pepper |
| ¼ | cup vinegar |

Blend dressing ingredients well and check seasonings.

Boil potatoes until just tender. Cube and add salt and pepper. Add eggs, pickles, celery, and parsley. Toss. Pour dressing over and mix well. Check seasoning. Garnish with olives and crumbled bacon.

# BLUEBERRY SALAD

*So good – can be a dessert!*

| | |
|---|---|
| 2 | small packages blackberry Jello |
| 2 | cups boiling water |
| 1 | 15–ounce can blueberries, drained |
| 1 | 8¼–ounce can crushed pineapple, drained |
| 1 | 8–ounce package cream cheese |
| ½ | cup sugar |
| ½ | pint sour cream |
| ½ | teaspoon vanilla |
| ½ | cup chopped pecans |

Dissolve Jello in boiling water. Drain blueberries and pineapple; measure liquid. Add enough water to make 1 cup; add to Jello. Stir in blueberries and pineapple. Pour in 2 quart flat pan and refrigerate until set. Combine sugar, sour cream, cream cheese, and vanilla. Spread over Jello layer; sprinkle pecans on top. Very sweet and rich, may also be used as a dessert.

# TOMATO ASPIC

1   large can tomato juice
3   packages plain gelatin
3   pods of garlic, crushed
1   bay leaf
6   cloves
1   Tablespoon onion, grated
1½  cups celery, finely chopped
1   small green bell pepper, finely chopped
½   cup parsley, finely chopped
½   cup sliced green olives, (optional)
1   Tablespoon lemon juice and the zest
½   cup Worcestershire sauce
1   teaspoon salt
1   teaspoon cracked black pepper

Dissolve gelatin in one cup of the tomato juice. Simmer the rest of the juice with the garlic, bay leaf, cloves, and onion. Strain the hot tomato juice and add to gelatin. Add the rest of the ingredients. Pour into greased ring mold and chill. Unmold on lettuce. You can fill the center with frozen green peas that you have cooked, seasoned, and chilled; or serve with a dollop of cream cheese – sour cream mixture; or fill with cottage cheese.

# HOLIDAY FRUIT DELIGHT

| | |
|---|---|
| 4 | ounces cream cheese |
| ¾ | cup sugar |
| 1 | large can pineapple tidbits, drained |
| 1 | 10–ounce package frozen strawberries (thawed and use juice) |
| 2 | bananas, sliced – cover with lemon juice and drain |
| ½ | cup chopped pecans |
| 1 | large carton Cool Whip |

Cream sugar and cream cheese. Add pineapple, strawberries and juice, bananas – drained, and pecans. Fold in Cool Whip. Freeze. You can cut this in squares or take out about 30 minutes before serving and mound in an ice cream dish. Top with a slice of kiwi and a strawberry. Can also be served as a dessert with a little cookie or as a fruit salad with your meal. Pretty in color – sort of reminds me of a sorbet. So easy and so good! Alpha Spence, has our Investment Club for lunch for the December meeting – her home is alive with Christmas spirit and she serves this for dessert.

# CRANBERRY CONGEALED SALAD

*(This is Laura Cage Wied's recipe. Mother of Mary Amanda and Katherine. Jesse's wife, Mike's daughter and my friend and it is good!)*

*Pretty for holiday entertaining!*

Serves 10.

1     **package Cherry Jello**
1     **cup hot water**
¾     **cup sugar**
1     **Tablespoon lemon juice**
1     **Tablespoon plain gelatin dissolved in**
1     **cup pineapple juice, then melted over hot water**
1     **cup ground raw cranberries**
1     **orange and rind, ground fine**
1     **cup crushed pineapple, drained**
1     **cup chopped celery**
½     **cup chopped pecans**
     **Lettuce**

Dissolve Jello in hot water; add sugar, lemon juice, and pineapple juice–gelatin mixture and stir until blended. Chill until partially set; add remaining ingredients; pour into ring mold. To serve, unmold on lettuce leaves, garnish with turkey or chicken salad, using grape halves in place of celery.

# CONGEALED LIME SALAD

*An Old Time Favorite!*

Serves 10.

2    packages lime Jello
1    cup water
1    3–ounce package
     cream cheese
½    cup mayonnaise
½    pint whipping cream,
     whipped
2    small cans crushed
     pineapple,
     undrained
1    cup pecans, finely
     chopped

Dressing:
1    cup mayonnaise
1    cup cream, whipped

Dissolve 1 package Jello in 1 cup boiling water; cool in refrigerator, then whip in mixer. Cream softened cream cheese and mayonnaise, add to Jello and beat slightly. Fold in whipped cream, pineapple and pecans. Stir together well, pour into a 9 x 13 inch pan and set in refrigerator overnight.

Glaze: Follow directions on the other package of lime Jello. When it cools pour over the SET mixture to form a clear lime top layer.

Dressing: Equal parts of mayonnaise and whipped cream. Garnish with cherries.

# AMBROSIA

5    or 6 large sweet
     oranges, peeled and
     sectioned
1    cup pecans, chopped
¾    cup frozen coconut
1    teaspoon sugar

Combine all ingredients. Chill and serve in a pretty crystal bowl. It would not be Thanksgiving without Ambrosia. Some people put crushed pineapple and maraschino cherries in theirs. I prefer it the other way.

# FRENCH DRESSING

*This is my all time favorite!*

| | |
|---|---|
| 1 | cup olive oil |
| ½ | cup vinegar |
| 1 | lemon juiced and the zest |
| 4 | pods garlic, crushed |
| 2 | teaspoons salt |
| 1½ | teaspoons pepper |
| ½ | teaspoon sugar |
| 1 | Tablespoon Dijon mustard |

In a small bowl add crushed garlic, salt, and pepper. Mash together making a paste. Add vinegar and transfer to a quart jar. Add oil, lemon juice, the zest, sugar and mustard. Shake vigorously. Check seasonings, you may need to adjust the oil, vinegar, etc. You want this highly seasoned. This keeps indefinitely in the refrigerator and doubles or triples easily.

# RENDEZVOUS DRESSING

*(Not really, but close)!*

| | |
|---|---|
| 1 | pint mayonnaise |
| 1 | Tablespoon anchovy paste |
| 4 | Tablespoons horseradish mustard |
| 1 | cup Sandwich Spread |
| 2 | hard–cooked eggs |
| ½ | medium onion |

Place all ingredients in blender or food processor and blend well. Serve this over green salad with Greek olives; or lettuce, tomatoes, Greek olives, anchovies, Duleito peppers, hard–boiled eggs, feta cheese and capers.

# HOMEMADE MAYONNAISE

3    egg yolks
1½   cups of Wesson oil
1½   cups olive oil
     Juice of 2 lemons
2½   teaspoons salt
¾    teaspoon cracked
     pepper
¾    teaspoon dry
     mustard
2    Tablespoons boiling
     water

This is important...Use a small, deep bowl (small at the bottom so you can beat the yolks better). Beat egg yolks until thick and lemon colored. Alternately add the oil and lemon juice, slowly at first. When the mayonnaise "begins to make" you may add the oil more freely. Add boiling water, beating well. It takes away the oily appearance.

# HELEN CORBITT'S POPPY–SEED DRESSING

Yield: 3½ cups.

1½  cups sugar
2   teaspoons dry
    mustard
2   teaspoons salt
⅔   cup vinegar
3   Tablespoons onion
    juice
2   cups salad oil
    (Wesson oil)
3   tablespoons poppy
    seeds

Mix sugar, mustard, salt, and vinegar. Add onion juice and stir it in thoroughly. Add oil slowly, beating constantly, and continue to beat until thick. Add poppy seeds and beat for a few minutes. Refrigerate. One of my favorite salads is avocado – grapefruit on shredded lettuce with Helen's poppy–seed dressing. Men love this!!

# SENSATION SALAD DRESSING

1  (½ pound) wedge
   Romano cheese,
   grated
1  pint Wesson oil
   Juice of 2 lemons
2  pods of garlic, grated
   Dash of salt &
   cracked black
   pepper

Combine ingredients in quart jar. Shake well. Check seasonings. Refrigerate. Allow to stand a few days before using.

# OLD FASHION COOKED DRESSING

*My Grandmother Lela's dressing!*

2    teaspoons dry
     mustard
3    Tablespoons sugar
1    teaspoon salt
1½   Tablespoons flour
1    cup milk
1    egg, well beaten
1    Tablespoon butter
¼    cup vinegar

Mix dry ingredients; add milk; stirring until smooth. Add egg and cook until mixture thickens. Remove from fire, add butter and vinegar. This is so good! A change from other dressings. Good for potato salad, slaw or just a good green salad or spinach.

# EGG SALAD DRESSING

5    hard–cooked eggs
½    cup salad oil
¼    cup lemon juice
1    teaspoon salt
½    teaspoon pepper

Mash egg yolks in a bowl. Add oil, and mix well. Add lemon juice, salt and pepper. Break egg whites in small pieces, and add. Stir well. Serve on lettuce wedges.

# HOT LOUISIANA PEPPER SAUCE

*A must for your peas and greens!*

2    **cups white distilled vinegar**
1    **teaspoon salt**
1    **teaspoon oil of sesame, optional**
1    **jigger vodka (pulls heat out of peppers)**
2    **cloves garlic**
     **Lots and lots of your favorite peppers (mix them or try just one variety, experiment and find the flavor you like)**

**Some of my favorite peppers are the:**

**Chinese Ornamental –** Hot, itty-bitty peppers on small round plant. Dries easy. Good border plant. Awfully hot!

**Birdeye Pepper –** Hot, small ¼ inch bead like pepper. I think this one grows wild in the southwest.

**Rat Turd –** Hot, small orange pepper shaped like name.

**Poinsettia Pepper –** Hot, upright clusters of 2–3 inch peppers. Compact plant, beautiful foliage, lots of peppers.

You will need a whisky bottle, I like to use the ½ pint Crown Royal bottle or a 10–ounce Worcestershire bottle works well! Pick a pretty one, because this pepper sauce looks really nice on your table or in your kitchen. Boil the vinegar, salt, and oil mixture. Pour over your peppers, garlic and add the vodka. Keep adding peppers until the bottle is full. Let this sit 2 or 3 weeks. Keep the top or stopper loose the first week so the gas can escape. Believe me I know, I got shot from behind in my own kitchen – scared me to death!

*(Continued on next page)*

*(Hot Louisiana Pepper Sauce, continued)*

<u>Purple Pepper</u> – Hot,
  lots of 1 inch purple
  peppers on purple
  plants. Ripens red.
  Real pretty plant!

One of my greatest fears! Have a guest ask for
"Tabasco" and not have it! It's almost un–American
not to have Tabasco! I have really got a lot to worry
about, don't I?

# PICO DE GALLO

*(Beak of the Rooster)*

5     medium tomatoes,
        diced (fresh is best)
        or 2 cans tomatoes
⅓     cup tomato sauce
¼     cup finely chopped
        purple onion
3     cloves garlic, minced
1     to 2 jalapeño peppers,
        seeded and minced
2     Tablespoons minced
        fresh cilantro or
        parsley
1     Tablespoon minced
        fresh oregano or 1
        teaspoon dried
        whole oregano
2     Tablespoons lime
        juice
1     teaspoon salt

Combine all ingredients, stirring gently; cover and chill. Serve with tortilla chips, fish, chicken or steak.

## CALIFORNIA SALSA

6    large avocados, cut
        in chunks
2    large tomatoes
        Fresh cilantro, cut
        up leaves
        Garlic salt
        Pepper
        Medium size jar
        picante sauce
2    lemons, squeeze
        juice over top
        Green onions, 1
        bunch, chopped
        Jalapeños to taste

Mix all ingredients. Chill.

## PEACH OR MANGO SALSA

1½  cups chopped mango
        or peaches
1½  cups jícama, chopped
1    small clove garlic,
        crushed
1½  teaspoons grated
        ginger
1½  small jalapeño
        peppers, seeded and
        minced
1½  teaspoons chopped
        fresh cilantro
2    teaspoons chopped
        parsley
¼    cup honey
½    cup sliced green
        onions
¼    cup white vinegar
2    Tablespoons lime juice
        Salt and pepper

Combine first 5 ingredients in a medium bowl; set aside.

Combine sugar and remaining ingredients in a saucepan; bring to a boil, stirring until sugar dissolves. Pour hot mixture over mango mixture, stirring gently; cover and chill. Serve with cooked ham, pork or Fajitas, with a hoisin sauce and grilled peppers and onions.

# RÉMOULADE SAUCE

1    cup vinegar
½    cup lemon
3    (6–ounce) jars Creole
     hot mustard
4    Tablespoons paprika
1    jar horseradish
½    cup mayonnaise
3    cups olive oil
     Salt and pepper to
     taste
3    bunches green
     onions, tops and
     bottoms, finely
     minced
1    bunch parsley, finely
     minced

Mix first six ingredients well. Add olive oil and beat vigorously. Add onions and parsley. This sauce keeps well refrigerated. The more it stands, the better it tastes. For a cocktail party, marinate in sauce, 5 to 10 pounds boiled shrimp. Serve ice cold or individually with 4 to 6 shrimp on a bed of shredded lettuce with the Rémoulade on top.

# HORSERADISH SAUCE

1    cup sour cream
1    cup mayonnaise
     Juice of 1 lemon
3    Tablespoons
     horseradish
¾    teaspoon salt
2    Tablespoons chopped
     chives

Mix ingredients together. Chill. Love this with a good roast beef.

# MARCHAND DE VIN SAUCE

Yield: 2 cups.

¾   cup butter
⅓   cup finely chopped
      mushrooms
½   cup minced ham
⅓   cup finely chopped
      shallots
½   cup finely chopped
      onions
½   cup finely chopped
      carrots
2   Tablespoons garlic,
      minced
2   Tablespoons flour
½   teaspoon salt
⅛   teaspoon pepper
      Dash cayenne
¾   cup beef stock
½   cup red wine
2   Tablespoons lemon
      juice and the zest

In a 9–inch skillet melt butter and lightly sauté the mushrooms, ham, shallots, onion and garlic. When the onion is golden brown, add the flour, salt, pepper, and cayenne. Brown well, about 7 to 10 minutes. Blend in the stock, wine and lemon and simmer over low heat for 35 to 45 minutes.

# HOLLANDAISE SAUCE

Makes 1 cup.

4   egg yolks
1½ Tablespoons lemon
      juice
½   pound butter, melted
¼   teaspoon salt
      Red pepper to taste

In top of double boiler, beat egg yolks. Add lemon juice. Cook slowly on low heat. Do not allow water in the bottom of the pan to come to a boil. Add melted butter a little at a time, stirring constantly with a wooden spoon. Add salt and pepper. Cook until thickened.

# BROWN SAUCE

4    large green onions,
      chopped
1    cup mushrooms,
      chopped
½    cup butter
2    Tablespoons flour
¾    cup beef bouillon
2–3 teaspoons Kitchen
      Bouquet
½    cup sherry, sweet or
      dry
      Salt, red and black
      pepper
      Tabasco

Sauté onions and mush-rooms in butter until tender not brown. Make a thin paste with flour and a little water. Gradually add bouillon stirring constantly. Add Kitchen Bouquet until rich brown color. Add sherry. Season to taste. Simmer 30 – 40 minutes.

# TARTARE SAUCE

1    cup homemade
      mayonnaise with
      olive oil base
1    teaspoon dry
      mustard
1    Tablespoon grated
      onion
2    Tablespoons minced
      parsley
1    clove garlic, pressed
2    Tablespoons minced
      dill pickle
2    Tablespoons drained
      capers
1    Tablespoon minced
      green onions

Combine all ingredients. Let mellow 30 minutes or so. The ingredients can be used with a commercial mayonnaise, but the home-made makes this especially delicious.

# BAR–B–QUE SAUCE

| | |
|---|---|
| 1 | onion, finely chopped |
| 2 | Tablespoons oil |
| 1 | large bottle Worcestershire Sauce |
| 1 | large bottle catsup |
| 1 | lemon, sliced |
| 2 | pods garlic, chopped |
| 1 | or 2 bay leaves |

Sauté onions in oil until soft. Simmer all remaining ingredients with onions. So good over any Bar–B–Que or smoked meats.

# BARBECUE SAUCE

| | |
|---|---|
| 1 | stick butter |
| 1 | cup apple cider vinegar |
| 1 | Tablespoon dry mustard |
| 1 | onion minced |
| 4 | Tablespoons Worcestershire Sauce |
| 2 | pints chile sauce |
| 1 | lemon, juice only |
| 1 | lemon, sliced |
| 3 | cloves of garlic |
| 2 | Tablespoons sugar |
| 1 | pint ketchup |
| 1 | pint water |
| | Tabasco to taste |

My son, George, gave me this recipe. Makes a lot – keeps well and is wonderful!

# JEZEBEL SWEET HOT SAUCE

*This is delicious with all meats, and keeps forever in the refrigerator. Love this with fried duck breast or ham!*

Makes 4 cups.

1   18–ounce jar pineapple preserves
1   18–ounce jar apple jelly
¼   cup dry mustard
1   5–ounce jar horseradish
    Cracked black pepper

In saucepan, combine pine-apple preserves and apple jelly. Heat, stirring with a whisk until melted and thoroughly mixed.

Gradually add mustard, blending well.

Remove from heat and add horseradish. Mix well. Refrigerate.

# CUCUMBER VERDE SAUCE

1   cup mayonnaise
1   Tablespoon mustard
1   cup sour cream
2   Tablespoons chives, chopped
4   Tablespoons parsley, chopped
2   cucumbers, peeled and chopped
1   teaspoon salt
1   teaspoon red pepper
2   teaspoons lemon juice

Combine all ingredients and mix well.

# HOT MUSTARD SAUCE

Makes 3 baby food jars.

| | | |
|---|---|---|
| 1 | cup sugar | |
| 1 | cup vinegar | |
| ½ | teaspoon salt | |
| 2 | cans Coleman's mustard | |
| 3 | eggs | |

Blend in mixer or blender. Cook in top of double boiler until thick. So good on ham, beef or turkey!

# BASIL PESTO SAUCE

| | |
|---|---|
| 4 | cups of compressed sweet basil leaves |
| 1 | cup olive oil |
| 1 | cup pine nuts (or pecans or walnuts) |
| 1 | cup fresh Parmesan cheese cut in small pieces |
| 6 | to 8 cloves of garlic |
| 2 | teaspoons salt |

Combine ingredients in Cuisinart or other food processor. Cut, chop and blend until mixture is consistency of a thick sauce. This is wonderful swirled in pasta. Pesto is also especially good on tomatoes. I like to slice tomatoes fairly thick and place the slices in a Pyrex baking dish and put thin pieces of mozzarella cheese on top of the tomatoes and a tablespoon of Pesto on top of the cheese. Run these in the over at 375 degrees for 15 minutes. Pesto can also be swirled into dough for homemade bread. This freezes well!

Free
Range

## MIGAS

Serves 6.

| | |
|---|---|
| 1 | **pound bacon; fried very crispy and brown** |
| 4 | **Tablespoons butter or bacon drippings (or 2 of each)** |
| 1 | **teaspoon Tabasco** |
| 8 | **eggs, lightly beaten** |
| 1 | **small onion, finely chopped** |
| 1 | **small bell pepper, finely chopped** |
| 2 | **hot peppers, chopped** |
| ¼ | **cup chopped cilantro** |
| 1½ | **cups grated Cheddar cheese** |
| 1 | **cup Tostados, crumbled** |

Melt butter or drippings in a large skillet. Sauté onions, peppers, and cilantro. Stir Tabasco into eggs and pour into skillet. When eggs are almost cooked, add cheese and Tostados and fold in. Serve hot with crispy bacon and a side dish of Salsa and plenty of warm flour tortillas. Just perfect for breakfast or brunch. Muy Bonita !!!

## CHALUPA CHARLIE

**Guacamole**
**Shredded lettuce**
**Chopped fresh tomato**
**Fresh Cilantro, chopped**
**Poached eggs (or fried)**
**Re–fried pinto beans or black beans**
**Grated yellow cheese**
**Corn tortillas**

Fry corn tortillas whole until crisp. Layer beans, Guacamole, cilantro, lettuce, tomato, egg, and top with cheese. Put under broiler until cheese melts. Serve with salsa.

# CHEESE STRADE

6    eggs, beaten
1½   cups milk
1½   cups half and half
¾    teaspoon salt
⅛    teaspoon pepper
1    Tablespoon dry
     mustard
⅛    teaspoon red pepper
½    teaspoon seasoned
     salt
2    green onions and
     tops, chopped
1    4–ounce can green
     chilies, chopped
10   slices bread (white
     sandwich, butter
     one side and trim
     crust and cube)
1    pound Sharp Cheddar
     cheese (shredded)

**Sauce for Cheese Strade:**
4    Tablespoons flour
4    Tablespoons butter
½    cup Half and Half
1    cup chicken broth
¾    cup grated cheese
     (half Monterey and
     half Swiss)
1    teaspoon salt (or
     more to taste)
1    can drained, sliced
     mushrooms

In bowl combine eggs, milk, half and half, salt, pepper, dry mustard, red pepper, and seasoned salt, green onions, and green chilies. Arrange layers of bread and cheese in 9 x 13 inch Pyrex dish. Combine other ingredients and pour over top of bread. Cover and chill overnight. Take out and let come to room temperature. Cook at 350 degrees for about 1 hour – until knife comes out clean. Cut into squares and serve with sauce.

Combine sauce ingredients like a white sauce. Add grated cheese and salt. At end of cooking add mushrooms. Make a night ahead and reheat slowly. Perfect for a brunch. Serve with Smoked Ham, Green Bean Horseradish, fresh or hot fruit, homemade rolls, and for dessert pass Lemon Loves, Caramel Squares and Pecan Loves, and of course, good hot coffee.

## CHEESE ENCHILADAS

*These enchiladas are my friend – Patricia Fullen Jarret's, from Eastland, Texas. They are the best!*

| | |
|---|---|
| 1 | package (20) corn tortillas |
| ¾ | cup Crisco |
| 1 | pound yellow cheese (grated) |
| 1 | small box Velveeta cheese (cut in small pieces) |
| 1 | onion, grated or chopped very finely |
| 1 | small can chopped green chilies or jalapeño peppers |
| 1 | or 2 chopped serrano peppers |
| 1 | can Wolf Brand chili or homemade chili |

In small skillet, heat oil, then dip each tortilla through the oil for about 5 seconds on each side. Set aside. Put a flat oiled tortilla on counter; spread about a tablespoon of grated onion and a handful of cheese. Roll tightly into a tube shape and place in a casserole dish. Stack them touching each other. Cover with plenty of both cheeses and chili. Bake in oven 350 degrees until hot and cheese has melted. Not too long or the tortillas will fry and be too crisp.

*The Velveeta makes these creamy like the ones in a restaurant.

## EGGS BENEDICT

| | |
|---|---|
| 2 | English Muffins |
| 2 | large thin slices ham, grilled |
| 2 | eggs, soft poached |
| ¾ | cup Hollandaise Sauce |
| | Red pepper and chopped parsley for sprinkling on top |

Cover English muffins with ham, then eggs, then Hollandaise Sauce. Top each egg with a dash of red pepper and garnish with chopped parsley. Serve immediately.

# EGGS SARDOU

Yield: 1 serving.

1    **cup creamed
     spinach, piping hot
     (I like to add 1 slice
     grilled ham,
     chopped)**
2    **artichoke bottoms,
     warmed in salted
     water**
2    **eggs, poached**
¾    **cup Hollandaise
     Sauce**
     **Salt and red pepper**

Make a base of spinach on serving plate, place artichoke cups on top. Put an egg in each and top with Hollandaise sauce. Serve with Caramelized Tomatoes and hot buttered English muffins.

# EGG AND ARTICHOKE CASSEROLE

*Marvelous for brunch!*

Serves 4 as a main dish.

1    **bunch green onions**
2    **6½ ounce jars
     marinated
     artichoke hearts**
1    **clove garlic**
4    **eggs, beaten**
8    **ounces medium
     Cheddar, grated**
6    **crackers, rolled**

Finely mince onions using half of the tops also. Cut artichokes in thirds and reserve oil. Sauté onions and garlic in the artichoke oil. Combine all ingredients. Bake in a greased 9 x 9 inch Pyrex dish at 350 degrees for 40 minutes. This recipe tripled serves 30 for brunch cut in 2 inch squares. It does not have to be kept hot while serving. Prepare a day ahead and refrigerate or freeze. Thaw and rewarm about 15 to 20 minutes in a 350 degree oven.

# WELSH RAREBIT

4     Tablespoons butter
1     teaspoon salt
½     teaspoon paprika
¼     teaspoon cayenne
        pepper
½     teaspoon prepared
        mustard
1     teaspoon
        Worcestershire
        sauce
1     pound sharp
        processed cheese,
        grated
        About 1 cup beer or
        ale
2     eggs, slightly beaten

In double boiler, melt butter, add seasonings and cheese. Stir until cheese is soft. Add some beer or ale tablespoon by tablespoon, stirring gently. Mix the slightly beaten eggs with a little of the beer and add last stirring until the rarebit is smooth. Serve on French bread cut rather thick and oven–toasted, or slices of broiled tomatoes.

# SCRAMBLED OKRA

Yield: 4 servings.

2     cups sliced fresh
        okra
1     teaspoon salt
½     cup cornmeal
4     slices bacon
½     cup sliced fresh
        mushrooms
3     eggs, beaten

Sprinkle okra with salt; add cornmeal, stirring until okra is coated. Set aside. Cook bacon in a 9–inch skillet until crisp; remove bacon, reserving drippings. Cover and cook over medium heat 10 minutes or until okra is tender. Stir in mushrooms; cook for 5 minutes, stirring often. Add eggs; cook over low heat until eggs are set but still moist. Sprinkle with bacon before serving.

# CHEESE SOUFFLÉ

3    Tablespoons butter
¼    cup flour
1⅞  cups milk
1    teaspoon salt
     A dash of cayenne
        pepper
1    teaspoon prepared
        mustard
2    drops Worcestershire
        sauce
1    cup grated American
        cheese, packed
6    eggs

Make a cream sauce by melting the butter and blending in the flour. Cook until bubbly. Add the milk, salt, cayenne, mustard, and Worcestershire sauce, and bring to a boil, stirring constantly. Boil 1 minute. "Time it!" Remove from heat and cool slightly. Add the cheese. Beat the egg yolks until thick, and add the cheese mixture, stirring constantly. Beat the egg whites until stiff. Fold into the cheese mixture carefully; pour into a well–buttered baking dish (three fourths full). Bake at 300 degrees in hot–water bath for 2 hours, or until a silver knife inserted into the center comes out clean. This soufflé keeps a day in the icebox after baking, so it can be a leftover successfully.

# SKILLET FRIED CHICKEN WITH GARLIC

Serves 4–6.

1   **large fryer, cut into serving pieces (remove most of skin and as much fat as possible)**
¼   **cup butter**
¼   **cup olive oil**
12  **small cloves of garlic**
    **Salt and cracked black pepper to taste**
    **Louisiana Gold Pepper Sauce to taste**
    **Granulated garlic to taste**
1   **sprig rosemary**
    **Paprika for color**
1   **cup chicken stock**

In a large bowl, season chicken generously with all of the ingredients except garlic and rosemary. Allow to marinate approximately one hour prior to frying.

In a large black iron skillet, heat butter and oil over medium heat. Sauté chicken until golden brown on both sides. Add garlic and rosemary and lower heat to simmer. Cover, turn occasionally and allow to cook approximately 30 minutes. The chicken will release its own juices in the pan, creating a natural sauce.

If you should wish to have more of a gravy once the chicken is fried, remove from skillet and add chicken stock. Bring mixture to a rolling boil and reduce to one half volume. Season to taste and serve along with chicken. Serve with rice and snap beans.

# FIESTA CHICKEN WITH CHEESE

*Ideal for Entertaining!*

*A beautiful entrée, Fiesta Chicken Breasts are a rainbow of colors and an appealing blend of flavors and textures. Serve on a bed of green spinach fettuccine with red peppers and a creamy Monterey Jack cheese sauce.*

Yield: 6 servings.

| | |
|---|---|
| 1 | 12 ounce package spinach fettuccine |
| 3 | Tablespoons butter |
| 3 | whole chicken breasts, split, skinned and boned |
| 1 | (7 ounce) jar roasted red peppers, drained, sliced into ½–inch strips |
| | Salt, pepper, and a little cumino |
| 2 | green onions, thinly sliced |
| ¼ | cup all–purpose flour |
| 1 | cup each chicken broth and milk |
| ¼ | cup dry white wine |
| 1½ | cups Shredded Monterey Jack or Mild Cheddar Cheese – low fat is fine |
| ¼ | cup chopped fresh cilantro |

Cook fettuccine according to package directions. Drain well and transfer to serving platter; keep warm. Meanwhile, melt butter in large skillet over medium heat. Add chicken; cook 4 to 5 minutes per side or until golden brown and cooked through, sprinkle with seasonings. Place chicken over fettuccine. Top with pepper strips; keep warm. Add green onions to drippings in skillet; cook 1 minute. Add flour; cook 1 minute, stirring constantly. Add broth, milk and wine; heat to a boil and cook until thickened, stirring constantly. Add Monterey Jack cheese; stir until melted. Pour evenly over chicken, peppers and fettuccine; sprinkle with cilantro.

# SOUTHERN FRIED CHICKEN

1   fryer chicken, cut up
2   teaspoons salt and 1
      teaspoon pepper
      and paprika
1   to 2 cups all–purpose
      flour
    Crisco (Shortening –
      not vegetable oil)

Frying: A Tablespoon or 2 of bacon drippings are good mixed with oil, but not necessary. Have chicken at room temperature, never fry cold chicken. Salt and pepper chicken generously. Shake well in flour (I put mine in a big brown paper bag). In a big black iron skillet, heat shortening just enough to cover about half of each chicken piece, maybe about 1½ cups over high heat – smoking hot but not burning—be careful. Add chicken pieces. Cover and bring back to a steady frying. Reduce heat to steady cooking and sort of shake skillet. In about 10 minutes turn chicken and leave top off and cook about 10 more minutes or until golden brown. Remove and drain on lots of paper towels. Hint: The secret to success with frying good chicken is to keep a constant frying temperature. A good fried chicken seasoning like McCormick's is really good to sprinkle over after it is cooked.

# ROASTED HOLIDAY TURKEY

*This is the best and oh, the wonderful aroma!*

1    **turkey**
      **Dry mustard**
      **Worcestershire sauce**
      **Olive oil**
      **Salt and pepper**
      **Vinegar**
1    **onion, cut in half**
      **Celery**
      **Parsley**
      **Bacon**
      **Butter**
2    **cups chicken stock**

The day before roasting, take a well thawed bird and rub inside and out with a paste which you make with the dry mustard, Worcestershire, olive oil, salt and pepper and vinegar. Place onion, celery and parsley in cavity. Across the breast lay 2 strips of bacon; between leg and breast, stick hunks of butter.

Soak an old dish towel in olive oil and lay over the turkey and put in an uncovered roaster; add about 2 cups stock. Cook turkey according to time table on your turkey–wrappings in a 300 degree oven. Baste 2 or 3 times during cooking. This is a beautiful brown, tender, juicy turkey. The juices make the best gravy.

A new study shows that modern–day turkeys take less time to cook than turkeys of a few years ago, mostly because of breeding techniques. I would adjust the time, maybe 3 to 5 minutes per pound – depending on size – you do not want to over cook it!

# CURRY SAUCE

*A Curry of Smoked Turkey or Chicken*

*Curry of Smoked Turkey is wonderful for using up the dark meat.*

| | |
|---|---|
| 2 | **Tablespoons chopped onion** |
| 2 | **Tablespoons chopped celery** |
| ½ | **cup butter** |
| ½ | **teaspoon salt** |
| 1 | **Tablespoon curry powder** |
| ½ | **cup flour** |
| 3 | **cups milk (or half milk, half chicken stock)** |
| 1 | **cup cream** |
| 2 | **Tablespoons sherry (may be omitted, but is good)** |
| 3 | **cups cooked chicken (or what you have) diced into large pieces** |

**Accompaniments:**
**Chutney, of the Major Grey variety**
**Diced crisp bacon**
**Finely diced hard-cooked egg whites and yolks, diced separately**
**Finely chopped salted peanuts or pecans or almonds**

Sauté onions and celery in the butter until onions are yellow; add salt and curry powder and mix thoroughly; add flour and cook until bubbly. Add milk and cream, stirring briskly until smooth and thick and cook until all the starchy flavor has disappeared. Add sherry and turkey or chicken and serve over rice.

With curry, the accompaniments are important. In India each accompaniment is served by a servant boy, so we call curry "Five–Boy", "Seven–Boy" or however many accompaniments we use. These are usual, and served in individual bowls.

Curry is so popular and easy – a fun party – lunch or dinner.

Serve along side with a bowl of cold, fine coleslaw with tissue–thin slices of onion on top, or maybe Spanish green onions and of course

*(Continued on next page)*

*(Curry Sauce, continued)*

Finely chopped
   French–fried onions
Shredded coconut,
   fresh if possible
Raisins
Green onions,
   chopped

the puppodums (an Indian flat bread). Years ago, I went to a beautiful curry party in Dallas at the home of Sir Victor Sassoon – Herman Lay (as in Frito Lay) was my dinner partner.

O, yes I did have fun!

# RED CHICK

*(A Cage Children's favorite!)*

1      fryer, cut up
½     cup sliced onion
½     cup sliced bell
         pepper
½     teaspoon garlic
         powder
1      bay leaf
½     teaspoon oregano
1      can tomato sauce
1      tomato sauce can of
         water
2      Tablespoons brown
         sugar
2      Tablespoons
         prepared mustard
2      Tablespoons
         Worcestershire
         sauce
1      teaspoon salt
¼     teaspoon pepper
¼     cup vinegar

Place fryer pieces side by side in a 9 x 13–inch casserole. Mix all other ingredients. Pour mixture over chicken. Cook at 350 degrees about 1½ hours, or until done. Turn chicken over at end of 45 minutes.

# CHILI CHICKEN SPAGHETTI

*Wonderful for a big, fun party!*

*In this recipe, a Tablespoon means a Large Kitchen Spoon*

Serves 12 people.

4   **pounds hen (or chicken) (boil, remove meat; save stock and when cool, refrigerate)**
3   **Tablespoons oil**
3   **Tablespoons (heaping) flour**
1   **large onion, chopped**
1   **clove garlic, chopped**
3   **stalks celery, chopped**
2   **cups stock**
1   **can tomato paste to which has been added a pinch of baking soda**
    **Salt**
    **Pepper**
1   **teaspoon sugar**
1   **bay leaf**
    **Lots of chili powder (try ½ bottle and taste)**
2   **cans whole mushrooms, drained**
    **Spaghetti**

Brown oil and flour in a deep heavy skillet. After flour is very brown, add onion and garlic. Add celery a few minutes later. Then add stock, one cup at a time, stirring. Add tomato paste, salt, pepper, sugar, bay leaf, chili powder.

Cover and simmer about an hour, stirring occasionally. Add another cup of stock if necessary. When cool enough to taste, check seasoning. When done, add mushrooms (drained) and chicken. Can be frozen. Serve over spaghetti or you can mix with spaghetti as the spaghetti will absorb the liquid, make sure you have enough stock. May have to add more.

Sophia Blanks has the best parties in town. Sometimes she served this, a big green salad, hot crusty French bread, and a good Cabernet Sauvingon. We always ended up dancing and having fun.

# CHINESE CHICKEN SPAGHETTI

Serves 8 to 10.

1  hen
2  large bell peppers, chopped
2  large onions, chopped
1  bunch celery, chopped
1  can pimentos, chopped
1  can whole mushrooms
   Chicken stock
1  package spaghetti
   Salt
   Pepper
   Accent
   Soy Sauce

Cook hen in seasoned water and leave in broth to cool. Debone hen when cooled and reserve stock. Cut meat into bite size pieces. Cook the bell pepper, onions and celery in 1 cup of chicken stock. Cook the spaghetti in rest of chicken stock until tender. You will find you absorb all the stock. Toss all together and add the pimentos and mushrooms. Season to taste with salt, pepper and Accent. This is very good and different chicken spaghetti. Pass soy sauce.

# CHICKEN AND ASPARAGUS CASSEROLE OLÉ

*A Real Crowd Pleaser! A Good Company Dish*

If large breasts are used this will serve 12.

| | |
|---|---|
| 6 | whole chicken breasts |
| 1 | medium onion, chopped |
| ½ | cup butter |
| 1 | 8–ounce can mushrooms |
| 1 | can cream of mushroom soup |
| 1 | can cream of chicken soup |
| 1 | 5⅓ ounce can milk |
| ½ | pound sharp Cheddar cheese, grated |
| ¼ | teaspoon Tabasco |
| 2 | teaspoons soy sauce |
| 1 | teaspoon salt |
| ½ | teaspoon pepper |
| 1 | teaspoon Accent |
| 2 | Tablespoons pimento, chopped |
| 2 | cans green tip asparagus |
| ½ | cup slivered almonds |

Boil chicken breasts in seasoned water until tender. Cool, debone and tear into bite size pieces. Set aside. Sauté onion in butter and add remaining ingredients, except asparagus and almonds. Simmer sauce until the cheese melts. To assemble; place a layer of chicken in a large casserole, a layer of asparagus and a layer of sauce. Repeat layers ending with sauce. Top with almonds. Bake at 350 degrees until bubbly. Do not add liquid even if it looks dry. Freezes well.

## CHICKEN SPECTACULAR

Serves 16.

3   cups cooked chicken
1   package Uncle Ben's
    Combination Wild
    and White Rice,
    cooked
1   can cream of celery
    soup
1   medium jar sliced
    pimentos
1   medium onion,
    chopped
2   cups French style
    green beans,
    drained
1   cup Hellmann's
    mayonnaise
1   cup water chestnuts,
    diced
    Salt and pepper, to
    taste

Mix all ingredients. Pour into a 2½ or 3 quart casserole. Bake 25 to 30 minutes at 350 degrees. Do not cook prior to freezing.

# KING RANCH CHICKEN

*A Mexican party must!*

*Serve with <u>Mexican Salad</u>, <u>Salsa</u> and Tortilla Chips*

Serves 8 to 10.

| | |
|---|---|
| 1 | **3 to 4 pound hen** |
| 1 | **onion** |
| 1 | **or 2 ribs celery** |
| | **Salt and pepper** |
| 1 | **onion, chopped** |
| ½ | **cup cilantro chopped** |
| 1 | **large bell pepper, chopped** |
| 1 | **can chopped green chilies** |
| 1 | **can mushroom soup** |
| 1 | **can cream of chicken soup** |
| ½ | **pound Cheddar, grated** |
| | **Chili powder** |
| | **Cumin** |
| | **Garlic salt** |
| 1 | **package corn tortillas** |
| 1 | **can Rotel Tomatoes and Chilies, undrained** |

Boil hen until tender in water seasoned with onion, celery, salt and pepper. Cut chicken into bite size pieces and reserve all defatted stock. Chop onion and bell pepper, combine soups and grated cheese. Just before putting casserole together, soak the frozen tortillas in boiling chicken stock until wilted. Start layering casserole in a 9 x 12 inch baking dish in this order: Tortillas "dripping with stock", chicken, onion, bell pepper, sprinkling to taste with chili powder, Cumin, and garlic salt, soup mixture and cheese. Repeat layers, being sure the tortillas are oozing with the stock. Cover the casserole with the Rotel tomatoes and all the juice. Juices in the casserole should be about half of the depth of the dish; if not, add a little more stock. May be made and frozen several days ahead, but always make at least one day

*(Continued on next page)*

*(King Ranch Chicken, continued)*

ahead and refrigerate so that the flavors will blend. Bake in covered casserole at 375 degrees for 30 minutes. Secret: a well seasoned stock. Do not over cook.

## CHICKEN DIVAN

5    **chicken breasts, cooked and deboned**
2    **10–ounce packages broccoli, thawed**
2    **cups cream of chicken soup**
1    **cup real mayonnaise**
1    **teaspoon lemon juice**
½    **to 1 teaspoon curry powder**
½    **cup sharp Cheddar cheese**
½    **cup soft bread crumbs**
1    **Tablespoon butter or margarine**

Barely cook broccoli in salt water 1–3 minutes. Drain. Grease an 11 x 7½ x 1½ inch baking dish. Place chicken on top of broccoli. Combine soup, mayonnaise, curry powder and pour over chicken. Sprinkle with cheese. Combine melted butter and bread crumbs. Sprinkle over dish. Bake at 350 for 30 minutes.

# CHICKEN TETRAZZINI

1  3 to 4 pound hen
1  onion
1  bay leaf
2  ribs celery
   Salt and pepper
1  stick butter
1  bunch green onion,
     chopped
1  bell pepper, chopped
1  large can mushrooms
½  cup chopped parsley
½  cup chopped celery
1  clove garlic, pressed
1  cup cream
1  cup stock
2  Tablespoons white
     wine or sherry
1  Tablespoon lemon
     juice
2  cans cream of
     chicken soup
1  cup sour cream
12 ounces thin
     spaghetti
   Parmesan cheese

Boil hen until tender with onion, bay leaf, celery, salt and pepper. Cool, debone and cut into bite size pieces. Melt butter in skillet and sauté all the vegetables until tender. About 10 minutes. Add cream, stock, wine, lemon juice, soups and sour cream. Cook spaghetti in left over chicken stock, just until done. Drain and combine with chicken mixture or all ingredients and place in a buttered casserole. Sprinkle with Parmesan cheese and bake uncovered in a 300 degree oven, about 30 minutes or until hot. This freezes well.

# CHICKEN–N–DUMPLINGS

Serves 4.

| | |
|---|---|
| 1 | **fryer, cut into pieces** |
| 1 | **medium onion** |
| 2 | **ribs celery** |
| | **Salt and pepper to taste** |
| 1 | **cup flour** |
| ¼ | **teaspoon salt** |
| ⅛ | **teaspoon baking powder** |
| 1 | **Tablespoon Crisco** |
| 1 | **egg yolk** |
| ¼ | **cup broth or milk** |
| 1 | **egg, hard boiled** |

Boil the chicken in water seasoned with onion, celery, salt and pepper. To make the dumplings, mix flour, salt, baking powder and Crisco together. Add egg yolk and mix well. Add ¼ cup broth or milk to make a dough. Roll the dough thin on a floured surface and cut into squares. Lay the squares on waxed paper for 30 minutes or more to dry out. Remove the chicken from the stock, bring the stock to a boil and drop the dumplings in. You may add a small amount of milk or a hard boiled egg to the broth. Return the chicken to the pot, cover and let cook for approximately 10 minutes or until dumplings are tender. I always serve my dumplings with Lady Peas, candied sweet potatoes and a green salad. A short, short, short cut and good – use flour tortillas cut in strips to make the dumplings.

# WHITE CHILI

Serves 8 to 10.

1    **pound white beans, soaked overnight**
6    **cups chicken broth**
2    **cloves garlic, minced**
2    **medium onions, chopped (divided)**
1    **Tablespoon oil**
2    **(4 ounce) cans chopped green chilies**
2    **teaspoons ground cumin**
¼    **teaspoon ground cloves**
1½   **teaspoons dried oregano**
¼    **teaspoon cayenne pepper**
4    **cups diced cooked chicken breasts**
3    **cups grated Monterey Jack cheese**

Combine beans (drained), chicken broth, half of the onions and garlic in large pot and bring to a boil. Simmer until beans are very soft. Add more broth if necessary. Sauté remaining onions in oil until tender. Add chilies and seasonings; mix thoroughly. Add to bean mixture. Add chicken and continue to simmer 1 hour. Serve with Monterey Jack Cheese and chopped green onions. This is Charlie Petty's, our San Antonio connection.

# GOURMET CHICKEN LIVERS AND ONIONS

*Perfect! Elegant! I love this for brunch or Sunday supper!*

| | |
|---|---|
| 3 | or 4 medium size white onions |
| 10 | to 12 chicken livers |
| 3 | large strips bacon |
| ¼ | to ½ cup sherry, or to taste |
| | Salt and pepper, to taste |

Slice the onions ¼ inch thick and arrange in a flat baking dish, 3 quart size or larger. On top of each onion, place 1 chicken liver and salt lightly. Cut strips of bacon in 4 pieces, if bacon comes in smaller strips, use enough for each onion and liver to be covered. Salt and pepper generously. Pour sherry over all. Bake, uncovered, in a moderate oven, 350 degrees. Baste occasionally with pan drippings, until bacon begins to crisp, about 45 minutes. This is a good way to use chicken livers when chickens have been used for a barbecue. Serve with grits and baked bananas.

# COQ AU VIN

*A Country French Chicken*

1   fryer, cut up (remove most of the skin and as much fat as possible)
½   cup flour
Salt and pepper
3   slices bacon
3   Tablespoons flour
Bacon drippings
1   large onion, sliced
1   cup mushrooms
½   teaspoon thyme leaves
1   bay leaf
½   cup chopped parsley
3   cloves garlic, chopped
4   or 5 carrots, halved
1   cup chicken broth
1   cup burgundy wine

Salt, pepper chicken and coat with flour. Fry bacon in a large skillet until crisp; remove and brown chicken in bacon fat. Remove. Add flour to drippings and brown. Add onion, mushrooms, thyme, bay leaves, parsley, and garlic. Mix well. Add broth, burgundy, carrots, and chicken. Cover and simmer about 1 hour. Check seasonings. Spoon off any fat. So, so good, and better the next day. A good do ahead dinner party...winner! Serve with lots of hot crusty French bread.

From
the
Hearth

LYoung

American Indians danced the "Bread Dance" for prosperity and good crops.

Break bread with friends.

# HOME–STYLE BREAD

*Enjoy when fresh...with lots of butter and Mayhaw jelly. Wonderful for sandwiches and toast.*

| | |
|---|---|
| 2 | **packages yeast** |
| ½ | **cup warm water** |
| ⅔ | **cup Crisco** |
| 2 | **cups scalded milk** |
| ½ | **cup sugar** |
| 1 | **Tablespoon salt** |
| 1 | **egg** |
| 7 | **to 9 cups flour (sometimes, I use half wheat!)** |

Dissolve yeast in lukewarm water. Melt Crisco; add scalded milk, salt and sugar. Cool to lukewarm. In large bowl of mixer, combine yeast, egg and milk mixture with enough flour to make a soft dough, about 2 to 3 cups. Beat until dough looks elastic. Add enough flour to make a stiff dough. Knead dough until it is smooth. Put in a greased bowl; cover and let rise until doubled. Grease three 9 x 5 inch pans. Shape the dough into three loaves. Brush top of loaves with melted butter; cover and let rise until doubled. Bake at 350 degrees for about 35 minutes or until done.

**Tips:** When kneading, punch your finger into dough, if the dough springs back out, it has been

*(Continued on next page)*

*(Home–Style Bread, continued)*

kneaded enough. When rising, if you punch your finger in it; it has risen enough. Remember...proof the yeast!

Proofing the yeast means testing it to make sure it is still active. To do this, pour the contents of the package into ½ cup of the warm milk (about 100 to 115 degrees), add the sugar, stir well, and set aside. After a few minutes the fermentation of the yeast will become apparent as the mixture swells and small bubbles appear here and there on the surface.

You can be a Star!

# GRAN MERE'S ICE BOX ROLLS

*Oh the smell of fresh baked bread...Mmm! Your whole dinner can be a disaster but if you have wonderful homemade breads, rolls or biscuits you are saved – praise the Lord!*

*These are the best – never fail!*

| | |
|---|---|
| 1 | package dry yeast |
| 1 | cup warm water |
| ½ | cup shortening |
| ¼ | cup sugar |
| 1 | egg |
| 1 | teaspoon salt |
| 3 | cups flour or half whole wheat |

Dissolve yeast in warm water. Cream shortening with sugar, beat in egg, add yeast mixture and beat until well mixed. Add salt and flour working in until a smooth dough is formed. Place in a bowl, cover with Saran Wrap and refrigerate until ready to use. Roll and form rolls. Let rise for 1½ hours. Bake in a 350 degree oven for 15 minutes.

**Egg Washes:**
1. Whole egg beaten with 1 teaspoon cream or milk gives a shiny, medium–brown glaze.
2. Egg yolk beaten with 1 teaspoon cream or milk gives the shiniest, brownest glaze.
3. Egg white beaten with 1 teaspoon water gives shine without browness.

# ANGEL BISCUITS

1 package dry yeast
¼ cup warm water
2½ cups flour
½ teaspoon baking soda
1 teaspoon baking powder
1 teaspoon salt
⅛ cup sugar
½ cup shortening
1 cup buttermilk

Dissolve the yeast in warm water, setting aside. Mix the dry ingredients in the order given, cutting in the shortening as you normally do for biscuits or pie dough. Stir in the buttermilk and the yeast mixture. Blend thoroughly and the dough is ready to refrigerate or roll out into biscuits.

When you're ready to make these delicious biscuits, turn the dough onto a floured board and knead lightly for regular biscuits. Roll out and cut with a biscuit cutter, placing them in a greased pan.

Let the dough rise slightly before baking in a 400 degree oven for about 12 to 15 minutes until lightly browned and done. If the dough is cold, you'll need to let it set a little longer to rise.

Great for breakfast, lunch and supper. Your family will love you for making these!

# CHALLAH

*(from Gottlieb's Bakery 100 year old recipe)*

1½ **cups warm water
     (120 – 130 degrees)**
3    **tablespoons yeast**
½    **cup sugar**
½    **cup vegetable oil**
2    **eggs**
1    **Tablespoon salt**
5    **to 6 cups unbleached
     flour**
     **Egg wash: 1 yolk
     mixed with 1
     Tablespoon of water**

Put 5 cups of flour in mixing bowl with yeast and mix for 30 seconds.

Add sugar and salt and mix for another 30 seconds. Next add all the water, egg and vegetable oil.

Mix until well blended with paddle attachment of mixer. When well blended, switch to dough hook and add another cup of flour. Knead dough for another 10 minutes. Place dough in a well oiled bowl, turning to coat all sides.

Cover with saran wrap that has been oiled and let rise until double in size in a draft–free place.

When the dough has doubled in size, punch down and divide in half.

Divide each half into 4 or 6 equal pieces and roll out like sausages. Now braid. If you can't braid with 4, 3 will do just fine.

Place on greased baking sheets, cover loosely with

*(Continued on next page)*

*(Challah, continued)*

plastic wrap. Spray the bread first with Pam before placing plastic wrap over it. Let it rise until double in size. Brush with egg wash and bake in a preheated 375 degree oven until golden brown and hollow sounding when tapped. Bake about 30 minutes. Cool on wire racks.

**Shabbat Shalom! Eat and Enjoy!**

Be gentle when you touch the bread.

Let it not lie uncared for, unwanted.

So often bread is taken for granted.

There is much beauty in the bread –

Beauty of sun and soil,

Beauty of patient toil.

Winds and rains has caressed it,

Christ often blessed it.

Be gentle when you touch the bread.

AUTHOR UNKNOWN

# RUSTIC COUNTRY BREAD

*This is Jane Sartor's bread and it is well worth the time. You think you are in the South of France dipping this hot crusty bread in extra virgin olive oil, or sopping up gravy from your Osso Buco or your Cassoulet...Unbelievable and fun to make! This bread is so pretty. My friend Shirley Brown likes to bake it and puts it in a big old wooden bowl for decoration in her beautiful South of France kitchen. Think how good her house smells when the bread is baking.*

## The Sponge:
½  teaspoon active dry yeast (not rapid–rise)
1  cup bread flour
1  cup whole wheat flour

## The Dough:
3½  cups bread flour
½  cup rye flour
2  Tablespoons honey
1  Tablespoon kosher salt or 2 teaspoons table salt
    Coarse cornmeal for sprinkling on peel

*For the sponge*, dissolve yeast into 1 cup tap water in medium–size bowl. Mix in flours with rubber spatula to create stiff, wet dough. Cover with plastic wrap; let sit at room temperature for at least 5 hours, preferably overnight. (Can be refrigerated up to 24 hours; return to room temperature before continuing with recipe.)

*For the dough*, mix flours, 1⅓ cups tap water, honey, and sponge with rubber spatula in the bowl of an electric mixer. Knead, using dough hook attachment, on lowest speed until dough is smooth, about 15 minutes, adding salt during final 3 minutes. Transfer dough to large, lightly oiled bowl.

*(Continued on next page)*

*(Rustic Country Bread, continued)*

Cover with plastic wrap; let rise until tripled in size, at least 2 hours.

Turn dough onto lightly floured surface. Divide into 2 balls. Lightly dust hands and top of dough with flour. Lightly press dough balls into a large disk. Fold toward center, overlapping edges slightly. Transfer dough, smooth side down, to colander or basket lined with heavily floured muslin. Cover loosely with large sheet of aluminum foil; let rise until almost doubled in size, at least 45 minutes.

As soon as dough begins to rise, adjust oven rack to low–center position and arrange quarry tiles on rack to form 18 x 12 inch surface (or larger). On lowest oven rack, place small baking pan or cast–iron skillet to hold water. Heat oven to 450 degrees.

Sprinkle coarse cornmeal liberally over entire surface of peel. Invert dough onto peel and remove muslin. Use scissors or serrated knife to cut three slashes on top of dough.

Slide dough from peel onto tiles. Carefully add 2 cups hot water to pan or cast–iron skillet. Bake until instant read thermometer inserted in bread registers 210 degrees and crust is very dark brown, 35 to 45 minutes, turning bread around after 25 minutes if not browning evenly. Turn oven off, open door, and let bread remain in oven 10 minutes longer. Remove from oven, then let cool to room temperature before slicing, about 2 hours. To crisp crust, warm in 400 degree oven for 10 minutes.

Whole wheat and rye flours contribute to this bread's full flavor, and extra oven time gives the bread its thick crust. Because of its high water content, the bread will be gummy if it is undercooked.

**Note:** To help ensure a good crust, preheat a pan; fill it with warm water, and set it on the oven's lower rack. Also, to check bread for doneness, remove it from the oven and use a digital thermometer to check the temperature.

## ASPHODEL BREAD

*Asphodel is a plantation home near Jackson, Louisiana. This light bread from the Asphodel kitchen is famous statewide.*

Makes 2 loaves

5    **cups Pioneer Biscuit Mix**
4    **Tablespoons sugar**
½    **teaspoon salt**
2    **envelopes yeast**
2    **cups warm milk**
4    **eggs**
¼    **teaspoon cream of tartar**

Into very large bowl sift the biscuit mix, sugar, and salt. Soften the yeast in warm milk. If the milk is too hot, it will kill the yeast. Beat egg with the cream of tartar. Combine milk and eggs and pour into the dry ingredients. "Stir," do not use a mixer. This is a heavy, sticky mixture that must be mixed well. Set in a warm place and cover with a damp dish towel, or seal with plastic wrap. When doubled in bulk, punch down and place into two greased 9 x 5 x 3 loaf pans. Let double in size before baking in a 350 degree oven. Serve very hot! This bread freezes well. Thaw completely before reheating.

# ENGLISH MUFFIN BREAD

1   **package dry yeast**
1¼ **cups warm water**
1   **Tablespoon sugar**
½   **teaspoon salt**
1   **Tablespoon cornmeal**
2½ **to 3 cups flour**

Mix yeast with 1 cup flour. Heat water, sugar and salt until warm. Mix liquid with flour and yeast until blended. Add the remaining flour ½ cup at a time until soft dough is formed. Place in large greased bowl; cover and let rise in a warm place for one hour. Punch the dough down and let rest for 10 minutes. Place dough in a greased casserole sprinkled with ¾ Tablespoon cornmeal. Sprinkle the top of the bread with the remaining cornmeal. Let rise for one hour. Bake in a 400 degree oven for 45 minutes. If the top browns too quickly, cover with foil.

# DILLY CASSEROLE BREAD

| | |
|---|---|
| 1 | package dry yeast |
| ¼ | cup warm water |
| 1 | cup creamed cottage cheese |
| 2 | Tablespoons sugar |
| 1 | Tablespoon instant minced onion |
| 2 | teaspoons dill seed |
| 1 | Tablespoon butter |
| ¼ | teaspoon soda |
| 1 | teaspoon salt |
| 1 | egg |
| 2¼ | cups flour |

Soften yeast in warm water. Heat cheese to lukewarm; combine in a mixing bowl with sugar, onion, dill, butter, salt, soda, egg and yeast. Add flour to form soft dough, beating well. Cover, let rise until double in bulk, about 1 hour. Beat down dough. Put in a greased 1½ quart round casserole. Let rise until light, 40 minutes. Bake at 350 degrees until golden brown, 40 to 50 minutes. Brush with melted butter, sprinkle with salt. Serve warm.

# RAISIN ZUCCHINI BREAD

Yield: 2 loaves.

| | |
|---|---|
| 2 | medium zucchini |
| 2 | cups sugar |
| 1 | cup oil |
| 3 | eggs, beaten |
| 1 | Tablespoon vanilla extract |
| 3 | cups flour |
| 1 | Tablespoon cinnamon |
| 1 | teaspoon salt |
| 1 | teaspoon baking soda |
| 1 | teaspoon baking powder |
| 1 | cup Del Monte Seedless Raisins |
| 1 | cup chopped pecans |

Finely shred zucchini to measure 2 cups; set aside. Cream sugar and oil. Add eggs, zucchini and vanilla; mix well. Combine flour, cinnamon, salt, baking soda and baking powder; mix well. Add raisins and nuts to dry ingredients. Combine with zucchini mixture; mix well. Pour into two greased and floured 9 x 5–inch loaf pans. Bake at 350 degrees for 1 hour or until tests done. Let stand 10 minutes; turn out on wire rack to cool.

# PUMPKIN BREAD
# OR SWEET POTATO BREAD

*Our daughter Sara bakes this pumpkin bread during the Thanksgiving and Christmas holidays and shares with all her friends and family. Glad I am on her list!*

3 eggs
1½ cups sugar
1½ cups pumpkin or
   sweet potato
1 cup plus 2
   Tablespoons
   Wesson oil
1½ teaspoons vanilla
2¼ cups flour
1½ teaspoons baking
   soda
1½ teaspoons baking
   powder
1½ teaspoons salt
1½ teaspoons cinnamon
¼ teaspoon cloves
¼ teaspoon ginger
¼ teaspoon nutmeg
1 cup chopped pecans

Beat eggs and sugar together well. Add pumpkin, oil and vanilla, mix thoroughly. Sift flour, soda, baking powder, salt and spices. Add to pumpkin mixture and beat. Add pecans. Bake at 350 degrees for one hour in two well greased loaf pans. This freezes well and is wonderful sliced thin and spread with softened cream cheese for tea sandwiches.

# POPOVERS

*These are always served at the Neiman Marcus Tea Room!*

2  eggs
1  cup milk
1  cup sifted flour
½  teaspoon salt
1  Tablespoon melted
   butter

Beat all ingredients 1 to 2 minutes. (I whip mine in the blender.) Cover and chill in blender for at least 2 hours. About ½ hour before you want to serve, beat or whirl batter vigorously, again. In a preheated 450 degree oven, place the well greased muffin tins until they become sizzling hot! Pour cold batter into <u>hot</u> greased tins – about ½ full. Bake at 450 degrees for 15 minutes. Reduce heat to 350 degrees and bake 10 to 15 minutes longer. A few minutes before removing from oven, prick each popover with a fork to allow steam to escape. Serve with plenty of butter and honey!

# LOUISIANA BLUEBERRY ORANGE MUFFINS

*Liz Cage makes the best muffins of all!*

Makes 24 muffins or 1 loaf.

3   cups all–purpose flour
4   teaspoons baking powder
¼   teaspoon baking soda
¾   cup sugar
1½  teaspoons salt
2   eggs
¾   cup milk
½   cup butter, melted
1   Tablespoon grated orange peel
½   cup orange juice
1½  Tablespoons lemon juice
1   cup fresh blueberries

Preheat oven to 425 degrees. Sift flour, baking powder, soda, sugar and salt. Add blueberries and toss until coated. In another bowl, mix remaining ingredients. Pour liquid mixture into dry ingredients and stir. Fill greased muffin tin ⅔ full. Bake for 20 minutes. Variation: pour batter into a 9 x 5 inch loaf pan and bake in a preheated 350 degree oven for 70 minutes.

# APPLE BRAN MUFFINS

*Like Grandmother said, an apple a day...*

*Although no food can ensure perfect health, apples can play an important role in a healthy diet. October arrives with its Red Delicious, Golden Delicious, McIntosh, Rome Beauty, Granny Smith, Jonathan, Winesap, and Arkansas Black. Aren't we lucky!*

Makes 24 muffins.

| | |
|---|---|
| 2 | **cups whole wheat flour** |
| 1½ | **cups wheat bran** |
| ½ | **teaspoon salt** |
| 1 | **Tablespoon grated orange rind – That is the zest (just the orange color – not the white – Egg head!)** |
| 1 | **cup chopped apple** |
| ½ | **cup blackstrap molasses** |
| 1¼ | **teaspoons baking soda** |
| ½ | **cup raisins** |
| ½ | **cup chopped nuts juice of 1 orange scant 2 cups buttermilk** |
| 2 | **beaten eggs** |
| 2 | **Tablespoons oil** |
| ½ | **teaspoon nutmeg** |

Preheat oven to 350 degrees. Toss flour, bran, salt, soda and nutmeg together. Stir in orange rind, apples, raisins and nuts. Pour the juice of 1 orange into a 2–cup measure and add buttermilk to make 2 cups. Add to eggs, molasses and oil; Stir thoroughly. Stir liquid ingredients into dry ingredients with a few swift strokes. Pour into greased muffin tins, filling them ⅔ full, and bake for 25 minutes.

Eating an apple gives you high fiber and cleans your teeth.

# OVERNIGHT COFFEE CAKE

*This recipe is Johnnie and Dick Nealy's of Ruston –*
*Debbie's Mama and Daddy!*

*If you have house guests or an early morning meeting*
*and need something wonderful. Try this! Just to die for –*
*so good – easy and pretty!*

1   **package (24) frozen dinner rolls**
½   **cup white sugar**
1½  **teaspoons cinnamon**
½   **cup chopped pecans**
½   **cup brown sugar**
1   **package (4 servings) dry butterscotch pudding mix (not instant)**
1   **stick plus 2 Tablespoons butter**

Grease Bundt pan, mix cinnamon and white sugar. Roll the frozen rolls in sugar and cinnamon. Place in Bundt pan. Combine brown sugar and pudding mix sprinkle over rolls. Sprinkle nuts over this and cinnamon and sugar that was left. Dot with butter. Cover and let rise overnight. Bake at 350 degrees for 35–45 minutes.

# MORAVIAN SUGAR CAKE

*(From my good friend Carol Cole Nies and her mother, Irene.)*

**Cake:**

| | |
|---|---|
| 1 | **package active dry yeast** |
| ½ | **teaspoon granulated sugar** |
| 1 | **cup warm (105–115 degrees F.) water** |
| 3½ | **cups all–purpose flour** |
| ¼ | **cup instant non fat dry milk** |
| ⅓ | **cup mashed potato flakes** |
| ⅓ | **cup granulated sugar** |
| ¾ | **teaspoon salt** |
| 2 | **eggs, room temperature** |
| ½ | **cup butter or margarine, softened** |

**Topping:**

| | |
|---|---|
| 1 | **Tablespoon milk** |
| 1 | **cup light brown sugar** |
| 1 | **teaspoon ground cinnamon** |
| ½ | **cup butter, melted and cooled** |

In a large bowl, dissolve yeast in water with ½ teaspoon sugar added. Add 2 cups flour, the milk, potato flakes, sugar, salt, eggs, and butter. With mixer set at medium speed, beat 5 minutes. Stir in remaining flour to make a very soft dough. Beat well. Cover and let rise in a warm place (85 degrees F.) until doubled, about 2 hours. (If you have time, beat down and let rise again, about 1 hour.) With floured hands, spread dough evenly in a greased 17 x 11 x 1–inch baking pan. Cover and let rise until light, about 1 hour.

Heat oven to 375 degrees F. Brush dough with milk. Combine brown sugar and cinnamon and sprinkle evenly on dough. With floured finger–tips make shallow indentions in dough 1 to 2 inches apart. Drizzle with butter. Bake at 375 degrees for 15 minutes.

# AUSTRIAN TWISTS

*From the files of Irene Cole, the best bread baker I know.*

Yield: 64 twists.

| | |
|---|---|
| 1 | package dry yeast |
| 3 | cups all purpose flour |
| 1 | cup butter, softened |
| 3 | egg yolks |
| 1 | (8 ounce) carton commercial sour cream |
| ½ | cup sugar |
| ½ | cup chopped pecans |
| ¾ | teaspoon cinnamon |
| | Powdered sugar glaze |

**Glaze:**

| | |
|---|---|
| 2 | cups powdered sugar |
| 3 | Tablespoons milk |

Combine yeast and flour; add butter, mixing well. Stir in egg yolks and sour cream. Shape dough into 4 balls; wrap in waxed paper, and refrigerate overnight.

Combine sugar, pecans, and cinnamon. Set aside. Work with 1 portion of dough at a time. Place on a lightly floured surface and shape into circles. Spread ¼ cup sugar mixture evenly over each circle and cut into 16 equal wedges. Roll up each wedge, beginning at wide end and rolling to point; seal points firmly. Place on greased baking sheet, point side down. Bake at 350 degrees for 18 minutes or lightly browned. Sprinkle and glaze.

# CORNBREAD

*(Light as a feather – Boo Payne does this best!)*

1   cup cream corn
1   cup sour cream
2   eggs
½   cup vegetable oil
1   cup self–rising
      cornmeal
2   teaspoons baking
      powder
1   teaspoon salt

Mix. Pour into a hot, well greased black iron skillet. Bake at 400 degrees for 30 minutes. So light — wonderful.

# THE ORIGINAL MEXICAN CORNBREAD

Makes one 10½ inch round – or you can do muffins.

1½  cups cornmeal
1   cup cream style corn
1   cup sour cream –
      light
¼   cup salad oil
2   eggs
3   teaspoons baking
      powder
1   teaspoon salt
3   or 4 Jalapeño
      peppers, chopped –
      – to taste
2   Tablespoons minced
      bell pepper
1   cup sharp cheese,
      grated

Mix in order listed, but do not mix cheese. Pour half of mixture in a hot, well greased iron skillet. Sprinkle ½ of cheese over this. Add remaining mix. Cover with cheese. Bake at 350 degrees for 35 or 40 minutes.

# BROCCOLI CORN BREAD

1   stick butter
4   eggs
1   large onion (chopped)
1   package frozen
      chopped broccoli or
      about 1½ cups
      fresh (cook just
      before done),
      drained well
1   teaspoon salt
1   cup cottage cheese
1   box Jiffy corn bread
      mix
    Tabasco

Melt butter in a 9 x 3 inch Pyrex dish in a 350 degree oven. Beat eggs. Add all ingredients in order. Mix well. Pour into the fairly hot Pyrex dish over the melted butter. Slowly stir in butter. Bake in a 350 degree oven for about 40 minutes or until done.

# CRAWFISH CORNBREAD

1½  cups yellow cornmeal
1   teaspoon salt
1   teaspoon baking
      powder
½   teaspoon baking soda
3   eggs
½   cup chopped
      jalapeño peppers–or
      to taste
½   cup chopped bell
      pepper
1   small onion, chopped
1   cup grated cheddar
      cheese
⅓   cup oil
1   large can cream–
      style corn
1   pound crawfish tails

In a large bowl combine dry ingredients. In a medium bowl, beat eggs thoroughly. Add other ingredients to eggs. Add egg mixture to cornmeal mixture. Mix well. Pour into a well greased, hot 9 x 13 inch baking dish. Bake at 375 degrees for 30 minutes or until golden brown.

**Note:** Can substitute with egg beaters and fat free cheese. This was made for a tailgate party—quick, easy, and a big hit. Good at room temperature!

# OLD FASHIONED HOT WATER HOECAKES

1   **cup cornmeal**
1   **cup boiling water**
    **cold water**
½   **cup finely chopped bell pepper and hot pepper**
½   **cup finely chopped green onions**
½   **teaspoon salt**

Pour hot water over meal and mix. Add enough cold water to make consistency desired. You may like individual drop cakes and or a hoecake (thin). I also use less cold water and make into small pones (about the size of small egg). Fry in hot skillet with about ½ inch of bacon drippings or other oil. Brown one side, then turn and brown other. Pones are turned until brown and crusty all over. Fine with vegetables or fish.

## MAMMY'S SPOON BREAD

1 cup cornmeal
4 cups milk
4 eggs, separated
1 Tablespoon butter or margarine
1¾ teaspoons salt

Heat milk. Add to cornmeal and salt. Stir till smooth. Cook 5 minutes stirring constantly. Add butter, then cool. Beat yolks until light and lemon colored. Add to meal mixture. Beat whites until stiff. Fold into cornmeal mixture. Pour into a greased 2–quart Pyrex dish. Bake at 400 degrees F. for 45 minutes over a pan of hot water. Serve hot, and serve at once. Very Southern – light as a soufflé.

## LOUISIANA BLUEBERRY CORNMEAL PANCAKES

Serves 6–8.

1 cup flour
1 cup cornmeal
½ teaspoon salt
2 Tablespoons baking powder
3 Tablespoons sugar
3 Tablespoons vegetable oil
1 beaten egg
1½ cups orange juice
1 cup fresh blueberries
Blueberry syrup

In a medium bowl, mix together flour, cornmeal, salt, baking powder and sugar. Add oil, egg and juice. Mix well. Fold in blueberries. Heat a lightly greased medium–size griddle to medium high. Pour batter onto griddle using approximately ¼ cup for each pancake. Cook until bubbles appear. Flip pancakes over and cook until done. Serve with hot blueberry syrup.

## JALAPEÑO HUSHPUPPIES

*"The World's Best"*

2   **cups cornmeal**
1   **cup flour**
2   **eggs, beaten**
3   **teaspoons baking powder**
1½  **teaspoons salt**
1   **small can cream style corn**
3   **jalapeño peppers, chopped**
¼   **bell pepper, chopped**
1   **small onion, minced**
    **Buttermilk**
    **Pinch of soda**

Mix all ingredients. Use enough buttermilk to make this the consistency of cornbread batter. Test batter by scooping up a portion on a spoon and with your thumb, push portion into medium hot grease. **The object of this recipe is to have light, fluffy, hushpuppies.** If heavy and do not rise enough, use more baking powder. If hushpuppies are greasy and break apart, add more flour. If you want more tang, add some jalapeño pepper juice.

If you can find David Beard's hushpuppies from Catfish King in the frozen food section of the grocery, they are wonderful!

What a time saver!

A Feast of Relishes Jelly & Preserves

L.Young

# PEAR CHUTNEY

*Fun to make and so good. Makes you proud!*

9   pounds firm, unripe pears, peeled, cored and chopped (about 30)
5   onions, chopped
5   garlic pods, chopped
1   quart cider vinegar
1   pound seedless, golden raisins
1   pound currants
1   pound light brown sugar
1   pound white sugar
2½  Tablespoons salt
1   teaspoon cayenne pepper
2   teaspoons paprika
4   ounces mustard seed
1   cup orange marmalade (or frozen orange juice, undiluted)
1   Tablespoon grated orange rind
2   limes (or lemons) sliced thin
2   Tablespoons curry powder
3   Tablespoons candied ginger, chopped
1½  teaspoons each of: cinnamon, cloves, allspice, and nutmeg

Simmer vinegar and sugar in large enamel pot for about 15 minutes, then add all above ingredients and cook slowly for 1 hour. Add ½ pound dried apples, chopped, and ½ pound dried apricots, chopped. Cook about 30 minutes until thick. The dried fruit thickens the chutney and gives it texture. 1 cup sherry wine may be added after chutney is off the fire, if desired. Put into sterilized jars and seal. This is perfect with Curry or roast beef, a pork roast, ham, or turkey. Let the rich flavor of this chutney crown your next meal.

## DILLED OKRA

1    teaspoon dill seed
1    hot red pepper
1    hot green pepper
2    cloves garlic
1    quart white vinegar
1    cup water
½    cup uniodized salt
     Okra – trim top, do
        not cut off

Place ½ teaspoon dill seed in bottom of each jar, then pack fresh washed okra in as tightly as possible, being careful not to bruise okra. Add ½ teaspoon dill seed, peppers and garlic. Bring to boil the vinegar, water and salt. Cover okra with mixture; seal jars and allow to stand 2 weeks. Serve icy cold.

## CARROT PICKLES

Yield: about 3 pints.

2    to 3 pounds small
        carrots
2    cups vinegar
1½   cups water
1    cup sugar
1    teaspoon salt
1    Tablespoon mixed
        pickling spices
1    stick cinnamon

Cook carrots until just tender. Drain and remove skins. Leave small carrots whole; cut larger ones into pieces as desired. Combine vinegar, water, sugar and salt. Tie remaining spices in a cheesecloth bag; add to vinegar mixture. Boil 5 to 8 minutes. Pack carrots into hot jars, leaving ¼–inch head space. Remove spice bag. Bring pickling liquid to a boil. Pour hot liquid over carrots, leaving ¼–inch head space. Remove air bubbles. Adjust caps. Process pints and quarts 30 minutes in boiling water bath.

# UNSEALED VIDALIA ONION PICKLES

*Dianne's, Friend of Arlene*
*Arlene's Husband*
*Gail's Cousin Marie*
*Harie's Neighbor*
*Bernadette's Friend Sara's*
*Husband Bob's Great–Grandfather's Recipe!!*

Makes 6 pints.

**Day One:**
4½   pounds Vidalia onions, sliced thinly and packed into 1–gallon jar (glass)
⅓   cup plain salt
    Boiling water to cover (leave unsealed)

**Mix:**
1   quart white vinegar
1   cup sugar
1   Tablespoon mustard seed
1   Tablespoon pickling spice (tie in muslin)
1   Tablespoon alum
1   Tablespoon celery seed

**Day Two:**
Drain. Do Not Rinse.

Bring vinegar, sugar, mustard seed, pickling spice, alum, and celery seed to boil. Pour over onions. Do Not Stir.

**Day Three:**
Add 1 cup sugar. Do Not Stir.

**Day Four:**
Add 1 cup sugar. Do Not Stir.

**Day Five:**
Add 1 cup sugar. Do Not Stir.

**Day Six:**
Add 1 cup sugar. Do Not Stir.

**Day Seven:**
Add 1 cup sugar. Do Not Stir.

**Day Eight:**
Stir Only. Transfer to pickle jars and store in a dark place... "Refrigerator".

# HOT SWEET PICKLES

*So easy and a favorite!*

1   gallon sour or dill
     pickles, drained
     and sliced
5   pounds sugar
     Crushed red pepper
     Garlic pods, sliced
     (5 or 6)

Alternate sliced pickles, sugar, red pepper and garlic. Let stand about a week, turning jar once each day until sugar dissolves.

# GREEN TOMATO RELISH

Yield: 6 pints.

6   green peppers,
     chopped
3   hot peppers, chopped
12  green tomatoes,
     chopped
6   onions, chopped
½   cup salt
3   cups sugar
1   quart vinegar
1   Tablespoon turmeric
¼   box whole mixed
     pickling spice

Soak peppers, tomatoes, onions and salt overnight in water to cover. Drain and wash off. In a pot, place sugar, vinegar, turmeric and spices tied in cheesecloth. Bring to a boil. Add the drained vegetables. Return to a boil. Spoon into jars and seal.

# HOT JALAPEÑO JELLY

Yield: Seven 1–pint jars.

1   medium red bell
    pepper
1   medium green bell
    pepper
½   cup jalapeño peppers
1½  cups white vinegar
6½  cups sugar
1   6–ounce bottle Certo

Chop all peppers very fine. Combine peppers, vinegar and sugar in kettle and bring to a rolling boil. Set aside for 10 minutes. Stir in fruit pectin. Let set 10 minutes. Pour into hot sterilized jars and seal.

# ROSY ACRE RELISH

Make 8 pints (or 9 or 10).

4   cups ground onion
1   medium head
    cabbage (4 cups
    ground)
10  green tomatoes (4
    cups ground)
12  green peppers
6   sweet red peppers
½   cup salt
6   cups sugar
1   Tablespoon celery
    seed
2   Tablespoons mustard
    seed
1½  teaspoons turmeric
4   cups cider vinegar
2   cups water

Grind vegetables using coarse blade. Sprinkle with half a cup salt; let stand overnight. Rinse and drain. Combine remaining ingredients; pour over vegetable mixture. Heat to a boil. Simmer 3 minutes. Seal in hot sterilized jars. Do not use aluminum pan. Yes!!

## CHILI SAUCE

30 large tomatoes
10 large onions
5 large sweet bell
    peppers
1 teaspoon cinnamon
1 teaspoon allspice
1 teaspoon cloves
3 Tablespoons salt
1½ cups sugar
2 cups vinegar

Peel tomatoes. Chop all vegetables medium size. Cook all ingredients for two hours. Pack in hot sterile jars and seal.

## FIG PRESERVES

4 pounds figs
1 cup Karo
1 cup water
1 Tablespoon cream of
    tartar
3 pounds sugar
1 lemon sliced thin
6 or so cinnamon
    sticks

Cut tips off fig stems. Wash with hot soda water, using 1 cup soda to 6 quarts boiling water. Let stand 15 minutes. Rinse well. Drain. Mix sugar, water, Karo, cream of tartar, lemon and cinnamon sticks. Let simmer 15 minutes. Add figs. Cook 2 hours. Allow to stand overnight to plump up. Pack in jars and water bath in boiling water for 10 minutes so as not to lose any from mold.

# MUSCADINE (OR MAYHAW) JELLY

*The old fashion way. A grape of the Southern United States with a musky flavor.*

1   **gallon muscadine grapes – you can mix Scuppernong. I like mostly muscadines for the pretty dark red color (or mayhaw berries)**
**Water to cover**
**Sugar**

Wash grapes. In a large pot, do not use aluminum, barely cover grapes with water, you want a very heavy concentrate of the juice. Bring to a boil and simmer about 45 minutes; press out juice through a colander – then strain. This juice freezes well until ready to use. For 1 recipe of jelly – 4 cups juice to 2 cups sugar; you want a strong tart flavor. In a deep stainless steel pot (mine is 7½ inches wide and 8 inches deep – perfect for jelly making), bring juice and sugar to a rolling boil, skim off foam. (Do not give it to the dog! It will make him go blind, but I don't think that is true.) Stir occasionally with a metal spoon for about 15 to 20 minutes, jelly will start to fall off spoon in drops that look like sheets. When ready to pour up, have hot sterile jars and new lids and rings in boiling water. Fill drained hot jars and seal immediately with hot lids and rings. Turn each jar upside down for a few minutes. I usually

*(Continued on next page)*

*(Muscadine or Mayhaw Jelly, continued)*

get about 3 half pints per 4 cups of juice.

This takes a little longer, when not using Sure-Gel and you get half the yield, but twice the flavor and consistency. I do my mayhaw jelly this way. The best.

# BLACKBERRY JAM

Yield: 8 cups.

2    **quarts blackberries**
1    **package pectin**
7    **cups sugar**

Crush blackberries in small amounts. Add pectin and bring to a boil. Add sugar and boil for 1 minute. Ladle into hot jars – seal – water bath for 5 minutes.

# ORANGE OR LEMON BUTTER

½   cup butter
3   Tablespoons
      powdered sugar
2   Tablespoons orange
      and lemon zest,
      grated

Blend all ingredients until smooth. Serve with warm <u>Scones</u>.

# STRAWBERRY BUTTER

Makes 2½ cups.

1   pint fresh
      strawberries, or 10
      ounces frozen,
      drained
½   pound unsalted butter
1   cup powdered sugar;
      if using frozen
      berries, ½ cup sugar

Put ingredients in blender in order given. Blend until smooth and creamy. If the mixture appears to curdle continue blending until creamy. Chill. Serve with toast, <u>Biscuits</u>, <u>Muffins</u>, or pancakes.

# CREOLE STUFFED EGGPLANT

| | |
|---|---|
| 4 | medium eggplant |
| 1 | large onion |
| 1 | sweet pepper |
| 1 | bunch green onions |
| 2 | cloves garlic |
| 1 | stick butter (can use half olive oil) |
| ½ | cup minced parsley |
| 2 | slices bread, soaked in water and squeezed out |
| 1 | pound shrimp, boiled and peeled |
| ½ | pound crab meat |
| 2 | eggs |
| ½ | teaspoon sugar and 1 teaspoon thyme |
| 1 | Tablespoon red pepper |
| 1 | teaspoon lemon pepper |
| | Salt and pepper to taste |
| | Bread crumbs |

Parboil the eggplant 20 minutes or until done. Cool. Halve and scoop out the pulp, leaving the shells intact. Mash the pulp and sauté with onions, pepper, garlic, in butter. Work in the bread, eggs, and seasonings. Fold in shrimp, crab meat, and parsley. Refill the shells. Dot with butter, paprika and minced parsley. Bake at 325 degrees for 30 minutes. Serve with a nice green salad and hot French bread! This freezes well!

# TOMATO BASIL PIE

*Best with summer tomatoes and fresh basil.*
*Good with a grilled steak or roast beef!*

*A Crowd Pleaser!*

| | |
|---|---|
| 1 | **prepared pie crust** |
| 3 | **or 4 medium tomatoes, sliced fairly thick** |
| 2 | **Tablespoons fresh basil, chopped** |
| 1 | **cup mozzarella cheese, grated** |
| ½ | **cup sharp Cheddar cheese, grated** |
| 1 | **cup Kraft mayonnaise** |
| ½ | **teaspoon red pepper** |

Brush bottom of pie crust lightly with butter and bake at 400 degrees for 5 minutes. Remove from oven and place tomato slices in bottom of crust; sprinkle with basil. Mix cheese, mayonnaise and pepper. Pat on top of tomato-basil. Bake in a 400 degree oven for 15 to 20 minutes. Serve warm.

You are in for a treat!

# CARAMELIZED TOMATOES

*Serve with steak, roast meats and omelets*

| | |
|---|---|
| 4 | **to 5 tomatoes, halved** |
| | **Salt and pepper** |
| 3 | **Tablespoons browned breadcrumbs** |
| 2 | **Tablespoons dark brown sugar** |
| 2 | **Tablespoons melted butter** |

Place tomatoes, cut side up, in a buttered baking dish; season and bake in a moderate oven (350 degrees) for 7 to 10 minutes. Mix breadcrumbs and sugar together and stir in the butter. Sprinkle this mixture over the tomatoes and continue baking in a hot oven (425 degrees) for 6 to 8 minutes or broil them until browned and the sugar is slightly caramelized.

## BAKED TOMATOES MARIE LOUISE

5   tomatoes, fresh and chopped (or 2 large cans of stewed tomatoes)
1   large onion, chopped
3   or 4 cloves garlic, chopped
2   or 3 sticks celery, chopped
½   cup parsley, chopped
½   stick butter
1   or 2 slices bread, broken up
2   or 3 slices of bacon, fried crisp
¼   cup brown sugar
1   teaspoon curry powder, optional
    Salt, black pepper and red pepper to taste

In a heavy, big pot, melt butter and sauté onion, garlic and celery just a few minutes. Add tomatoes and parsley. Cook about 5 minutes. Add sugar, salt and pepper. Cover and cook slowly, about 20 minutes. Stir in bread and sort of mash into mixture. Add crumbled bacon and check seasonings. Pour in a buttered shallow Pyrex baking dish. Bake at 350 degrees about 30 minutes.

## SUMMERTIME TOMATOES

Fresh tomatoes, sliced
Bacon, fried and crumbled
Parsley
Salt

Place thick slices of sweet fresh tomatoes on a big platter. Chill. Just before serving, crumble dry very crisp bacon over. Garnish with parsley and a little salt.

## STUFFED TOMATOES OR SWEET ONIONS

*To make filling, see* Spinach Madeline *or* Oysters Rockefeller Casserole.

**Tomatoes or onions**
**Desired filling**
**Bread crumbs**
**Butter**
**Salt**

Scoop centers out of tomatoes or onions, enough to put a good dollop of the spinach mixture. Place in a baking dish; sprinkle with bread crumbs; dot with butter and bake at 400 degrees, tomatoes – 20 minutes. Onions 40 to 50 minutes or until onion is tender. You can also cover the onion with Saran wrap and microwave about 4 minutes. Always check seasonings. Sprinkle with salt before serving. Suzanne Wolff does these best!

## TOMATO, OKRA AND CORN

Serves 6.

| | |
|---|---|
| 2 | **Tablespoons butter or bacon drippings** |
| ½ | **cup chopped onion** |
| 2 | **cups sliced okra** |
| 2 | **cups peeled tomatoes** |
| 1 | **cup corn, cut from the cob** |
| 1¼ | **teaspoons salt** |
| ½ | **teaspoon paprika** |
| ¼ | **teaspoon curry powder** |
| 2 | **teaspoons brown sugar** |

Sauté onions in butter until brown. Add okra, and sauté for 5 minutes. Add other ingredients, and simmer until vegetables are tender.

# SPINACH MADELINE

2    **packages frozen,
     chopped spinach**
4    **Tablespoons butter**
2    **Tablespoons flour**
2    **Tablespoons chopped
     onion**
½    **cup evaporated milk**
½    **cup vegetable liquor**
½    **teaspoon black
     pepper**
¾    **teaspoon celery salt**
¾    **teaspoon garlic salt**
     **Salt to taste**
1    **6 ounce roll of
     Jalapeño cheese**
1    **teaspoon
     Worcestershire
     Sauce**
     **Red pepper to taste**

Cook spinach according to directions on package. Drain and reserve liquor. Melt butter in saucepan over low heat. Add flour, stirring until blended and smooth, but not brown. Add onion and cook until soft. Add liquid slowly, stirring constantly to avoid lumps. Cook until smooth and thick. Add seasonings and cheese which has been cut into small pieces. Stir until melted. Combine with the cooked spinach. Put into a casserole and top with buttered bread crumbs, or sliced tomatoes. Bake at 350 degrees for approximately 30 minutes. This freezes well.

## SPINACH SOUFFLÉ

Serves 6.

2   packages frozen
      spinach
1   can mushroom soup,
      undiluted
3   eggs, separated
1   small minced onion
½   teaspoon ground
      nutmeg
1   teaspoon lemon juice
1   cup sour cream
      Salt to taste
      Red pepper to taste

Cook spinach, drain. Mix with chicken soup, beaten egg yolks, onion and nutmeg. Beat egg whites until stiff. Fold into spinach mixture. Pour into greased 6½ cup soufflé dish or casserole. Bake at 400 degrees for 30 minutes. Garnish with dabs of sour cream and sprinkle with nutmeg.

## HOLIDAY BROCCOLI

Serves 8 to 10 or double and serve 50 to 60 as a dip.

2   (10–ounce) packages
      frozen, chopped
      broccoli
1   roll of garlic cheese
1   (10–ounce) can
      cream of mushroom
      soup
1   stick oleo
1   onion, chopped
2   stalks celery,
      chopped
1   (8–ounce) can whole
      button mushrooms,
      drained
      Bread crumbs
      Salt
      Red pepper

Cook broccoli according to package directions. Drain. Heat soup and cheese until cheese is melted. Sauté onion and celery in oleo. Mix all ingredients and place in casserole. Top with bread crumbs. Bake at 350 degrees until hot and bubbly. Very rich but delicious. Pretty in a Chafing Dish. Serve with melon rounds.

# BROCCOLI AND RICE

Serves 8.

1   large onion, chopped
¼   cup green bell
      pepper, chopped
      (optional)
½   cup celery, chopped
½   stick oleo
1   (10–ounce) can
      cream of mushroom
      soup
1   (10–ounce) can
      cream of chicken
      soup
1   (8–ounce) roll
      Jalapeño cheese
2   (10–ounce) packages
      frozen broccoli,
      cooked and drained
3   cups rice, cooked
      Salt and pepper to
      taste

Sauté onion, green pepper and celery in oleo. Add soups and cheese. Cook over low heat until cheese melts. Fold in broccoli and rice and add salt and pepper to taste. Put into greased casserole. Sprinkle with paprika or top with grated cheese. Bake at 350 degrees for 25 to 30 minutes or until bubbly.

# SKILLET CABBAGE

Serves 6.

4   cups shredded cabbage
1   green pepper, shredded
2   cups diced celery
2   large onions, sliced
      thinly
2   tomatoes, chopped
¼   cup bacon fat or oil
2   teaspoons sugar
1   teaspoon Accent
      Salt and pepper to
      taste

Combine ingredients in large skillet. Cover. Cook over medium heat for 15 minutes or longer, if needed.

# CREAMY SQUASH CASSEROLE

Yield: 8 servings.

1    medium–size yellow
     squash, sliced
1    medium onion,
     chopped
4    slices bacon, cooked
     and crumbled
¼    cup butter or
     margarine, melted
2    eggs, beaten
1    cup milk
1    Tablespoon sugar
1    cup cracker crumbs
     or 1 cup fine, dry
     breadcrumbs
1    cup (4–ounces)
     shredded Cheddar
     cheese
½    teaspoon salt
¼    teaspoon pepper
     Dash of hot sauce
1    teaspoon
     Worcestershire
     sauce

Cook squash and onion in a small amount of boiling water 5 to 7 minutes or until squash is tender; drain well. Place vegetables in container of electric blender, and process until smooth. Combine squash mixture and remaining ingredients; mix well and spoon into a lightly greased 2–quart shallow casserole. Bake, uncovered, at 350 degrees for 35 minutes.

# BAKED CUSHAW OR SQUASH

2    **pounds squash or 1 medium cushaw**
½    **cup brown sugar**
¼    **cup white sugar**
6    **Tablespoons butter**
      **Ground cinnamon, nutmeg and cloves to taste**
      **Salt**

Peel medium cushaw. Cut into 2–inch squares. Place in small amount of salted water. Bring to a boil and cook until tender enough to mash. Drain and mash with fork or use an electric mixer. Add remaining ingredients. Season to taste. Pour into buttered baking dish and bake at 350 degrees until bubbly. Alex Hunt of Ruston has the most wonderful vegetable garden and the prettiest cushaws in North Louisiana. He slices and scoops seeds out, sprinkles the above mixture over slices and bakes on the half shell. Good and so pretty to serve.

# CREAMED CAULIFLOWER AU GRATIN

Serves 4 to 6.

1   head cauliflower
2   Tablespoons butter
2   Tablespoons flour
1½  cups milk
½   teaspoon salt
¼   teaspoon pepper
2   Tablespoons chopped
      pimento (optional)
½   cup green onions,
      chopped (optional)
¼   cup buttered bread
      crumbs
¼   to ½ cup grated
      cheese

Cook the cauliflower in boiling, salted water for about 20 minutes. Drain. Break cauliflower into flowerets (or you can leave the cauliflower whole) and place in baking dish. Melt butter in small pot. Add flour and stir until blended. Gradually add milk, stirring until smooth and thick. Add salt, pepper, pimento and green onions. Blend well. Pour over flowerets. Sprinkle with grated cheese and bread crumbs. Bake in 375 degree oven for 20 minutes or until slightly browned.

# GREEN BEANS HORSERADISH

Serves 8.

2  #303 cans whole
   green beans
1  large onion
   Several bits of ham,
   bacon or salt meat
1  cup mayonnaise –
   light
2  hard cooked eggs,
   chopped
1  heaping Tablespoon
   horseradish
1  teaspoon
   Worcestershire
   sauce
   Salt, pepper, garlic
   salt, celery salt,
   and onion salt to
   taste
1½ teaspoons parsley
   flakes
1  lemon, juiced

Cook beans with meat and sliced onion for 1 hour or more. Blend mayonnaise with remaining ingredients and set aside at room temperature. When beans are ready to serve, drain and spoon mayonnaise mixture over beans. These are excellent left over, cold. The green beans are so different. My favorite Sunday Brunch menu includes: Ham, Biscuits, Mayhaw Jelly, Fig Preserves, Green Beans Horseradish, Cheese Grits and Curried Fruit.

# GREEN BEAN BUNDLES

2    **cans whole green beans**
½    **pound bacon, cut in half, cooked in microwave until just half–done (still limp and workable), pat with paper towel**

**Sauce:**
3    **Tablespoons butter**
½    **cup Worcestershire sauce**
¼    **cup any left–over jelly**
    **Salt and pepper to taste**

Combine all and bring to a boil. Reduce heat and simmer. Pour over cooked green beans and serve.

Beans: Drain and rinse beans in cold water. Divide into bundles of approximately 5 beans each. Wrap prepared bacon around beans and secure with a toothpick. Broil on a rack until the bacon is cooked. Pour Sauce over beans. This can be made ahead of time, just reheat. These are so pretty and good for a big cocktail party. I like to put them in a big silver Chafing dish or tray close to my grilled tenderloin – makes a pretty table!

# GREEN BEANS SUPREME

Serves 6 to 8.

2   cans green beans
    Salt pork
1   medium onion,
       chopped finely
2   Tablespoons butter
1   teaspoon salt
2   teaspoons soy sauce
⅛   teaspoon Tabasco
2   Tablespoons
       Worcestershire sauce
1   can mushroom soup
1   5 ounce can water
       chestnuts, sliced
       and drained
¾   pound sharp Cheddar
       cheese, grated
1   can fried onion rings

Cook beans and juice with salt pork. Drain beans. Sauté onion in butter. Add seasonings and soup. In a 1½ quart casserole layer beans, chestnuts, sauce and cheese. Repeat the layers. Bake at 350 degrees for about 30 minutes or until hot and bubbly. Top with onion rings and heat 10 more minutes.

# SPANISH GREEN BEANS

2   strips bacon,
       chopped
¼   cup onion, chopped
2   Tablespoons green
       pepper, chopped
1   Tablespoon flour
2   cups canned
       tomatoes, drained
1   cup canned green
       beans, drained
    Salt and pepper to
       taste

Fry bacon, onion and green pepper in heavy skillet until bacon is crisp and onion and pepper are brown. Add flour.

Stir and add tomatoes and green beans; salt and pepper to taste. Place in a casserole and bake at 350 degrees for 30 minutes. Mama use to take these up the river, to go along with the bar–b–que...a family favorite!

## CARROTS HORSERADISH

1½ pounds carrots
2 cups mayonnaise
 (can use light)
2½ heaping Tablespoons
 horseradish
1½ teaspoons
 Worcestershire
 sauce
1½ teaspoons lemon
 juice
 Salt and pepper to
 taste
⅛ cup carrot water
6 or 8 Saltine crackers,
 crushed
 Little butter
 Paprika
 Parsley

Peel carrots and cook just until tender. Drain and reserve a little of the water. Cut carrots into sticks about the size of your little finger. Line them in a big, greased Pyrex dish – two or three rows, single layer. Mix next six ingredients and spread over carrots. Top with crushed crackers. Dot with butter, sprinkle with Paprika and parsley. Bake at 350 degrees about 25 to 30 minutes. The first time I had this was at Pat Wolff's. It is just wonderful and pretty on your plate and so different! I love to serve it with a roast beef or lamb. Everyone has a fit over it and you can make this the day ahead...so easy!

## SPICY BABY CARROTS

1½ pounds carrots,
 steamed
2 Tablespoons brown
 sugar
1 Tablespoon mustard
1 Tablespoon vegetable
 oil
1 teaspoon soy sauce

Steam carrots and drain. Add to sauce and toss carrots. Place in single layer and broil approximately 8 to 10 minutes or until browned.

# BAKED CARROT RING SOUFFLÉ

Serves 8.

12   medium carrots,
       cooked and mashed
½    to 2 Tablespoons
       prepared
       horseradish
½    cup mayonnaise
2    Tablespoons finely
       minced onion
3    eggs, well beaten
½    teaspoon salt

Mix all ingredients and pour into lightly oiled ring mold. Place in pan of hot water and bake at 350 degrees for 40 minutes. Turn out on serving platter and fill center with cooked fresh English peas or creamed mushrooms. Serve immediately.

# ARTICHOKE CASSEROLE

Serves 6.

3    artichokes
1    large onion, chopped
1    stick butter
1    can mushroom soup
1    can mushrooms,
       drained
½    cup buttered bread
       crumbs
     Lemon slices

Boil artichokes in seasoned water. Scrape meat from leaves and cut up the heart. Sauté onion in butter. Add mushrooms and soup. Blend in all artichoke meat. Put in a baking dish. Top with buttered bread crumbs and lemon slices. Bake 45 minutes in a 350 degree oven. This freezes well. It is also good as a dip with melba rounds.

# STUFFED ITALIAN ARTICHOKES

*This is Josephine Cascio's...Victor and Marie's mother...you know they are good!*

4 **large artichokes**

**Stuffing:**
1 **cup Progresso bread crumbs**
6 **ounces grated Parmesan cheese**
4 **cloves garlic, minced**
4 **to 5 ounces olive oil**
   **Lemon juice**
   **Parsley**

Trim tops of artichoke leaves to remove pointed tips. Soak artichokes in salted water about 15 minutes. Drain. Mix the stuffing ingredients. Fill the artichoke leaves with stuffing. Stand stuffed artichokes on a rack in the bottom of a Dutch oven. Put a small amount of water in the container, but do not let the water touch the artichokes. Cover and steam slowly, adding several drops of olive oil over the stuffing about every 15 minutes. Continue to steam until artichokes are done; when the leaves pull out easily, about 1 hour. Sprinkle lemon juice and parsley on top. The secret to this recipe is in the use of the olive oil. Do not use too much.

# ASPARAGUS WITH TARRAGON LEMON SAUCE

2   **pounds medium asparagus, trimmed and peeled**
½   **cup mayonnaise**
½   **cup sour cream or plain yogurt**
1   **Tablespoon minced fresh tarragon or ½ teaspoon dried**
2   **teaspoons fresh lemon juice**
1   **teaspoon finely grated lemon zest**
½   **teaspoon Dijon mustard**
    **Salt and freshly ground pepper**

Bring a large skillet of salted water to a boil. Add the asparagus and cook until tender, 3 to 5 minutes. Cool.

In a medium bowl, whisk together the mayonnaise, sour cream, tarragon, lemon juice, lemon zest and mustard. Season with salt and pepper.

Arrange the asparagus on a large platter and serve the lemon sauce alongside for dipping.

# ASPARAGUS CASSEROLE

Serves 6.

2   **cans asparagus**
2   **eggs, hard boiled**
1   **can mushroom soup**
1   **Tablespoon liquid from asparagus**
½   **teaspoon celery salt**
    **Salt and pepper**
1   **Tablespoon butter**
1⅓  **cups grated cheese**
    **Crumbled Ritz crackers**

Drain asparagus reserving a small amount of liquid. Butter a 1 quart casserole and arrange half of the asparagus on the bottom. Cover with the sliced eggs. Heat soup with the seasonings; pour half over the eggs and sprinkle with ⅔ cup of cheese. Repeat with asparagus, soup and cheese. Top with crumbled crackers. Bake in a 350 degree oven until brown and bubbly.

# ASPARAGUS AND ENGLISH PEA CASSEROLE

Serves 6 to 8.

1    can English peas
1    can asparagus tips
½    cup chopped water chestnuts
½    stick oleo
½    cup milk
1    can cream of mushroom soup
1    cup grated American cheese

Drain peas and asparagus tips. Chop water chestnuts. Place in casserole. Melt oleo and add milk and soup. Heat and cover vegetables with sauce. Top with American cheese. Brown until cheese melts, about 20 minutes at 300 degrees.

# SOUTHERN SUMMER PEAS

1    quart fresh shelled purple–hull, crowder, or lady peas
1    whole onion, peeled
2    teaspoons salt
1    teaspoon black pepper
1    to 2 teaspoons sugar
2    slices bacon or 1 ham hock
5    to 6 cups water

Clean peas and rinse thoroughly. In a large sauce pan, place all ingredients and bring to a boil. Reduce heat and simmer uncovered for 2 hours. At the end of cooking time you may separate onions into pieces and let sit covered until serving time. When summer peas are plentiful – buy a bushel; blanch and freeze. A special treat in winter. Serve with garden fresh, sliced tomatoes.

# MUSTARD OR TURNIP GREENS

*August through September plant you a little green patch and multiplying onions. You can get greens year round, but I cook them only when they are in season. So much fun and good to pick the young tender ones out of your own garden.*

2   to 3 bunches of turnip tops or mustard greens
1   ham hock (optional to cut fat, but you loose the flavor)
¼   cup sugar or Sweet & Low
   Salt

Stem and pick the greens; wash several times until you have clear water...no grit, please. In a large pot boil your ham hock or salt meat in two cups water. Add greens, they will cook down. Sprinkle with sugar and boil. Reduce heat, cover and cook until greens are tender. You may need to add a little more water. Season to taste with salt and pepper. While cooking, sometimes I add chunks of turnips. These freeze well. Serve greens with hot, buttered cornbread, Louisiana Beauregard sweet potatoes, and country pork backbone. The liquid in the greens is the famous "Pot Likker" and with family folks, the cornbread is often dunked therein. So good – makes you feel warm, healthy and safe or maybe just satisfied!

# UPTOWN COLLARDS

Yield: 8 to 10 servings.

2    **bunches of fresh
     collards**
1    **medium onion,
     quartered**
1    **cup water**
1    **cup Chablis or other
     dry white wine**
1    **Tablespoon sugar**
1    **Tablespoon bacon
     drippings or ham
     hock**
1    **small sweet red
     pepper, diced**

Remove stems from greens. Wash leaves thoroughly, and cut into 1–inch–wide strips; set aside. Combine onion and next 4 ingredients in a large Dutch oven; bring to a boil. Add greens and red pepper; cover and cook over medium heat 45 minutes to 1 hour or until greens are tender, adding additional water, if necessary.

Note: Collards are best after the first frost. That is the only time I cook them.

## WHIPPED TURNIP PUFF

4    medium turnips
1½  teaspoons sugar
1½  teaspoons salt
½   teaspoon pepper
½   to ¾ stick butter
     Sugar to taste
     Salt and pepper to
        taste

Peel and dice turnips. Boil with sugar, salt, and pepper until tender. Rinse and set aside in a colander to drain thoroughly. Melt butter; add to turnips and mash. Season to taste with more sugar, salt and pepper. Butter is the secret to this recipe. Wonderful for your dinner parties! You can take a few of the small turnip tops, cook them in bacon until very tender, chop and swirl in your whipped turnips. It is pretty and an added touch!

## TURNIP AND CHEESE BAKE

*Cook those greens – but save the turnips for this!*

Serves 6.

1½  pounds turnips,
        pared and sliced,
        4 cups
2    Tablespoons butter
2    Tablespoons flour
½   teaspoon salt
     Pepper to taste
1    cup milk
½   cup shredded sharp
        cheese
     Snipped parsley
     Paprika

Cook turnips in boiling salted water until tender; drain. In a sauce pan melt butter. Blend flour, salt and a dash of pepper. Add milk; stir until thickened. Reduce heat, stir in cheese until melted. Combine cheese sauce and turnips; turn into a 1 quart casserole. Cover and bake in 350 degree oven for 15 to 20 minutes. Sprinkle with parsley and paprika.

# CORNBREAD DRESSING

*"Over the river and through the woods to Grandmother's we go... My children's favorite.*

| | |
|---|---|
| 1 | **big black iron skillet of cornbread, any recipe (be sure the cornbread is well browned)** |
| 1 | **cup bread crumbs or left over biscuits or rolls, crumbled** |
| 1 | **cup onions, chopped** |
| 1 | **cup celery, chopped** |
| ½ | **cup bell pepper, chopped** |
| 1 | **cup green onions, chopped** |
| ½ | **cup parsley, chopped** |
| 1 | **cup whole kernel corn, drained (optional)** |
| 1 | **stick good margarine** |
| 2 | **boiled eggs, chopped Chicken stock (lots of it) – defatted of course – you can use canned or chicken bouillon Salt and pepper, to taste** |
| ½ | **to 1 teaspoons sage to your taste, but be careful (you never want one seasoning to over power)** |
| 3 | **beaten eggs or egg beaters** |

This is the way my Mama and Grandmothers made their dressing, but I have cut the fat out of it and it is just as wonderful! I do my chicken stock one day – let it get cold and defat it – put your dressing together the next day. It freezes well.

Crumble your cornbread and bread crumbs in a big pretty wooden bowl. Sauté your vegetables in margarine – just until soft. Add to cornbread mixture and corn and seasonings. Moisten with lots of hot stock. Check seasonings. Add beaten eggs – you want this well moistened – almost like a cake batter (but not quite). It will come together after it bakes. Bake at 350 degrees for 30 to 40 minutes until brown on top – do not over bake! When my children were at LSU and in apartments I used to make this dressing and add chicken or turkey and gravy, freeze it in small tin casseroles and send a can of cranberry sauce and LeSueur peas. Do you think they love their Mama?

# FRESH SWEET CORN LOUISIANA STYLE

*If you ever have this fresh, you will understand why you put sweet corn up in the summer for those long winter days. There is no substitute.*

3   **cups summer sweet corn, cut off the cob and milked**
¼   **cup sugar**
¼   **cup flour**
½   **stick butter**
¾   **cup water**
    **Salt and pepper**

In a heavy black iron skillet add corn, sugar, butter and bring to a slow boil. Add water and sprinkle flour, stirring constantly to avoid lumps. Bring back to a slow boil, add salt and pepper. Turn heat to low, cover and cook slowly, about 20 minutes or until thick. Serve immediately or bake in a greased Pyrex dish about 30 minutes.

# INDIAN CORN CASSEROLE

1   **can whole kernel corn**
1   **can cream style corn**
½   **cup cornmeal**
3   **eggs, beaten**
2   **strips bacon**
½   **onion, chopped**
¼   **cup chopped bell pepper**
1   **cup cheddar cheese, grated**

Fry bacon in oven–proof skillet; remove from grease. Sauté onion and peppers in bacon drippings. Pour in corn, crumble bacon over top; add cornmeal and stir well. Add eggs and cheese. Bake in 325 degree oven until set firm in the center, about 35 minutes.

# DIRTY RICE

Serves 12 to 15.

| | |
|---|---|
| 1 | package chicken necks |
| ½ | pounds chicken livers |
| ¾ | pound chicken gizzards |
| 1½ | cups minced green onions |
| 2 | white onions |
| 6 | large ribs celery |
| 1 | large bell pepper |
| 2 | or 3 hot peppers, chopped |
| ½ | cup fresh parsley |
| 2 | cups rice |
| 1 | stick butter |
| | Salt |
| | Pepper |
| | Seasoned salt |
| | Garlic powder, optional |
| | Red pepper |

Boil necks and gizzards until tender in salted water. Save stock broth and meat. Reserve at least 6 cups of broth. Boil livers. Drain. Mash the livers and set aside. Finely mince all vegetables and the meat. The more finely these ingredients are minced, the better the recipe. Do not grind the vegetables as they become too watery. Cook rice as usual in broth. Sauté all chopped vegetables in the butter until very soft. Mix rice and giblets into the sautéed vegetables. Cook and stir adding about 2½ cups of reserved broth to moisten mixture. Season with salt, pepper and optional garlic. Continue cooking and stirring about 30 minutes. Place in a baking dish and reheat when ready to serve. Definitely best when made the day before and refrigerated. A marvelous freezer dish also. You can mix in one can mushroom soup for a more creamy consistency.

# RICE CONSOMMÉ

1   cup raw rice
1   can beef consommé
1   can water
¼   cup butter
½   package onion soup
      mix
1   small can sliced
      mushrooms
1   small can water
      chestnuts (optional)

Combine all ingredients together in casserole dish. Cover and bake in preheated oven at 350 degrees for 1 hour, stirring every 15 minutes. Be sure oven is preheated.

# INDIAN RICE CASSEROLE

*You will like this one; it is pretty to serve, low fat and lots of fiber.*

1   cup wild rice –
      cooked
1   cup brown rice –
      cooked
1   cup raisins
½   cup pine nuts,
      toasted lightly
¼   cup chopped parsley
2   Tablespoons grated
      orange zest
¼   cup olive oil
2   Tablespoons fresh
      orange juice
    Salt and freshly
      ground pepper to
      taste
1   teaspoon curry
      powder (optional)
    Freshly grated
      Parmesan cheese

In a large bowl, mix the two rices. Add remaining ingredients except Parmesan cheese. Toss! Transfer mixture to a shallow baking dish. Cover tightly with foil and bake in a 350 degree oven 20 to 30 minutes. Sprinkle with freshly grated cheese and serve. You will love the wonderful orange essence. So good with any game, ham or roast beef. Enjoy!

# GRITS SOUFFLÉ

*I like to use this recipe for my hash, beef bourguignonne, and grillades.*

| | |
|---|---|
| 1 | cup grits |
| 2 | cups water |
| 2 | cups milk |
| 1 | Tablespoon salt |
| 2 | Tablespoons sugar |
| ½ | cup cream |
| 2 | eggs, separated |

Cook grits in boiling water, milk, salt and sugar. Remove from heat and cool slightly. Add beaten egg yolks and cream. Fold in stiffly beaten egg whites. Pour into a lightly greased Pyrex baking dish. Bake at 350 degrees for 40 minutes.

# GRITS DRESSING

| | |
|---|---|
| 1 | cups grits |
| 4 | or 5 cups well seasoned, defatted chicken stock |
| 3 | Tablespoons butter |
| ½ | cup celery, chopped |
| ½ | cup onion, chopped |
| ½ | cup bell pepper, chopped |
| ¼ | teaspoon sage |
| 2 | eggs, lightly beaten |
| ¼ | teaspoon thyme |
| 1 | can cranberry sauce, pureed |

Cook grits in well seasoned chicken stock with vegetables you have sautéed in butter. Add seasonings and beaten eggs. Pour in a well greased large Pyrex dish. Top with puree of cranberry sauce. Bake at 350 degrees for 30 minutes. Instead of cranberry sauce, you can top with fresh grated Parmesan cheese.

# HOT CHEESE GRITS

*Barbara Cattar's are the best!*

Serves 12 to 14.

1   **cup grits**
5   **cups water**
2   **teaspoons salt**
1   **roll jalapeño cheese, grated**
1   **cup cheddar cheese, grated**
4   **eggs, beaten**
1   **teaspoon garlic powder, optional**

Stir grits into boiling salted water. Cover and cook slowly 25 to 30 minutes. Add all cheese except ¾ cup and stir until melted. Blend a small amount of grits into beaten eggs, then stir eggs into grits. Add garlic powder if used. Pour into a greased 2 quart casserole, sprinkle with remaining cheese and bake 20 minutes at 350 degrees.

# GOURMET HOMINY BAKE

*A delicious dish to serve with charcoaled foods.*

2   **1 pound, 13 ounce cans white hominy**
2   **4 ounce cans green chilies, minced**
    **Salt and cracked pepper to taste**
    **Butter**
    **Sour cream**
½   **cup heavy cream**
1   **cup shredded Monterey Jack cheese**

Drain and rinse the hominy. Generously butter a 2½ to 3 quart casserole. Layer the ingredients in the following order: hominy, green chilies, season with salt and pepper, dot with sour cream and butter. Repeat the layers, ending with a layer of hominy. Dot the top with butter and pour the cream over all. Sprinkle with cheese. Bake at 350 degrees for 25 to 30 minutes. Serve piping hot.

## ROASTED POTATOES

| | |
|---|---|
| 4 | large or 6 medium potatoes |
| ½ | cup olive oil |
| ¼ | stick butter (optional) |
| | Salt and pepper |
| | Paprika |
| ½ | cup finely chopped parsley |

Peel potatoes. Cut in large chunks. Parboil in salted water for about 10 minutes. You want them firm. Drain well. Place in a 9 x 13 casserole. Pour olive oil and melted butter over potatoes, coating all. Sprinkle with salt, pepper and paprika. Bake at 450 degrees about 30 minutes or until golden brown. Sprinkle with parsley and serve. Sometimes I add bell pepper slices, onions and garlic. Perfect with your roast lamb or roast beef.

## POTATO CASSEROLE WENDY

| | |
|---|---|
| 2 | pounds Ore Ida Brand frozen hash browns (thaw just enough to mix with ¾ stick melted butter) |
| ¼ | teaspoon salt and pepper |
| 1 | can cream of chicken soup |
| 1 | 8–ounce carton sour cream |
| ½ | bunch green onions, chopped |
| 2 | cups grated cheese |

Mix all ingredients. Bake at 350 degrees for 1 hour or longer in an ungreased casserole.

# CRUSTY POTATO SOUFFLÉ

3    cups mashed
     potatoes
4    Tablespoons butter,
     softened
16   ounces small curd
     cottage cheese
½    cup sour cream – low
     fat
2    eggs, beaten
2    teaspoons salt
⅛    teaspoon cayenne
     pepper
½    cup finely chopped
     green onions (tops
     and bottoms)
½    cup chopped bell
     pepper
¼    cup grated Parmesan
     cheese
     Chopped fresh
     parsley, or chopped
     chives, or paprika

In a large bowl, blend potatoes and butter. Beat in cottage cheese, sour cream, eggs, salt, cayenne, and onions. Pour into a 2–quart soufflé dish. Sprinkle with cheese and bake 50 minutes in a 400 degree oven. Garnish with parsley, chives, or paprika.

## SWEET POTATO SHELLS

5    oranges, unpeeled
3    cups sweet potatoes
½    cup sugar
½    cup butter
     Dash of cinnamon
       and nutmeg
1    teaspoon vanilla
1    teaspoon salt
1    Tablespoon grated
       orange peel

Topping:
⅓    cup melted butter
1    cup brown sugar
½    cup flour
1    cup chopped pecans

Halve oranges, scoop out pulp (save for your Ambrosia). Boil and mash potatoes. Mix in remaining ingredients. Stuff into your orange shells.

Topping: Melt butter and mix in remaining ingredients. Sprinkle on top of potato mixture. Bake at 350 degrees for 20 to 30 minutes.

## FRIED SWEET POTATOES

3    or 4 baked sweet
       potatoes
½    stick butter
½    cup sugar
     Cinnamon
     Lemon juice
     Salt

Slice cold baked potatoes about ¼ inch thick. Melt butter in a heavy black iron skillet. Lightly fry on both sides. Sprinkle sugar, cinnamon, lemon juice and salt over. Cook a few minutes more. Transfer to a shallow baking dish. When ready to serve, bake in a 350 degree oven about 20 to 30 minutes. Wonderful with pork or game.

# BAKED BANANAS

| | |
|---|---|
| 8 | bananas |
| ¼ | cup lemon juice |
| 1 | stick butter, melted |
| ¾ | cup sugar |
| | Cinnamon and |
| | nutmeg |

Peel and slice in half lengthwise. Please in a shallow baking dish. Sprinkle with lemon juice and pour butter over. Sprinkle with sugar and a little cinnamon and nutmeg. Bake for 25 to 30 minutes. I love to serve this with my lamb and roast beef.

# CURRIED FRUIT BAKE

| | |
|---|---|
| 2 | bananas |
| ½ | cup pitted black cherries |
| 1 | No. 303 can cling peaches |
| 1 | No. 303 can pineapple slices |
| 1 | No. 303 can pear halves |
| ½ | cup copped pecans |
| ⅓ | cup butter |
| ¾ | cup light brown sugar, packed |
| 4 | teaspoons curry powder |

Day before: heat oven to 325 degrees. Drain fruits after cutting in bite size pieces. Dry fruit on paper towels, then arrange in 1½ quart casserole. Melt butter, add sugar and curry powder. Spoon over fruit. Bake 1 hour uncovered. Let cool and then refrigerate overnight. When ready to serve, reheat casserole in 350 degree oven for 30 minutes.

# A BLACKENED PEPPER GARNISH

3 green bell peppers, sliced
1 red bell pepper, sliced
1 yellow bell pepper, sliced
2 large onions, sliced
2 jalapeños, chopped
3 cloves garlic, chopped
3 Tablespoons olive oil
Salt and pepper

In your big black iron skillet, heat oil over medium heat. Add onions and cook about 5 minutes. Stir in peppers, garlic and parsley. Cool until slightly limp (about 5 more minutes). Add salt and pepper. Cook until some are pretty brown, sort of candied or as the French say; "caramelized". I like to serve this with my fajitas – hot dogs (talk about good) steak, and lamb. It's good on anything but ice cream!

# ROASTING GREEN CHILIES

*Bob and Carol Cudd introduced us to the world of chilies and the flavors of the southwest on our visits to New Mexico.*

Green chilies

Place chilies on a baking sheet; broil 5 to 6 inches from heat, turning often with tongs until chilies are blistered on all sides. Immediately place in a heavy–duty plastic bag; fasten securely, and let steam 10 to 15 minutes. Remove peel of each chili (chilies will be limp). Split chilies, and carefully remove stem and seeds. Drain on paper towels.

# CHILI RELLENOS CASSEROLE

| | |
|---|---|
| 2 | cans green chili peppers or 8 fresh chilies, peeled |
| 1 | cup Monterey Jack cheese |
| 1 | cup Ricotta cheese |
| 2 | eggs |
| 1 | cup milk |
| ¼ | cup flour |
| ¼ | teaspoon chili powder |
| ¼ | teaspoon cumin |
| ¼ | teaspoon red pepper |
| | Salt |

In an oiled baking dish, place chilies single layered. Spread combined cheeses over chilies. Mix eggs, milk, flour and seasonings. Pour over the peppers and bake 25 to 30 minutes at 350 degrees. Wonderful with a good grilled steak!

# BEANS, BEANS FULL OF HEALTH

Note to Dieters: Beans are good for weight control because they let your body use less insulin. A rise in insulin triggers hunger. A lunch "full of beans" helps prevent overeating later in the day.

Newest News: Beans are rich in folic acid, a B vitamin. New research shows folic acid depresses homocysteine, an amino acid that promotes artery clogging, strokes and heart disease. Folic acid also deflects cancer. Smokers deficient in folic acid are at greater risk for lung cancer; high–risk women low in folic acid have greater odds of cervical cancer. Deficiencies are tied to psychiatric problems, including depression. So beans may be good for your mood.

The More You Eat...Dried beans and peas, known as legumes, are seeds from the plant family Leguminosae. They pack more protein than any other plant food, plus lots of fiber, B vitamins, zinc, complex carbohydrates, potassium, magnesium, calcium and iron–with no cholesterol and very little fat.

Legumes include: These beans: adzuki, black, cannellini, fava, garbanzo (chickpeas), Great Northern, lima, kidney, navy, pinto, soybeans, Also lentils, black–eyed peas and, surprisingly, peanuts.

Folk Facts: Humans have been eating dried beans for about 10,000 years. The ancient Greeks held "bean feasts" to honor the god Apollo. The Egyptians put beans in the tombs of the Pharaohs as food for the afterlife.

# BEANS, BEANS MUSICAL FRUIT...

*With a Southwest Flavor*

Serves 10 to 12

4   slices bacon
2   onions, chopped
1   cup bell pepper,
      chopped
1   hot pepper, chopped
1   cup parsley, chopped
1   cup celery, chopped
2   cloves garlic, pressed
1   can pork and beans
1   can pinto beans
1   can white beans
1   can Rotel tomatoes
1   can stewed tomatoes
1   can pimento,
      chopped
1   Tablespoon prepared
      mustard
1   teaspoon chili
      powder
1   Tablespoon cumin
1   Tablespoon cilantro,
      chopped
    Salt and pepper to
      taste

Fry the bacon strips crisp; remove from drippings and set aside. Sauté all of the fresh vegetables in the bacon drippings until tender. Add beans, tomatoes, pimentos, seasonings and crumbled bacon. Place in a casserole or bean pot and bake at 300 degrees for 1½ hours.

# BAKED BEANS

4   cups pork and beans
½   pound bacon, fried
     crisp
1   cup ketchup
1   Tablespoon
     Worcestershire
     sauce
1   cup chopped onions
¾   cup chopped bell
     pepper
½   teaspoon minced
     garlic
2   Tablespoons,
     prepared mustard
¾   cup cane syrup
¼   cup brown sugar
1   teaspoon black
     pepper

Topping:
1   cup crumbled bacon
3   Tablespoons plain
     flour
¾   cup brown sugar

Sauté vegetables in ½ cup bacon drippings or oil until tender. Pour beans into 2–quart baking dish and add remaining ingredients. Bake in 300 degree oven for 2 hours. Remove from oven and cover with topping made by mixing bacon, flour and brown sugar. Return beans to oven and bake an additional 15 minutes. Place under broiler for 3 to 5 minutes so topping will get bubbly and crisp. Watch closely to prevent burning.

# RED BEANS OR PINTO BEANS AND RICE–A MIKE CAGE FAVORITE!

*So good for you! Full of fiber.*

| | |
|---|---|
| 1 | **pound red kidney beans** |
| ¼ | **cup chopped ham** |
| 2 | **large onions, chopped** |
| 1 | **bell pepper, chopped** |
| 2 | **ribs celery, chopped** |
| 2 | **cloves garlic, finely chopped** |
| | **Salt and pepper to taste** |
| | **Pinch of sugar** |
| 1 | **bay leaf** |
| 2 | **pounds link spicy sausage** |
| ¼ | **cup parsley, chopped** |
| 3 | **cups cooked rice** |

Soak beans overnight. Rinse. Cover with water and cook with ham (fat trimmed off), onion, bell pepper, celery, garlic, salt, pepper, sugar, and bay leaf. While beans are cooking, slice sausage into ½ inch thick pieces and fry in skillet; drain and set aside. Cook beans until fork tender; then add fried sausage. Serve over hot fluffy rice with good green salad and hot French bread or cornbread.

# BLACK BEANS WITH TOMATO, BELL PEPPER, AND CILANTRO

5   cups dried black
     beans
12  cups water
1   small red onion,
     chopped
1   green bell pepper,
     chopped
3   large bay leaves
½   cup olive oil
4   cups chopped
     tomatoes
1   small onion, chopped
1   fresh cilantro bunch,
     chopped
¼   cup chopped garlic
1   Tablespoon ground
     cumin
     Salt and pepper

Place beans in large pot with enough cold water to cover by 3 inches. Soak overnight. Drain.

Return beans to pot. Add 12 cups water, red onion, bell pepper and bay leaves and bring to boil. Reduce heat to medium and cook until beans are tender, stirring occasionally, about 1½ hours. Drain. Transfer to bowl.

Heat oil in pot over medium heat. Add remaining ingredients; sauté 2 minutes. Add beans; stir to heat thoroughly.

# BLACK BEAN CAKES

Yield: 4 servings.

2   (14 ounce) cans black beans, rinsed and drained
2   Tablespoons unbleached flour
4   scallions, chopped
1   clove garlic, minced
½   teaspoon red pepper
1   teaspoon salt
1   teaspoon ground cumin
1   teaspoon chili powder
4   cups cooked rice
1   cup salsa
½   cup nonfat sour cream
    Chopped cilantro
    Green onions

Place beans, flour, scallions, garlic, salt, pepper, cumin and chili powder in a food processor and process until blended but not pureed. Form the black bean mixture into 4 patties. Heat a large nonstick frying pan over medium heat. Coat patties with nonstick cooking spray and add them to the hot pan. Cook the patties, turning once, for about 10 minutes or until they are heated through. Serve each patty on a bed of rice. Top with salsa, sour cream, chopped cilantro and green onions.

If you do not know how to care for your game, as in shooting, cleaning, and freezing properly, just skip this section because you don't have a chance in preparing something wonderful and special. All I can say is shame on you!

Birds, or any game, should not be kept over a year. Enjoy while it is nice and fresh!

## WILD DUCKS WITH GREENS N TURNIPS

2   **wild ducks**
1   **bunch mustard greens**
1   **bunch turnip greens**
1   **pound turnips**
    **Sweet potato**
6   **strips of bacon**
    **Sugar**
    **Salt and pepper**

Wash greens well, peel and slice turnips. In a big Dutch oven, layer up greens, turnips, cubes of bacon, salt, pepper and a sprinkle of sugar—repeat layers, till pot is full. Salt and pepper ducks well, inside and out. Stuff cavity with a whole turnip or sweet potato. Place ducks on top of greens, sprinkle with about 2 tablespoons sugar, cover each duck with a strip of bacon. Add about 1 cup and a half of water. Cover and bake about 250 degrees 3½ hours. Check to make sure you have plenty of liquid. Serve with sweet potatoes and hot corn bread. At the duck camp, we would fix this the night before the big hunt. Early the next morning, as we would leave for the duck blind, we would put this in a slow oven and it was just right, when we came in from the morning hunt. Serve with Boo's Cornbread.

# PLANTATION SQUIRREL PIE

*(This is Mama Sherman's – as in Sherman Shaw's Grandmother! She was a cutie pie!)*

3    or 4 squirrels, quartered
1    large onion, chopped
2    ribs celery, chopped
3    or 4 hot peppers, chopped
     Salt and pepper to taste
3    or 4 carrots sliced and cooked just till done
1    box frozen peas, cooked and drained
1    cup mushrooms, drained
1    cup sliced black olives
½    cup parsley, chopped
2    boiled eggs, sliced

Gravy:
¼    cup oil
¼    cup flour
2    to 3 cups squirrel broth
1    cup milk
     Salt and pepper to taste

Crust:
2    3 ounce packages cream cheese – light
1    cup butter or margarine
2    to 3 cups flour

Make a light roux. Add hot broth, milk, salt and pepper and make a well seasoned thin gravy.

Mix crust ingredients well and roll two crusts to the size of a large baking dish (one for the bottom and one for the top). Boil squirrels in seasoned water, with onions, celery and peppers until very tender. Cool, save the stock for your gravy. Remove the bones. Line a large baking dish with half the crust. Layer squirrel meat, carrots, peas, mushrooms, olives, parsley and boiled eggs. Pour about half the gravy over this. Repeat layers and add the rest of the gravy. Top with crust. Slit top of crust 3 or 4 times. Bake at 320 degrees for 45 minutes to an hour. Serve with candied sweet potatoes and a nice green salad.

# FRIED SQUIRREL

**Young squirrels**

Always save the little young squirrels for frying—cook like your fried chicken, just not as long! If you fry the older, bigger squirrels, be sure to par boil in seasoned water until tender, then fry!

# SMOTHERED SQUIRREL OR DOVES

2   **squirrels or 6 to 8 doves**
   **Salt and pepper to taste**
2   **Tablespoons flour, more if needed**
¼   **pound slab bacon, diced**
1   **medium onion, chopped**
   **Water**
2   **Tablespoons chopped shallot tops**
1   **Tablespoon chopped parsley**

Cut squirrels into pieces. Salt and pepper. Sprinkle with flour. Dice slab bacon and cook slowly in a heavy skillet until brown. Remove bacon, and brown squirrels in drippings. Remove squirrels, add onion, and cook until transparent. Return squirrels to skillet, add a small amount of water, cover and simmer until tender, about one hour. Add shallot tops, parsley and bacon bits. Add additional water if needed and cook a few minutes while stirring. Makes a wonderful gravy! Served with lots of hot fluffy rice and buttered carrots, sweet green peas and hot biscuits. O, yes!

# DUCK LA LOUISIANA
# WITH ORANGE SAUCE

3    **wild ducks**
      **Salt, pepper, garlic salt, whatever you have**
3    **Tablespoons flour**
3    **Tablespoons oil**
1    **cup each onion, celery, bell pepper**
2    **cloves garlic**
½    **cup Lea and Perrins**
1    **cup red wine or Orange Curaçao or Calvados (just use whatever you have; if I use Orange Curaçao, I stuff my ducks with oranges, and if I use Calvados, stuff with apples)**
1    **cup jelly, any kind**
3    **strips bacon**

Brown ducks in a 500 degree oven. Make a roux with oil and flour. Add ½ vegetables and wilt. Blend in other seasonings and stir in water. Stuff cavity with celery, apples, oranges or any thing you happen to have on hand. Sprinkle with seasonings again. Put a dollop of jelly on top of breasts; place remaining vegetables on top of jelly, then criss cross with a strip of bacon. Pour wine over. Cover and bake at 300 degrees 2 to 3 hours or until tender. Baste a couple of times. When leg is tender, your ducks are just right. Serve with wild rice, gravy, little green peas, curried fruit, and homemade rolls with a sweet butter.

# CHAFING DISH DUCK

Cook ducks as directed above. Bone. Make a good gravy; add sliced mushrooms, chopped green onions and parsley. Serve with party rolls. Be sure and season this well with salt, pepper, red pepper, and thyme.

# DUCK PÂTÉ

3   or 4 mallard ducks
½   pound chicken livers
1   cup celery, chopped
1   cup green onions,
      chopped
1   bell pepper, chopped
3   or 4 hot peppers,
      chopped
2   cloves garlic,
      chopped
1   cup chopped parsley
2   strips bacon
½   stick butter
    Salt and cracked
      black pepper
½   teaspoon nutmeg
½   teaspoon mace
2   Tablespoons brandy

Cook the ducks any way you wish, till they almost fall apart. Remove all bones and skin. Sauté vegetables in bacon until tender. In food processor, grind ducks and sautéed vegetables. Add butter and seasonings. Check seasonings. Mold out on lettuce leaves. Garnish with extra parsley.

# FRIED DUCK BREAST

*(Oh, so good!)*

**Ducks**
**Buttermilk**
**Seasoned flour**
**Peanut oil**
**Jezebel Sauce**

Breast your ducks (save the legs and carcass for gumbo or a good stock). Cut in about ¾ inch pieces. Dip in buttermilk then shake in seasoned flour. Fry in hot peanut oil 4 to 5 minutes. Drain well and serve immediately with Jezebel Sauce.

## MIKE'S GRILLED JALAPEÑO STUFFED DUCK BREAST

*(Mike's son, Mike, who is an avid hunter, does these and they are a favorite of his family, Michele, Taylor and Jordan. He shares with us. Thanks Mike; we enjoy!)*

4   **duck breasts (8 halves)**
8   **strips of Jalapeño pepper**
4   **slices bacon, cut in half**
    **Wishbone or marinade of your choice**

Roll each breast half around pepper then wrap bacon strip around roll. Secure with toothpick. Marinate over night, if possible. Grill over hot white coals, basting 10 to 12 minutes. Don't over cook; you want them pink. Serve as an hors d'oeuvre or a main course with dirty rice, green beans and copper pennies.

## CINNAMON GRILLED DUCK BREASTS

*(As good as beef tenderloin)*

½   **stick butter**
½   **cup Worcestershire**
    **Juice of 1 lemon**
¼   **cup of any jelly**
    **Salt and pepper**
4   **wild ducks**
4   **slices bacon, cut in half**
    **Cinnamon**

Combine first 5 ingredients. Bring to a boil and simmer 10 minutes. Set aside. Remove each duck breast half as intact as possible, also the skin. Wrap each breast half in bacon and secure with toothpick and sprinkle generously with cinnamon. Cover with sauce and marinate 3 or 4 hours in refrigerator. Grill over hot coals 3 to 4 minutes on each side for rare to medium. Duck is best when pink and juicy. Slice thin!

# GRILLED VENISON ROAST

*Always work with venison or any wild game that has been shot, field dressed, aged and processed properly. You are wasting your time if you don't!*

**1    boneless venison roast with all fascia, blood vessels, lymph nodes and tendons cut out**

It is nice if you have someone like Mike Cage to do this for you...a master surgeon! All you want is the muscle. Marinate in Worcestershire, a little jelly, lemon juice, salt and pepper and any old wine or liqueur you want to get rid of, for 1 to 3 days. Make a heavy duty foil boat. Charcoal grill should be fiery hot. Place roast over red hot coals for about 8 to 10 minutes (depending on size of roast). Remove, place roast in heavy duty foil. Pour marinade over roast. Move to far side of hot coals. Close the top of your pit, cook 30 to 40 minutes more. It should be pink. Remove. It will still cook a little. Sprinkle with salt. Slice thin and enjoy! I love to grill one of these and just put it up on my chopping block with a sharp, pretty knife and watch my guests carve and enjoy! An elegant appetizer!

# VENISON BACKSTRAP, STUFFED

1     **venison backstrap**
2     **green onions, finely chopped**
1     **can sliced mushrooms**
1     **clove garlic, pressed**
1     **Tablespoon chopped parsley**
     **Worcestershire sauce**
     **Cracked black pepper**
     **Salt**
     **Lemon juice**
     **Butter**

In 4 tablespoons butter, sauté the onion, mushrooms, garlic and parsley. Slit the backstrap (be careful not to cut all the way through) and add the vegetables. Close the slit with toothpicks. Brush with melted butter, a little Worcestershire and lemon juice. Broil on the barbecue pit until the desired degree of doneness is obtained. On a fairly hot grill, about 15 to 20 minutes you will have a nice rare backstrap. Serve this with Spinach Madeleine, Rice Consommé, a nice green salad and hot French bread with sweet butter.

# FROG LEGS OVER CHARCOAL OR FRIED

*(I like the small ones)*

10  to 20 pair of frog
    legs, (Allow 2 pair
    per person)
1   stick butter
½   cup Worcestershire
    Juice of 1 lemon
    Salt and pepper

In a sauce pan, combine butter, Worcestershire, lemon juice, salt and pepper. Bring to a boil and simmer 10 minutes. Cool. Pour over frog legs and marinate 2 to 3 hours. Grill over hot white coals 3 to 4 minutes on each side–do not over cook. You can fry them as you would the quail, but only 4 to 5 minutes in hot peanut oil. A wonderful hors d'oeuvre to pass. Frog legs are the lowest of all in fat count. If you ever get to Paris, be sure to go to Roger La Grenouille on the left bank!

# RABBIT IN MUSTARD SAUCE – TOMMY GODFREY'S

1   whole 3– to 4–pound rabbit cut into 6 pieces
¼   cup extra–virgin olive oil
1   small onion, peeled and sliced
1   cup dry white wine
2   to 3 heaping Tablespoons Dijon mustard, or to taste
2   cups chicken stock (preferably homemade)
    Thyme, rosemary or other fresh herbs, to taste
2   Tablespoons flour
1   cup heavy cream
1   head garlic, cut in half
    Salt and freshly ground pepper

Preheat oven to 375 degrees. Sauté rabbit in olive oil until dark brown. Push pieces of rabbit aside; sauté onion until soft and lightly colored. Add white wine and reduce until it's completely evaporated. Then add Dijon mustard, chicken stock, herbs, flour, cream, garlic, and lightly season with salt and pepper. Cook, stirring, for a few minutes until ingredients blend. Pour sauce over rabbit; bake 40 minutes. Check seasonings. Serve rabbit with fettuccine and steamed, buttered broccoli.

# STEAK DIANNE

*I Love That Name!*

Serves 4.

**4    sirloin steaks (½ inch thick, 4 inches in diameter)**
**Salt and pepper**
**2    Tablespoons butter**
**½    cup good cognac, warmed**

<u>**Sauce:**</u>
**4    Tablespoons melted butter**
**4    Tablespoons chopped green onions, (include tops)**
**2    Tablespoons finely chopped parsley**
**2    Tablespoons A–1 sauce**
**4    Tablespoons good sherry or Madeira**
**2    Tablespoons Worcestershire sauce**

Combine sauce ingredients and heat gently for 30–45 seconds. Melt 1 tablespoon butter in a carefully controlled skillet. Season the steaks with salt and pepper. Cook 2 steaks at a time, 1½ minutes on each side. Pour half the sauce over the steaks; cook until bubbly. Prepare remaining steaks in the same way. Add the warmed cognac, light it and spoon the mixture over the steaks. Serve immediately.

# BOEUF BOURGUIGNONNE

3   cups cubed steak or
    roast beef, that you
    have left over or
    you can just use a
    lean boneless beef
1   chopped onion
½   cup chopped celery
1   sweet bell pepper
2   cloves garlic
1   cup sliced
    mushrooms
1   cup small cubed
    carrots
2   Tablespoons bacon
    drippings
2   Tablespoons flour
¼   cup red wine
    Salt, pepper, lemon
    pepper, garlic salt,
    etc.

If you have a steak or roast bone, boil in a seasoned water, and make a nice rich stock. Meantime, sauté onion, celery, bell pepper, and garlic in bacon drippings, until limp. Stir in flour. Brown. Add your meat, mushrooms, and carrots. Slowly add your hot stock until you get the right consistency (a little thin, because you want to bake this). Add seasonings, fresh herbs, if you have some. Don't forget the wine. Check seasonings. If this is not dark brown, this is cheating, but we won't tell – add a little Kitchen Bouquet. You want a pretty color. Sprinkle with lots of chopped parsley. Bake at 350 degrees for about 30 minutes or until hot. Serve with grits and homemade biscuits, and mayhaw jelly. A nice crisp green salad with riced, hard boiled eggs and homemade mayonnaise.

# RIB EYE ROAST–PINK IN THE MIDDLE

8 to 9 pounds rib eye
    roast
Cracked black pepper
Salt

Rub the rib eye all over with pepper and place it in a shallow pan. Preheat the oven to 500 degrees. When the oven is hot, put the roast in the oven and close the door. Do not open the door for 2 hours and then the roast is ready to serve. The roast should be cooked 5 minutes a pound at 500 degrees and then the heat should be turned off. If the roast weighs 8 pounds, you cook the roast 40 minutes and turn the oven off. From the time you start the roast until it is ready to slice the time is 2 hours. Pour part of the fat out of the pan and add some water and salt for a delicious natural gravy. The roast will be pink in the middle every time. Never fail – perfect! An Allen Barham special.

# BLACKENED TENDERLOIN

**Beef or Pork
Tenderloins**

Rub with Kitchen Bouquet and cracked black pepper. In a hot black iron skillet, heat a little olive oil and blacken about five minutes on each side. Check desired doneness. Do not over cook. Move to a warm platter. Add brandy (your choice) and hot water, parsley, green onions, salt, and lemon juice to the hot skillet. Reduce sauce, pour over meat. Wonderful! You can flame this with "Booker's" Batch 124 proof.

# LEG OF LAMB

*As told by my children's Grandmother, "Cook".*

1    **6 pound leg of lamb**
     **Salt and pepper**
     **Worcestershire sauce**
     **Chopped celery**
1    **whole onion**
⅓    **cup chopped parsley**
2    **or 3 chopped green**
     **onions**
1    **to 1½ cups water**

**Gravy:**
1    **Tablespoon flour**
2    **Tablespoons bacon**
     **grease or lard**
     **Seasonings (such as**
     **onion, celery,**
     **garlic, green onion**
     **and parsley)**
     **Drippings from lamb**
     **plus water (2 cups**
     **liquid total)**

Hers was the very best! "I do not like the strong taste of lamb and anytime that I buy a leg of lamb, I stick a good clove of garlic in it as soon as I get home from the grocery. I take about a 6 pound leg of lamb and rub it thoroughly with salt, pepper and Worcestershire sauce. Then I put it in the oven, a very hot oven set up almost to broil, in an uncovered roast pan and let it brown for about 20 minutes and then turn it over. Meanwhile, take 1 piece of chopped celery, 1 whole onion, one–third cup of chopped parsley, and 2 or 3 chopped green onions and sprinkle this over the leg of lamb. Then cover the pot, having added to it a good cup or 1½ cups of water and turn the heat down to 300 degrees. For a 6 pound leg of lamb, I cook it at least 2 hours or more, and sometimes 2½ hours because I don't like rare leg of lamb.

For Gravy: I always start off with a roux made of 1 big tablespoon of flour to 2 level tablespoons of bacon

*(Continued on next page)*

*(Leg of Lamb, continued)*

grease and browned on top of the stove and then add to this my seasonings and stir until limp and brown. Add drippings from lamb and water – about 2 cups of liquid in all. Reduce and serve with lamb and a good <u>mint jelly</u> is nice with this."

## EGGPLANT WITH LAMB AND PINE NUTS

*These rounds of eggplant covered with a flavorful sauce not only look fantastic but taste of the summer nights on the desert.*

| | |
|---|---|
| 1 | **pound ground lean lamb** |
| 1 | **medium yellow onion, peeled and chopped** |
| 2 | **cloves garlic, crushed** |
| 4 | **Tablespoons olive oil** |
| | **Salt and pepper to taste** |
| ½ | **cup tomato sauce, canned** |
| ¼ | **cup red wine** |
| ½ | **teaspoon cinnamon** |
| ½ | **teaspoon allspice** |
| 3 | **Tablespoons pine nuts** |
| 1 | **eggplant** |

Brown the lamb along with the onion in the garlic and oil. Add the salt, pepper, tomato sauce, red wine, cinnamon, allspice, and pine nuts. Cook for about 15 minutes until the sauce reduces a bit. Cut the eggplant into ½–inch thick slices. Lightly brown them in a frying pan with just a touch of olive oil. Turn, and brown the other sides. Do not overcook. Place the slices of eggplant on a baking sheet, and spread with lamb mixture. Bake at 300 degrees for 30 minutes.

# GRILLED LAMB OR VEAL CHOPS

*(Should be rare to medium rare; never over cook them!)*
*Outstanding!*

8    **1½ inch chops**
     **Kitchen Bouquet**
     **Cracked black pepper**

**Sauce:**
½    **stick of butter**
½    **cup jelly – any kind**
1    **lemon, juiced and**
     **the zest (if you**
     **have time)**
½    **cup Worcestershire**
     **sauce**
½    **cup fresh herbs**
     **chopped fine**
     **(rosemary, parsley,**
     **basil, etc.)**

In a sauce pan, melt butter. Add jelly, lemon juice, Worcestershire and herbs. Bring to a boil, stirring well. Reduce heat and simmer about 10 minutes. Have your pit smoking hot. Rub chops with Kitchen Bouquet and cracked pepper. Place chops on hot grill – baste generously. Close top of pit – time it three minutes. Turn chops, baste, cook three more minutes and move off hot coals for about 5 minutes. Check doneness. Sprinkle with salt. Reduce remaining sauce and pour over chops. Serve with rice, Spinach Madeline, baked bananas, carrots, horseradish, homemade rolls and mayhaw jelly.

# FAJITAS

Beef skirt steak
Salt and pepper to
   taste
Minced garlic
Fresh lime juice

Cut steaks into pieces 6 inches long. Season with salt and pepper and minced garlic. Arrange a single layer in a glass dish; cover with lime juice to marinate 30 minutes. Grill very quickly 3 to 4 minutes, turning often. Slice into thin strips. Serve with sautéed onion and bell pepper, salsa, sour cream and guacamole. Wrap in flour tortilla and enjoy.

# FIESTA FAJITAS

¾   cup oil
¼   cup soy sauce
¼   cup honey
2   Tablespoons vinegar
2   Tablespoons chopped
      green onion
1   large clove of garlic
1½  teaspoons ginger
1   flank steak (1½
      pounds), not scored

Combine first seven ingredients; add steak and marinate at least 4 hours. Drain. (Marinade may be saved for future use.)

Barbeque meat over hot coals, basting with marinade. Turn one time. Five minutes on each side will cook the steak medium. To serve, cut crosswise to grain. Serve with warm tortillas, <u>peach or mango salsa</u>.

# SONTERRA CHILI

*This is almost like a thick soup.*

*Sonterra Country Club, in San Antonio, is famous for their chili and it is served everyday. I think it is a first place winner and __heart__ __healthy__ to boot!*

| | |
|---|---|
| 2 | pounds, lean ground meat (you can use venison) |
| ½ | cup of a good oil (I use olive oil) |
| 8 | ounces pinto beans, cook according to directions, or 2 cans pinto beans, undrained |
| 1 | large onion, chopped |
| ½ | cup finely chopped green pepper |
| 1 | can chopped green chilies |
| 1 | or 2 chopped hot peppers, I use chili piquin |
| 6 | cloves garlic, minced |
| 4 | Tablespoons chili powder |
| 2 | Tablespoons cumin |
| 1 | Tablespoon oregano |
| 1 | to 2 Tablespoons salt |
| 1 | Tablespoon black pepper |
| 1 | large can (48 ounces) of V8 juice |

In a Dutch oven, brown meat; drain in a colander and run under hot water – get that fat off! Use a little of your seasonings on this and set aside. Heat oil and sauté onion, peppers and garlic until limp; sprinkle in flour and stir well. Add ground meat and seasonings, stir well. Add V8 juice and cook slowly. Add half of the cooked beans – the other half puree in the food processor and add to mixture. Stir well. Cover and simmer about 1 hour. If too thick, add a little hot water. Check seasonings. This chili is like a thick soup and has a distinctive cumin flavor. Serve in big bowls and garnish with lots of chopped onions, and grated sharp cheese. Tostitos and a good cold beer go well with this.

## SMOKED HAM

| | |
|---|---|
| 1 | **6 to 8 pound cooked ham, bone in** |
| 1 | **part brown sugar** |
| 1 | **part lemon juice** |
| 1 | **part dark molasses** |
| 2 | **cans diced or crushed pineapple, with juice** |

Smoke ham on grill away from coals for 1 to 1½ hours. Remove and wrap in foil to prevent drying. Return to grill, still on opposite end from coals for another 2 to 3 hours. Unwrap again and score top and sides deeply. Pour mixture of sugar, lemon juice and molasses over ham and rewrap. Return to grill for ½ hour. Ham should be cooked by this time. Unwrap once more and surround ham with pineapple, pouring juice over top. Wrap and heat 15 minutes, just enough for pineapple to heat but not wilt. This is just wonderful and so pretty for a big Christmas or Easter party. For a Sunday Brunch serve this with Yeast Biscuits and Mayhaw Jelly!

# HOLIDAY STUFFED HAM

Serves 20 to 25.

1    **10 to 12 pound ham, boned**
3    **Tablespoons shortening**
1    **cup celery, minced**
1    **cup shallots, minced**
1    **cup bell pepper, minced**
½    **cup pecans, minced**
½    **cup parsley, minced**
    **Salt to taste**
    **Tabasco, to taste**
    **Herbs of your choice: marjoram, cumin, savory, etc., to taste**
1    **package frozen chopped spinach, thawed and undrained**
1    **cup cooked rice**
½    **cup mushrooms, coarsely chopped**
1    **cup mixed dried fruit, coarsely chopped**
2    **or 3 cans beer**
    **Cloves**
    **Blackberry jam**
    **Dark brown sugar**

Have the butcher bone the ham and take off the rind. Save for other seasoning purposes. In 3 Tablespoons shortening smother celery, shallots, bell pepper, pecans, parsley and seasonings. When the mixture is soft, but not brown, add the spinach and blend well, stirring constantly. Add cooked rice, mushrooms and chopped fruits, again stirring until the mixture is blended, but not cutting up the mushrooms. Set aside and reserve. Wipe ham well inside and out. Stuff dressing into cavity and tie securely in several places, if necessary. Place in a 350 degree oven, bake 20 minutes to a pound, planning so the ham will be done about 20 minutes before serving time. Pour a can of beer over the ham and baste from time to time with the mixture of beer and drippings. Add more beer gradually to make up for evaporation. Forty minutes before the ham is done take the pan from the oven, stud

*(Continued on next page)*

*(Holiday Stuffed Ham, continued)*

the fat side with cloves, brush with jelly and hand–pack the sugar over the top, to glaze the ham. Baste with the beer–jelly–fat drippings as before. Serve hot or cold. Strain fat from pan drippings before serving with the meat. Fabulous and beautiful! I have also done this with a fresh pork ham.

# HAM

**Smoked ham**
**Cold water to cover**
**Brown sugar**
**Whole cloves**

Soak plain smoked ham overnight in cold water or for at least 3 hours. Add fresh water in a pot large enough to hold the ham and all of the seasonings to taste. Simmer the ham: 12 pound ham for 3 hours, 16 pound ham for 4 hours. Let the ham cool off in the water. Remove the ham and skin it. Score the fat on the ham crossways and rub with brown sugar and stud it with cloves. Bake at 400 degrees for 30 minutes. This ham is hard to beat and it never dries out. It is always juicy.

# SMOKED TONGUE

*From Marie Louise Snellings – as told! One of my favorites.*

*(Don't overlook this one!)*

|   |   |
|---|---|
|   | **Smoked tongue** |
|   | **Water to cover** |
| 1 | **onion, cut in half** |
| 1 | **lemon** |
|   | **Celery** |
|   | **Parsley** |
|   | **Red pepper** |
|   | **Garlic** |
|   | **Piece of bay leaf** |
| 1 | **small box pickling spice** |

This recipe was given Marie Louise by her mother and it is one that has never failed to please everyone who tasted it. First, obtain a smoked tongue, can use a fresh one. Soak it overnight in cold water. Pour this water off and put the tongue in a large boiler with ample lukewarm water to cover it well and add to the tongue and water an onion cut in half, a lemon, a piece of celery, some parsley, a piece of red pepper, a bit of garlic, a piece of bay leaf, and if you have it, a small box of pickling spice (just add about 1 tablespoon) and boil it gently for about 4 hours. Then remove the tongue, let it cool, and take your hands and peel off the leathery peeling which will peel off quite easily just like a stocking. Then set your tongue in a bowl and pour over it a <u>French Dressing</u>. Put about 1½ cups dressing over the tongue and then

*(Continued on next page)*

*(Smoked Tongue, continued)*

layer on the top of the tongue about 1 cup of mixed raw celery, green onion, onion and parsley chopped fine and then let your tongue soak in this for a day or two and it is even better after 3 or 4 days. When you slice the tongue, put a bit of this garnish and French dressing on each slice and it is truly a treat.

## CORNED BEEF

3    **to 4 pounds corned beef brisket or round**
1    **onion, quartered**
2    **ribs celery and tops**
1    **bay leaf**
1    **teaspoon Lawry's seasoning salt**
4    **whole cloves**
1    **carrot**
1    **teaspoon brown sugar**
1    **teaspoon cracked pepper**

Cover meat with cold water and seasonings. Bring to a boil, reduce heat and simmer about 3 hours or until meat is tender. Test. When fork easily pierces as with a baked potato, the meat is done. Overcooking dries meat and prevents you from slicing well. For a boiled dinner, remove meat, and boil cabbage, new potatoes, carrots and such in the beef stock. After boiling, the brisket may also be rubbed with mustard and brown sugar and baked in the oven about 30 minutes at 350 degrees or until glazed.

## OLD FASHION CHUCK ROAST – A FAMILY FAVORITE!

*Serve with rice, gravy from the roast, snap beans and hot biscuits with* <u>Mayhaw Jelly</u>.

| | |
|---|---|
| 1 | Chuck Roast (not over 4 pounds) |
| 2 | or 3 pods garlic |
| | Salt and pepper, to taste |
| | Flour to coat roast |
| ½ | cup oil |
| 3 | Tablespoons flour |
| 1½ | cups boiling water |
| ½ | cup left over wine – any kind will do |
| 2 | Tablespoons Kitchen Bouquet – for a pretty color |
| 2 | Tablespoons Worcestershire sauce |
| 2 | onions, sliced |
| 1 | bell pepper, cut in strips |
| 6 | to 8 carrots, cut in half |
| | New potatoes – little bitty – if you can find them – do not peel |
| ½ | cup chopped parsley – fresh – I like the flat leaf Italian – better flavor |

Stud roast with slivers of garlic. Salt and pepper and lightly flour. In a Dutch oven, or a big heavy skillet, heat oil and brown roast. Remove. Add flour to drippings and brown. Add boiling water, stirring well on high heat for 2 or 3 minutes. Add wine, Kitchen Bouquet, Worcestershire sauce. Check seasonings. You want a thin gravy – may need to add more water. Place roast in thin gravy. Top with onions and bell pepper. Cover and bake in a 300 degree oven about 2 hours. Add carrots, potatoes, and parsley. May need to add a little water. Cook another hour or until fork tender. Check seasonings and enjoy. This would be wonderful for a dinner party. You can go anywhere for a fancy dinner, but where can you go for an old fashion family favorite? That is what folks like!

A Gift of
the Waters

L Young

# CRAWFISH C'EST BON

12 main course servings.

3    pounds peeled
     crawfish tails
     Creole seasoning
1    cup vegetable oil
¾    cup flour
2    large onions,
     chopped
1    green bell pepper,
     chopped
1    stalk celery, chopped
1    bunch green onions,
     chopped
1    cup parsley, chopped
4    cloves garlic,
     chopped
2    dashes hot pepper
     sauce
1    Tablespoon Red
     pepper
     Salt and pepper to
     taste
1    lemon juiced and the
     zest
1    8-ounce package
     cream cheese
2    Tablespoons
     cornstarch
1½   cups water

Sprinkle crawfish with Creole seasoning. In a big pot, make a roux with oil and flour by cooking over medium–low heat, stirring constantly, until the color of peanut butter. Add onions, bell pepper, celery, green onions, parsley, garlic, and hot pepper sauce and sauté until vegetables are tender. Add crawfish and cook 5 minutes. Add cream cheese and stir until melted. Mix cornstarch with water and add to crawfish. Cook on low heat for 15–20 minutes.

This is wonderful in so many ways – as a dip in a chafing dish, over pasta or rice, or simply on patty shells – like the name says, "Crawfish Everything".

# CRAWFISH FETTUCINI

Serves 4–6.

1    heaping Tablespoon
        flour
1    stick butter
        Pinch salt
        Dash Tabasco
1    cup milk
2    cups green onions,
        chopped
1    pound crawfish tails
        and fat
½    pint whipping cream
12   ounces egg noodles

Make a roux with flour and ½ stick butter, salt, and Tabasco. Cook slowly until almost brown; add milk, stir, and simmer. Meanwhile, sauté green onions in another pan with remaining butter until soft. Add crawfish tails and fat. Simmer for about 8 minutes; then add to roux with the cream. Simmer for another few minutes while stirring. Cook noodles in lots of boiling salted water until they are "al dente" (just barely done). Drain and serve with crawfish mixture. Garnish with chopped parsley.

# CRAWFISH STEW

| | |
|---|---|
| 2 | pounds crawfish tails |
| 1 | stick butter |
| ½ | cup flour |
| 1 | large onion, chopped |
| 1 | pod garlic, chopped |
| 1 | bell pepper, chopped |
| 3 | sticks celery, chopped |
| 1 | small can tomato sauce |
| 1 | cup hot water |
| 1 | cup parsley and shallots, chopped |
| | Salt and pepper |
| | Red Pepper |

Make a roux with flour and butter. Cook until golden brown. Add vegetables; cook until soft, about 10 minutes. Stir in tomato sauce, salt and pepper. Cook 25 minutes. Add crawfish tails and fat. Cook for 15 minutes, covered. Add water according to desired thickness of gravy. Let simmer, about 10 minutes. Add parsley and shallots, add salt and pepper too. Cook 10 minutes. Serve on a bed of hot rice with a green salad and hot French bread.

# BROILED LEMON FLOUNDER

*(Any good fresh fish would be fine to use).*

| | |
|---|---|
| 2 | large flounder |
| ½ | lemon, sliced thin |
| 1 | stick butter, melted |
| ¾ | Tablespoon poultry seasoning |
| | Salt and pepper |
| | Juice of 1 large lemon |
| 1 | Tablespoon parsley, minced |
| 3 | green onions, diced, tops and bottoms |

Score flounder. Lay lemon slices into the slits. Melt butter. Add poultry seasoning, salt, pepper, lemon juice, parsley, and diced onions. Broil flounder in center of oven, basting with sauce. Broil about 15 minutes or until fish is done. Fish should be moist, but flaky when done. Do not over cook.

# TROUT ALMANDINE WITH FRESH PARSLEY

*(Always use fresh trout)*

*Helen Corbitt, once, many years ago was passing through Monroe, on her way to Atlanta, for the opening of the new Neiman Marcus store. She was traveling with our good friends from Dallas, the Tony Briggles. We were to have them for dinner. We were working on Cotton Country Collection at the time, so with the help of my friends, Marilyn Irby, Suzanne Wolff, and others, we served this trout, parsley new potatoes, Suzanne's stuffed tomatoes and <u>Floating Island</u> for dessert.*

Serves 4.

| | |
|---|---|
| 8 | **Tablespoons butter** |
| ½ | **cup slivered almonds** |
| 4 | **fresh trout fillets (5–6 ounces each)** |
| 1 | **cup buttermilk** |
| 2 | **teaspoons black pepper** |
| 1½ | **teaspoons garlic powder** |
| | **Salt to taste** |
| | **Flour** |
| | **Juice from 1 lemon** |
| 2 | **Tablespoons fresh parsley** |

In a skillet, melt 1½ tablespoons butter. Simmer almonds in butter until golden brown. Remove and set aside. Season the buttermilk with salt, pepper and garlic powder. Dip fish in buttermilk, then roll in flour coating both sides. Shake excess flour from fillets. Melt 5 tablespoons of butter in a skillet and sauté fillets until golden brown. Remove fish. Place on warm serving plates and keep hot. In the same skillet, add the lemon, 1½ tablespoons butter and almonds. Sauté for 1 minute until hot. Pour over fish, sprinkle with parsley and serve.

# CATFISH PARMESAN

| | |
|---|---|
| 2 | pounds farm raised catfish fillets |
| 1 | cup sour cream |
| ¼ | cup Parmesan cheese |
| 1 | Tablespoon lemon juice |
| 1 | Tablespoon grated onion |
| ½ | teaspoon salt |
| | Dash hot pepper |
| | Paprika |

Place catfish fillets in a single layer in a well greased 13 x 9 x 2 baking dish. Combine remaining ingredients except paprika. Spread sour cream mixture over fish. Sprinkle with paprika. Bake at 350 degrees for 20 to 25 minutes. Do not over cook.

# CALIFORNIA FISH TACO

Fresh fish – any kind will do (I like catfish, bream, perch or bass)

Shredded red cabbage

Homemade Tartar Sauce

Flour tortillas, warmed

Lemon wedges for garnish

Cut fish in finger–size strips. To fry see Southern Fried Fish. These are just wonderful and different. Put several pieces of hot, crispy fried fish in flour tortilla. Top with a generous dollop of tartar sauce. Layer with cabbage. You are going to want another!

# SOUTHERN FRIED FISH

*What a treat!*

**Fresh fish, whole or fillets (I like the small ones)**
**Prepared mustard**
**Cornmeal fish fry, well seasoned with salt, pepper, and red pepper**
**Fresh peanut oil for frying**
**Lemon slices, for garnish**
**Homemade tartar sauce**
**Hushpuppies, mixed up**

For thin fried fish, place fillet between two flat yard sticks, have a very sharp knife, and try for three slices from each fillet or get your butcher to slice them. Pat dry.

In a big wooden bowl, dip fish in lots of mustard, sort of shake off excess and add to seasoned cornmeal. Shake well to coat all pieces. Do a few at a time. Fry in hot peanut oil. Do not over cook. When it just begins to float, it's usually done. Drain on paper towel. Fry your hushpuppies in same oil. Serve with lemon slices and tartar sauce. The secret is good fresh fish and keeping the oil consistently hot. I love this fish cold the next day. Great with pasta salad or cole slaw and of course Summer Time Tomatoes, sliced, and purple onions.

# OVEN POACHED BIG FISH

*So pretty for a cocktail party! Serve with toast points and a homemade dill sauce...very elegant!*

1   **15 pound (approximately) red snapper, salmon, black bass, or your choice of fish**
**Seasoning salt**
**Poultry seasoning**
**Chopped parsley**
**Chopped green onions**
**Lemon juice and zest**
**Butter**

The hardest part of cooking fish is knowing when it is done and not over cooking. A good rule to follow is cook 10 minutes for each inch of depth. Measure depth at the thickest part of the fish, lying flat on its side. If you are cooking rolled stuffed fillets, measure after stuffing. Buy a 15 pound or so red snapper, salmon, black bass or your choice. Clean well and season with a good season salt like Ole Bay's or Tony's, poultry seasoning, chopped parsley, chopped green onions, lemon juice and the zest, and lots of butter. Lay the fish on ample (several layers) sheets of heavy foil. Don't skimp. Wrap and seal the fish. Bake on the rack of a preheated 450 degree oven for ten minutes to the inch plus ten minutes to let the heat penetrate. Place fish on a big platter. Sprinkle with salt and garnish with last of fresh parsley and lemon slices. Serve with toast points and a <u>Dill Dressing</u> or <u>Cucumber Verde</u> <u>Sauce</u>.

# CRAB CAKES

*These are Pat Godfrey's and they are the best ever!*

1   **pound fresh lump crabmeat**
4   **Tablespoons celery, chopped**
4   **Tablespoons green onions, chopped**
1   **Tablespoon bell pepper, chopped**
4   **Tablespoons parsley**
1   **Tablespoon mayonnaise**
1   **large egg, beaten**
6   **Tablespoons Italian bread crumbs**
1   **teaspoon dry mustard**
¼   **teaspoon red pepper**
¼   **teaspoon black pepper**
1   **teaspoon seasoned salt**

**Dijon Sauce for Crab Cakes:**
¼   **cup mayonnaise**
½   **cup plain yogurt (may use non–fat)**
3   **tablespoons Dijon mustard**
2   **to 3 Tablespoons green onions, chopped**
2   **Tablespoons capers**
2   **teaspoons balsamic vinegar**

Sauté the celery, green onions, bell pepper and parsley in olive oil. Mix mayonnaise and egg together. Mix the bread crumbs, mustard, red pepper, black pepper and seasoned salt together.

Fold the sautéed vegetables and the egg mixture into the crabmeat. Slowly spread the dry ingredients over the crabmeat and gently fold in. Chill for half an hour. Form into flat cakes. Sauté in olive oil until golden brown. Drain on paper towels.

Mix Dijon Sauce ingredients together. Serve at room temperature.

# CRAB N SHRIMP CASSEROLE

1    pound crabmeat,
     lump
½    pound shrimp,
     cooked and shelled
½    pound fresh
     mushrooms, sliced
     Salt, pepper and red
     pepper
½    stick butter, gently
     melted
½    cup green onions,
     chopped
½    cup fresh parsley,
     chopped
2    teaspoons lemon
     juice and zest
4    Tablespoons flour
2    teaspoons
     Worcestershire
1    pint half & half
¼    pound sharp Cheddar
     cheese, grated
     Buttered bread
     crumbs

Sauté mushrooms and onions in butter. Add flour and seasonings. Slowly add the half & half. Then add seafood, mushrooms, and cheese. Stir until melted. Place in a buttered 2½ or 3 quart casserole. Sprinkle the top with the crumbs. Bake, uncovered, for 30 to 45 minutes at 350. This is wonderful to use as a filling for crêpes.

# OYSTER UGLESICH'S (BUT BETTER!)

| | |
|---|---|
| 1 | Tablespoon butter |
| 1 | Tablespoon olive oil |
| 1 | Tablespoon bacon drippings (optional, but oh! the flavor) |
| 1 | large onion, coarsely chopped |
| 1 | large bell pepper, coarsely chopped |
| 1 | or 2 hot peppers, coarsely chopped |
| 5 | large pods garlic, coarsely chopped |
| ½ | cup parsley (Italian flat leaf) |
| 1 | Tablespoon flour |
| ½ | gallon oysters, drained. Check for shells, reserve a little liquid |
| 4 | or 5 new potatoes, chunked small and cooked just till done |
| 1 | Tablespoon Herbsaint or Pernod, (a licorice based liqueur) |
| | Salt and pepper |
| | Lemon pepper |
| | Creole seasoning |
| | Sprinkle of thyme |
| | Paprika |

In a big black iron skillet, heat butter, oil and drippings until smoking hot. Add chopped vegetables, cooking on high till light brown and limp. Sprinkle in flour, stirring well. Turn heat down to medium and add drained oysters. Cook on low about 5 minutes. Check seasonings. Oysters will draw water, but if you need more, you may add a little of the liquid from the oysters (be careful adding as oysters will continue to produce water). Add potatoes, Pernod and seasonings. Check seasonings and serve hot with crusty French bread.

# OYSTER GRAVY

½   **cup bacon drippings, butter or Canola oil**
¾   **cup flour**
1   **cup finely chopped onion**
½   **cup finely chopped celery**
1½   **cups finely chopped bell pepper (hot pepper, optional)**
1   **cup finely chopped green onions**
½   **cup finely chopped parsley**
2   **cloves garlic, chopped**
4   **pints oysters, drained on paper towels**
½   **cup oyster liquid (if needed)**
    **Salt and pepper to taste**
1   **teaspoon sugar**
¼   **cup Worcestershire sauce**
1   **lemon, juiced, and the zest**
    **Artichoke hearts**
    **Pepperidge Farm frozen pastry shells or rice**

Make a very dark roux with flour and drippings. Add next 6 ingredients. Sauté until onion becomes transparent. Add oysters, salt, pepper, sugar, Worcestershire, lemon juice and zest. Cook, stirring occasionally, until oysters begin to curl. If too thick add a little of the oyster liquor, but be very careful as oysters will create liquids of their own. You do not want this too thin. Can add a few well seasoned bread crumbs. Check seasonings. Serve as an entrée over hot fluffy rice with a good green crispy salad or in pastry shells or over artichoke hearts. This is wonderful for a big party served in a silver chafing dish with pieces of hot crusty, buttered French bread or if you have plates, serve with rice.

# OYSTER AND ARTICHOKE CASSEROLE

Serves 6 to 8.

6   to 8 boiled
    artichokes
1   stick butter
2½  cups finely chopped
    green onions
½   cup finely chopped
    celery
1   10–ounce can cream
    of mushroom soup
1   Tablespoon
    Worcestershire
    sauce
1   teaspoon salt
¼   teaspoon Tabasco
1   Tablespoon grated
    lemon rind
¼   teaspoon pepper
4   pints oysters,
    drained on paper
    towels
½   cup bread crumbs
    Lemon slices
    Parsley

Preheat oven to 350 degrees. Scrape artichoke leaves; mash scrapings with fork. Keep artichoke hearts whole. In a heavy skillet, melt butter; sauté onions and celery. Reduce heat; add soup, Worcestershire sauce, salt, Tabasco, lemon rind, and pepper; simmer 10 minutes. Add artichoke scrapings and oysters to mixture and simmer 10 minutes. Arrange artichoke hearts on bottom of 2–quart casserole. Pour oyster mixture over hearts and top with bread crumbs. Bake 30 minutes. If necessary, spoon off excess liquid. Broil 3 to 5 minutes, or until bread crumbs turn brown. Garnish with lemon slices and parsley. Can be made ahead.

# BAKED OYSTERS ITALIAN

1¼ sticks butter
½ cup olive oil
½ cup chopped green onions
¼ cup chopped fresh parsley
2 Tablespoons minced garlic
1⅓ cups seasoned bread crumbs
½ cup grated Parmesan cheese
1 teaspoon salt
½ teaspoon black pepper
¼ teaspoon cayenne pepper
1 teaspoon basil
1 teaspoon oregano
4 pints oysters, drained on paper towels

In a large skillet, heat butter and oil. Sauté onion, parsley, and garlic. In a bowl, combine bread crumbs, cheese, salt, black pepper, cayenne, basil, and oregano. Add to skillet and mix well. Remove from heat and add oysters. Stir gently; put into a 2–quart baking pan. Bake 15 minutes, or until brown and crusty.

## OYSTER DRESSING

3    large onions,
     chopped fine
1    bell pepper, chopped
     fine
1    bunch green onions,
     chopped
4    ribs celery, chopped
     fine
     Bacon drippings or
     margarine to sauté
     vegetables
3    cloves garlic, pressed
½    bunch parsley,
     chopped
     Salt to taste
     Red pepper and black
     pepper to taste
½    teaspoon sugar
6    dozen oysters
1    loaf week–old French
     bread
2    or 3 eggs

Finely chop onions, bell pepper, green onions and celery. Sauté in bacon drippings until tender. Add garlic, parsley, salt, pepper, sugar and simmer until wilted. In a separate pan, heat oysters in their juice and let simmer until the edges curl. Remove and cut into pieces. Break the bread into small pieces and soak them in the hot oyster liquid. Squeeze out the excess liquid. Add the eggs, starting with two, and mix well. Check for seasonings, adding more salt and pepper if desired. Bake at 350 degrees in a casserole until browned and crusty, about 45 minutes. This is Alice de Ben's recipe – Sallie's Mother and Max's best friend!

# OYSTER ROCKEFELLER

*This is from the files of Marie Louise Snellings via Antoine's French Restaurant – the very best.*

1    **pound butter**
1    **pint oysters, drained and chopped, save liquid**
4    **boxes chopped frozen spinach, thawed and drained, save 1 cup of liquid**
2    **bunches green onion, chopped**
4    **stalks celery, chopped**
1    **cup parsley, chopped**
1    **cup bread crumbs**
½    **cup absinthe**
4    **Tablespoons Worcestershire sauce**
     **Salt, pepper, red pepper**
     **Tabasco**
1    **lemon, juiced, and the zest**
1    **Tablespoon anise seed (if you have it)**

In a large pot, melt butter. Add vegetables and chopped oysters. Sauté slowly about 20 minutes. Add crumbs, absinthe, Worcestershire, salt and peppers, Tabasco and lemon. Cook a little longer. Check seasonings. I like lots of red pepper and maybe a little more absinthe. Cool and in small batches, put mixture through blender to a smooth consistency. This freezes really well. When ready to serve, have your baking sheet pan covered with rock salt. Place oyster shells on top, place in oven and heat until very hot. Then place oysters in hot shell. Put a big dollop of sauce, which you have heated in a double boiler, over each oyster. Bake in a very hot oven about 10 minutes. Serve immediately.

# OYSTERS BIENVILLE

Serves 2.

1  dozen oysters on half
    shell
1  bunch green onion,
    chopped
1  Tablespoon butter
1  Tablespoon flour
½  cup chicken broth
½  cup shrimp, chopped
⅓  cup chopped
    mushrooms
1  egg yolk
⅓  glass white wine
½  cup bread crumbs
    Paprika
¾  cup grated American
    cheese
    Ice cream salt

Follow Oyster Rockefeller baking instructions on page 238.

Sauce: Cook shallots in butter until brown. Add flour, stir and heat until brown. Add chicken broth, shrimp, and mushrooms. Beat egg yolk with wine and slowly add to sauce, beating rapidly. Season to taste. Simmer for 10 to 15 minutes, stirring constantly. Pour sauce over each oyster; top with combined bread crumbs, paprika, and grated cheese. Place in oven to brown, about 12 minutes.

## BOILED SHRIMP

1   gallon water
6   ounces liquid crab
    boil
2   lemons, halved
1   large onion, halved
3   bay leaves
1   Tablespoon cayenne
    pepper
36  large unpeeled raw
    shrimp, deveined
1   gallon (16 cups) cold
    water
¾   cup salt

Combine water, crab boil, lemons, onion, bay leaves and cayenne in 8–quart stockpot and bring to boil over medium–high heat. Boil rapidly 15 minutes. Add shrimp; cover and return to boil, cooking until shrimp are pink, about 1 to 2 minutes. Meanwhile, combine cold water and salt and stir until salt is dissolved. Drain shrimp and drop into cold salted water. Add ice and let stand 10 minutes, or until shrimp are well chilled. Drain completely and refrigerate in covered container until ready to use. Be careful – do not over cook.

# BAR–B–QUED SHRIMP

1   **pound shrimp**
**Olive oil**
**Cracked black pepper**
**Salt**
**Lemon juice**
**Tabasco**
**Lea & Perrins**
**Butter**

Place whole shrimp, keep shells on, in single layer in oven proof dish. Drizzle olive oil on top of shrimp. Pepper shrimp until they are black; when you think you have enough pepper, add more. Add lots of salt, lemon juice, Tabasco and Lea and Perrins. Remember you are seasoning through the shells. Cut up butter on top of shrimp and broil until shrimp are cooked, 15 to 20 minutes. Be sure and taste to see if they are done. Serve these with newspaper on the table and lots of napkins. Have French bread to sop up the oil and encourage guests to eat the shells, as well, if river shrimp are used. With cold beer and green salad, you have the makings of a great informal party. Base the amount of shrimp on the number of guests. About ½ pound per person is a good guideline.

# A LEMON BUTTERY – BROIL OF SHRIMP

2    **pounds large raw shrimp, shelled (leave the tail on, wash and pat dry)**
1½   **sticks melted butter**
¼    **cup olive oil**
2    **lemons, juiced and some of the zest**
     **Cracked black pepper**
     **Salt**
     **Parsley, chopped**

Preheat oven to broil. Arrange shrimp in shallow baking dish and coat with butter and oil. Sprinkle generously with pepper and salt. Broil 5 to 8 minutes. Sprinkle with parsley and additional salt. Serve hot with steamed asparagus, new potatoes and hot crusty French bread. Wonderful for dipping bread in the sauce. A nice glass of Chardonnay or a good ice cold beer is perfect for the occasion.

# COMPANY SHRIMP CASSEROLE

*(This is a Nancy Snellings Inabnett Special!)*

Serves 6.

2    **to 3 pounds shrimp, cooked, peeled and cleaned**
1    **cup rice, cooked**
1    **cup sharp cheese, grated**
1    **can mushroom soup**
½    **cup chopped green pepper**
½    **cup chopped green onion**
½    **cup chopped celery**
1    **stick butter**
8    **lemons, sliced very thin**

Mix first four ingredients together. Sauté green peppers, green onions, and celery in butter. Add to shrimp mixture. Put in long flat casserole and completely cover top with sliced lemons. Cook covered about 20 minutes at 375 degrees. May be frozen ahead. Delicious served with salad, French bread and dessert.

# SHRIMP AND SAUSAGE JAMBALAYA

1    pound smoked
     sausage, thinly
     sliced
3    Tablespoons olive oil
⅔    cup chopped green
     pepper
2    cloves garlic, minced
¾    cup chopped fresh
     parsley
1    cup chopped celery
2    16–ounce cans
     tomatoes
2    cups chicken broth
1    cup chopped green
     onions
1½   teaspoons thyme
2    bay leaves
2    teaspoons oregano
1    Tablespoon Creole
     seasoning*
½    teaspoon salt
¼    teaspoon cayenne
     pepper
¼    teaspoon black
     pepper
2    cups long grain
     converted rice,
     washed
3    pounds raw shrimp,
     peeled

In 4–quart heavy pot, sauté sausage; remove with slotted spoon. Add oil to drippings and sauté green pepper, garlic, parsley, and celery 5 minutes. Chop tomatoes and reserve liquid. Add tomatoes with liquid, broth, and onions. Stir in spices. Add rice. Add sausage and cook 30 minutes, covered, over low heat, stirring occasionally. After most liquid has been absorbed by rice, add shrimp and cook until pink. Transfer mixture to an oblong baking dish; bake approximately 25 minutes.

*A mixture of salt, red pepper, black pepper, chili powder, and garlic powder.

# ANGEL HAIR PASTA AND SHRIMP WITH BASIL AND GARLIC SAUCE

Serves 2 to 4.

½ cup olive oil
2½ garlic cloves, minced
1½ Tablespoons unsalted butter
1 onion, Minced
½ cup minced fresh basil leaves or 2 Tablespoons dried basil
½ cup minced fresh parsley
¾ teaspoon salt
½ teaspoon cayenne pepper
¼ teaspoon white pepper
¼ teaspoon black pepper
¼ teaspoon dried thyme leaves
¼ teaspoon dried oregano leaves
1 pound large shrimp, shelled and deveined
2 cups heavy cream
9 ounces angel hair pasta

In large skillet, heat garlic, oil and butter over moderate heat until butter is melted. Add minced onion, stirring for 3 minutes or until onion is softened. Add salt, peppers, thyme, oregano, basil and parsley; cook over moderate–low heat, stirring 2 minutes. Add shrimp and cook for 1 to 2 minutes on each side or until they are pink and just cooked through. Transfer shrimp with a slotted spoon to a plate and keep them warm. To the skillet add the cream; boil the mixture, stirring until it coats the back of the spoon. Remove from heat and return shrimp to the mixture. Pour over prepared angel hair pasta. Add Parmesan cheese.

These are health conscious, calorie conscious, and fat conscious times. When committing dietary sin, do it well – Enjoy!

Low fat desserts just don't compare. Indulge in something decadent! In other words, if you are going to sin, do it well.

ENJOY!

# MY FAVORITE DESSERTS

*When I really want to impress someone, I choose from this section.*

# FIGS–N–CREAM

*I serve this only in the Summer.*

Serves 6.

18   **large fresh figs (3 per person)**
¼   **cup fresh lemon juice and the zest**
1   **8–ounce package cream cheese (low fat)**
3   **Tablespoons sour cream (low fat)**
3   **Tablespoons honey Lemon rind curls Fresh sprigs of mint Nasturtiums – if you have any blooming**

Stand figs upright, slice from stem end into 3 wedges, do not cut through bottom, gently separate wedges. Drizzle with lemon juice. Set aside. Beat cream cheese, the zest, sour cream and honey until fluffy. To serve, place 3 prepared figs on a dessert plate. Put a small dollop of mixture onto center of each fig. Garnish with lemon curls, mint and a Nasturtium. I like to pass a plate of Ice Box Cookies or Tea Cakes and following with a pure cup of coffee.

## VENICE PEACHES

*Your dinner guests will be impressed! This requires an excellent fresh ripe peach! So easy and very dramatic.... Wonderful!*

8 ripe fresh peaches, room temperature
1½ cups chopped pecans
1 cup jelly. I like to use mayhaw or a good wild plum
1½ cups 100 proof brandy or rum
½ stick butter
½ cup sugar
Fresh mint

Cut peaches in half; sprinkle with lemon juice. Arrange peach halves on a pretty platter. Mix jelly and pecans. Fill center of peaches with the jelly–pecan mixture. Just before serving, in a small sauce pan, melt butter and sugar. Add brandy. Heat to the point of ignition. Light. Pour over the peaches. Quick...turn the lights down and run to the dining room and serve it flaming! Spooning the juice over the peaches again and again until the flame goes out. Serve at the table on crystal dessert plates. Garnish with a sprig of mint. (I know you have a mint bed – if not, start one now!)

# PEARS IN A FRENCH RED WINE SAUCE WITH MERINGUE BASE

*The most elegant dessert and you can have most of this done 3 or 4 days ahead! The night of your dinner party, all you have to do is assemble this dramatic presentation.*

Makes 12 tarts, 70 tartlets, 1 pie shell or 3 meringue discs.

| | |
|---|---|
| 4 | **pears** |
| ½ | **bottle of red wine** |
| ¾ | **cup of brown sugar** |
| 1 | **piece of stick cinnamon** |
| | **Juice of one lemon** |
| | **Sliced almonds – toasted** |

**Meringue:**

| | |
|---|---|
| 4 | **egg whites, at room temperature** |
| ¼ | **teaspoon cream of tartar or 1 teaspoon vinegar** |
| | **Pinch salt** |
| 1 | **teaspoon vanilla** |
| 1 | **cup sugar (preferably super fine, or can use half confectioner's sugar sifted with other sugar)** |

Peel pears leaving stems on. Boil the wine with the brown sugar, the lemon juice and the stick cinnamon. Put in pears and let cook slowly for 20 minutes (a slow simmering boil). Remove pears when done and cook the syrup down until it thickens slightly. Sprinkle almonds on top as garnish.

Combine egg whites, cream of tartar, salt and vanilla in a large bowl. Beat at low speed until eggs begin to foam, then at medium speed until egg whites hold soft peaks. Gradually add ¾ cup sugar, 1 Tablespoon at a time, while beating on high speed. Beat until meringue is very stiff, dull and no longer grainy. Gently fold in remaining sugar. Meringues should be dried rather than baked to obtain the proper texture. Shape meringue according to

*(Continued on next page)*

*(Pears in a French Red Wine Sauce with Meringue Base, continued)*

recipe. Line large baking sheet with parchment paper or a brown paper bag, lightly coated with a cooking spray, to ensure easy removal of meringues. Place in preheated 200 degree oven for 1 hour. Turn heat off and let meringues remain in oven for at least 4 hours or overnight. When completely dry, meringues may be kept covered in a dry airy place for several weeks or frozen. If frozen, uncover to thaw and place in oven on very low heat if they feel moist in any way.

For egg whites to mound their highest, no oil or grease should be on the bowl or beaters; the egg whites should be at room temperature; a little acid should be added in the form of cream of tartar, lemon juice or vinegar; the egg whites must be absolutely free from even a speck of egg yolk; the bowl should be slightly warm.

Custard Sauce: For the custard, I use my Floating Island custard recipe. You can make this 3 or 4 days ahead, keep in the refrigerator. To serve, on each dessert plate pour about ½ cup custard. Place meringue shell on top of custard. Place poached pear in shell. Top with the syrup. Sprinkle toasted almonds on top. This is pretty with a sprig of fresh mint on the plate.

# ORANGES IN CARAMEL

*This is a wonderful "do ahead" light dessert, and very beautiful to serve. Bob Cudd loves this one!*

8    **large sweet oranges (navel are good but the best are from Plaquemines parish in South Louisiana... if you are lucky enough to have some)**
1½   **cups sugar**
1    **cup Orange Curaçao – heated**

Cut peel from oranges, getting as much pith and outer membrane from oranges. I like to use a serrated edge knife. Slice in 3 or 4 circles. Arrange on a platter.

Caramelize sugar in a small black iron skillet by stirring over low heat until sugar melts and forms a syrup. Add hot Curaçao. Mix well and pour over oranges. Chill. Garnish with fresh mint! O, Yes!

# PUMPKIN CHEESE DELIGHT

**Crust:**
1½   **cups flour**
1½   **sticks oleo, melted**
¾    **cup chopped nuts**
**Filling:**
½    **large carton Cool Whip**
1    **8 ounce package cream cheese**
1    **can pumpkin (I used pumpkin pie filling)**
1    **cup sugar**
½    **teaspoon each, cinnamon, nutmeg, cloves**

Combine crust ingredients and press into 11 x 7 baking dish. Bake at 375 degrees for 25 minutes or until brown. Cool.

Cream together filling ingredients and put in cooled crust. Top with remaining Cool Whip. Garnish with chopped nuts, if desired.

## FLOATING ISLAND

Serves 8.

6    egg yolks
½    cup sugar
3    cups milk, scalded
1    Tablespoon vanilla or
       rum to taste
6    egg whites
2    Tablespoons sugar
1    cup milk
½    cup sugar, optional

Custard may be prepared ahead, but meringues should be prepared only an hour or two before serving as they tend to disintegrate somewhat after poaching. Beat egg yolks with sugar, scald milk and add slowly to the egg yolks mixture. Cook over hot water in a double boiler until it coats a silver spoon. Cool and stir in flavoring. Refrigerate, covered. Whip egg whites until frothy. Gradually beat in 2 Tablespoons sugar. Heat one cup of milk in skillet till bubbles appear around edges. Drop meringues by large spoonfuls on top of milk. Poach for a minute or two. Remove with slotted spoon. Store briefly in the refrigerator. If desired, melt sugar in a black iron skillet until caramelized. Drizzle or spin over meringues. Float the meringues on the custard in a big crystal bowl. Serve on dessert plates and garnish with fresh raspberries. Give the left over milk to your dog or cat!

# CARAMEL CUSTARD MOLD

1    cup sugar
6½ cups milk
9    eggs
5    egg yolks
1½ cups sugar
¾    teaspoon salt
1    teaspoon almond
      extract
1    teaspoon vanilla
      Boiling water
¾    cup heavy cream

Place 1 cup sugar in black iron skillet, set over high heat and watch! When it begins to melt, tilt pan back and forth to keep sugar moving. When sugar is melted and light brown, quickly pour into a 2½ quart ovenproof soufflé dish. In large kettle, scald milk. Beat eggs and egg yolks with 1½ cups sugar. Add about half of the scalded milk to the egg yolks. Pour all back into the remaining milk and mix well. Add the extracts and salt. Pour into the carameled soufflé dish. Place in pan, a roaster works well, and fill to within ½ inch of the top of the dish with boiling water. Bake in a preheated oven at 325 degrees for 1 hour and 10 minutes or until knife comes clean. Cool on wire rack and refrigerate. To serve, have cream whipped and set aside. Run spatula around dish, place serving platter over custard and invert. Spoon off ¼ cup caramel syrup and fold into the cream which has been whipped.

# NEW ORLEANS BREAD PUDDING

Serves 12.

| | |
|---|---|
| 1 | loaf French bread (about 7 cups) |
| 1 | quart milk |
| 4 | large eggs, beaten |
| 2 | cups sugar |
| 2 | Tablespoons vanilla |
| 1 | teaspoon cinnamon |
| ½ | teaspoon nutmeg |
| 1 | cup raisins |
| ½ | cup pecans (optional) |
| 3 | Tablespoons butter |

**Whiskey Sauce:**

| | |
|---|---|
| 1 | stick butter |
| 1 | cup sugar |
| 1 | egg beaten |
| ½ | cup bourbon |

Preheat oven to 375 degrees. In a large bowl, break bread into bite–size pieces. Cover with milk and soak 1 hour. Mix well. Add eggs and sugar. Stir in vanilla, cinnamon, and raisins. Melt butter in a 13 x 9 x 2 baking dish, tilting to coat all sides. Pour in pudding and bake 1 hour.

To make sauce, in a double boiler, melt butter and sugar. Gradually whisk egg. Cool slightly. Add bourbon. If serving right away, pour warm sauce over pudding. If not, warm sauce slightly before serving and serve in a sauce boat.

Variations: Separate the 4 eggs, reserving the whites. Add yolks and sugar. Stir in vanilla, cinnamon and raisins. Beat egg whites until stiff and gently fold in. Continue with directions. I bake my soufflé over a pan of hot water. I think this is better than Commanders Palace. Just wonderful and so easy!

# MILE HIGH PONTCHARTRAIN ICE CREAM PIE

Makes 2 cups sauce.

1   **10 inch baked pie shell**
1   **quart vanilla ice cream**
1   **quart coffee ice cream**
5   **egg whites**
1   **teaspoon vanilla extract**
½   **cup sugar**

Soften ice cream and spread in the pie shell. Freeze. Beat whites and vanilla until soft peaks form. Add 2 Tablespoons of sugar at a time and beat until stiff. Spread over frozen ice cream. Broil 5 to 6 inches from heat until golden brown. Return to freezer. Serve pie in wedges with Hot Fudge Sauce. See recipe below for the best easy chocolate sauce.

# HOT FUDGE SAUCE

*Just right for your ice cream and desserts!*

Recipe makes 1 cup and may be doubled or tripled.

4   **heaping Tablespoons cocoa**
¾   **cup sugar**
½   **cup milk, or little more**
⅓   **stick butter**

Mix cocoa and sugar together, stir in the milk and cook over low heat. Blend in butter. Continue to cook until you reach desired consistency. Store in the refrigerator. This even freezes beautifully.

# FROZEN SURPRISE

Serves 18.

½  gallon vanilla ice
    cream
1   cup chopped pecans
1   cup chopped
    chocolate chips
½  gallon Neapolitan ice
    cream
        or
4   quarts sherbet,
    different flavors
1   pint heavy cream,
    whipped

Soften vanilla ice cream. Stir in nuts and chocolate chips. Spread vanilla mixture 1 inch deep in an angel food cake pan. Closely arrange balls of ice cream or sherbet, alternating colors on top of vanilla mixture. Continue layering vanilla mixture. Freeze solid. Remove from pan onto serving plate. Frost with whipped cream. Return to freezer until solid. Remove about 15 minutes before serving. Slice cake. This is a big cake and so colorful!

*This is from the files of my good friend, Joan King.*

# OLD FASHION HOMEMADE ICE CREAM

Makes 3 quarts.

6    eggs
3    cups sugar
1    big can of Carnation
     milk
1    small can of
     Carnation milk
1    Tablespoon vanilla
1½  quarts whole milk
2    quarts strawberries
     or 6 fresh peaches,
     optional

Mix first five ingredients. Pour in freezer. Add whole milk until freezer is ¾ full; leave room for expansion. If using strawberries or peaches, allow room. The Tex Kilpatrick's always serve this. What a treat, but what do you expect from someone as sweet as Carole Kilpatrick! If you don't know her, you have missed a treat!

## MINT SHERBET

*Just the very best!*

Makes 1½ gallons.

2  **big handfuls of mint**
2  **small cans of frozen orange juice**
¾  **cup lemon juice**
1  **pint whipping cream**
1  **pint half & half**
4  **cups sugar**
4  **cups water**

Wash mint thoroughly and chop fine. Add 3 cans of water to the 2 cans of frozen concentrated orange juice. Then add ¾ cup lemon juice. Bring sugar and water to a boil and allow to boil 5 minutes. Let this syrup cool. Mix syrup with orange juice and lemon juice mixture. Soak the chopped mint in this overnight. Next morning strain mint out. Whip the whipping cream and fold in the half & half. Add drops of food coloring. Stir cream in orange juice mixture. Freeze in your ice cream freezer. Serve this with thin lemon tea cakes or ice box cookies.

## MANGO SORBET

You should get about 3 cups.

| | |
|---|---|
| 4 | to 5 medium ripe mangoes |
| 1¼ | cups sugar |
| 3 | Tablespoons lemon juice |
| 1 | Tablespoon cognac |

Peel the mangoes; remove and discard the pits. Cut mangoes into large pieces and puree in a blender, in batches, until smooth. Strain the puree through a sieve, pushing with the back of a wooden spoon to obtain as much puree as possible. Stir in the sugar, lemon juice and cognac. Stir to dissolve sugar. Freeze in an electric ice–cream maker following manufacturer's instructions. Serve right away or freeze in an airtight container. It will not freeze very hard, so you can serve it straight from the freezer.

## CHERRIES JUBILEE

| | |
|---|---|
| 1 | cup black Bing cherry juice |
| 1 | Tablespoon cornstarch |
| ¼ | cup sugar |
| ½ | cup black Bing cherries |
| 1 | Tablespoon butter |
| 2 | Tablespoons kirsch |
| 2 | Tablespoons brandy |

Bring juice to a boil. Mix cornstarch, sugar, and a little of the juice and add to the boiling mixture. Boil 1 minute. Add the cherries. Remove from heat; add the butter, kirsch, and brandy. Serve hot over vanilla ice cream. If you wish to ignite it, pour good cognac over and light.

## TIPSY PARSON

*Another Mrs. Don Irby (Marilyn) extravaganza! Marilyn is the Queen of "Cotton Country Collection", one of the most popular Junior League cookbooks in the country. She was our leader and guru – the Julia Child of the South! Thank you...Marilyn!*

| | |
|---|---|
| 1 | angel food cake |
| 3 | cups milk |
| 1 | 2 inch vanilla bean |
| 6 | egg yolks |
| ⅔ | cup sugar |
| 1 | Tablespoon flour |
| | Sherry |
| 3 | cups toasted slivered almonds |
| 3 | cups heavy cream, whipped |

Prepare favorite angle food cake flavored with vanilla and almond extract. Make custard: Scald milk with vanilla bean, remove from heat and let stand 10 minutes. In a bowl, beat egg yolks until they are light; gradually beat in sugar until smooth and creamy. Stir in flour. Pour some of the scalded milk slowly over egg mixture stirring constantly. Return all to heavy pan and cook over low heat, stirring constantly, until it coats the back of a silver spoon. Stir with whisk and refrigerate. To assemble: slice cake into 3 layers. Place bottom slice in shallow bowl larger than cake so there will be adequate room for the custard sauce. Sprinkle the layer generously with sherry and chopped toasted almonds; top with custard. Repeat layering of cake, sherry, almonds and custard. Sprinkle top layer with sherry. Spread top and

*(Continued on next page)*

*(Tipsy Parson, continued)*

sides with whipped cream. Sprinkle remaining almonds on top and pat on sides. Pour remaining custard around cake in bowl and when serving, generously spoon on custard. It makes the dessert!

# SHERRY TRIFLE

1   **Sponge Cake**
    **Sherry**
    **Mayhaw jelly or a**
    **   raspberry jam**
    **Custard (1 recipe)**
    **Whipping cream,**
    **   whipped**

First make a Sponge Cake; make this in a long cookie sheet and cut it with a knife to the size you wish. Line a bowl (the bottom of it) with your cake and pour over this, sherry to taste, generously! Spread raspberry jam over this, then add a light Custard layer. Repeat these layers – sponge cake, sherry, raspberry jam and custard. Top with layer of cake and add a little bit of sherry. Put bowl in the icebox and allow it to stand at least 4 or 5 hours. Turn out in a pretty mold and top with whipped cream. Very English! Way back when, this was the Arch Bishop of Canterbury's favorite dessert!

# TIRAMISU (TEAR–UH–ME–SOO)

*This dessert dates back to the 18th century. The foreign word literally translated means "pick me up". With the coffee–laced flavor, you know why!*

Yield: 10 to 12 servings.

6    egg yolks
1¼   cups sugar
1¼   cups mascarpone
       cheese*
1¾   cups whipping cream
¾    cup water
2    teaspoons instant
       coffee granules
1½   tablespoons brandy
       or rum or Kahlúa
2    (3–ounce) packages
       ladyfingers (or my
       Sponge Cake)

Combine egg yolks and sugar in top of a double boiler; beat at medium speed of an electric mixer until thick and lemon colored. Bring water to a boil; reduce heat to low, and cook 8 to 10 minutes, stirring constantly. Remove from heat. Add mascarpone, and beat until smooth.

Beat whipping cream in a medium bowl until soft peaks form; fold into cheese mixture.

Combine water, coffee granules, and brandy; brush on cut side of ladyfingers. Line sides and bottom of a trifle bowl or 3–quart soufflé dish with 36 ladyfingers; pour in half of filling. Layer remaining ladyfingers on top; cover with remaining filling. Garnish, if desired; cover and chill 8 hours. Garnish with shaved unsweetened chocolate.

*(Continued on next page)*

*(Tiramisu [Tear–uh–me–soo], continued)*

**Berry Tiramisu:**
1    **cup raspberries or strawberries**
¼    **cup sugar**
1    **teaspoon vanilla**
     **Juice of one small lemon and the zest**

For the Berry Tiramisu, serve sauce alongside. In your processor or blender, whirl berries, sugar, vanilla, lemon juice and zest. Chill and serve on the plate. Garnish with whole berries and fresh mint!

*Note: Mascarpone is a soft, rich, buttery cheese – the key to many Italian desserts. If you can't find it in your market, as a substitute, combine 2 8–ounce packages cream cheese, ⅓ cup sour cream and ¼ cup whipping cream; beat well. Not quite as good, but good.

# HUGUENOT APPLE TORTE

4    **eggs**
3    **cups sugar**
8    **Tablespoons flour**
5    **teaspoons baking powder**
½    **teaspoon salt**
2    **cups tart cooking apples**
2    **cups chopped pecans**
2    **teaspoons vanilla**

Beat eggs in mixer. Add sugar, flour, baking powder and salt. Mix well. Add apples, pecans, and vanilla. Pour into 2 well greased 8 x 12 pans. Bake at 325 degrees for 45 minutes. With a spatula, remove to a warm plate. Place on top of each other – hard crust on the top. Serve warm with whipping cream. So good and a Charleston, South Carolina special!

# CRÊPES SUZETTE

*Freezes well.*

**Basic Crêpe Recipe:**
1   **cup flour**
3   **eggs**
    **Pinch of salt**
1½  **cups milk**
4   **Tablespoons butter**

In a large bowl, place flour and make a well in center. Add eggs, salt and ½ cup milk. Beat, starting from center until batter is thick. Gradually beat in remaining cup milk until batter is consistency of light cream; it should just coat a spoon. Refrigerate at least 2 hours, or preferably overnight. Stir well. If needed, add more milk to bring it back to light cream consistency. In a 6–inch skillet, melt butter. Pour butter into batter and stir well. Wipe pan with paper towels and heat until a drop of water bounces. Spoon in 1 tablespoon batter and just enough to cover bottom of skillet. Turn when top looks dry, or cook only on one side. Stir batter frequently. To freeze: stack with waxed paper in between each crêpe, and wrap tightly in plastic. Thaw to room temperature.

*(Continued on next page)*

*(Crêpes Suzette, continued)*

**Filling:**

1   **8–ounce jar orange marmalade**
4   **Tablespoons butter**
¼   **cup fresh orange juice**
1   **ounce brandy, warmed**
3   **teaspoons sugar**

In center of each crêpe, place 1 tablespoon marmalade and fold into quarters. In a large skillet or chafing dish, melt butter; add remaining marmalade and juice. Simmer until blended. Place crêpes in sauce, arranging in an overlapping circle around skillet. Can be made several hours ahead up to this point. Before serving, pour in brandy and flame. Spoon sauce over crêpes and sprinkle tops with sugar.

# DATE DESSERT

*This is a beautiful Christmas dessert!*

Serves 9.

¼   **cup flour**
1   **teaspoon baking powder**
1   **cup chopped pecans**
1   **cup chopped dates (not pre–chopped type)**
4   **egg whites**
1   **cup sugar**
1½  **teaspoons vanilla**
1   **cup whipping cream, whipped**

Sift flour and baking powder over pecans and dates and toss well. Beat egg whites stiff, adding sugar gradually, then vanilla. Fold in date mixture. Bake in an 8 or 9–inch square pan that has been thoroughly greased and floured at 350 degrees for 40 minutes. Cut in squares and top generously with sweetened whipping cream.

# CREAM PUFFS OR PROFITEROLES

**Puff Pastry:**
| | |
|---|---|
| 1 | cup water |
| 4 | Tablespoons butter |
| 1½ | cups sifted flour |
| 2 | Tablespoons sugar |
| ½ | teaspoon salt |
| 4 | eggs, room temperature |

In a saucepan, boil water; add butter and melt. Combine flour, sugar, and salt; add to water all at once. With a wooden spoon, mix thoroughly and cook over medium heat about 4 minutes until mixture leaves sides of pan to form a soft dough. Cool 5 minutes. Add eggs, one at a time, beating well after each addition until pastry is smooth and shiny. Onto a lightly greased baking sheet, mound puffs with a spoon or a pastry bag to form either 2–inch cream puffs or 1–inch profiteroles, leaving 2 inches between each puff. Bake in a 450 degree oven 15 minutes; reduce heat to 325 degrees and bake 20 minutes until puffy and browned. Remove and slit each puff horizontally. Turn oven off and return puffs 2 minutes, leaving door ajar to dry out puffs. Cool on rack; store in air–tight container until ready to fill.

*(Continued on next page)*

*(Cream Puffs or Profiteroles, continued)*

**<u>Cream Puff Filling</u>:**
2    **cups milk**
3    **egg yolks**
⅔    **cup sugar**
1    **Tablespoon butter,**
     **softened**
½    **teaspoon salt**
⅓    **cup sifted flour**
2    **teaspoons vanilla**
2    **teaspoons Grand**
     **Marnier**

In top of a double boiler, scald milk. In a bowl, beat egg yolks until lemon colored. Add sugar and butter; blend until light and fluffy. Mix in salt and flour. Slowly add milk to egg mixture, blending with a wire whisk. Return to double boiler and cook 6 to 8 minutes until creamy and thick, stirring constantly. Add vanilla and Grand Marnier. Cool. Cover and chill until ready to fill puffs with custard and/or my <u>Fudge Sauce</u>. These are also wonderful filled with a spicy shrimp or chicken salad – pretty to pass at your parties.

# STRAWBERRIES DIANNE

*An absolute beautiful presentation. I make this only when the strawberries are at their peak!*

½ gallon vanilla ice cream
2 pints fresh, sweet strawberries
½ stick butter
1 lemon, juiced and the zest
¾ cup sugar
½ cup 100 proof liquor– I use Jim Beam's Bookers, 126.5 proof – talk about flaming!
¼ cup rum

In a large skillet, melt butter and sauté berries (if small leave them whole – cut the large ones in half) with sugar and lemon juice and zest. Cook on high heat about 3 minutes. Pour 100 or better proof liquor and flame stirring constantly. Add rum. Cook a few minutes more. The sauce will slightly thicken. Serve over ice cream. Garnish with a sprig of mint.

# BANANAS FOSTER

1 stick butter
8 heaping Tablespoons dark brown sugar
6 bananas – sliced in half
2 Tablespoons banana liqueur
2 Tablespoons rum
2 Tablespoons brandy
Cinnamon
Vanilla Ice Cream

In a large skillet, melt butter, add sugar. Stir until sugar melts. Add sliced bananas and cook just until tender. Add liqueur. Shake your skillet around. Sprinkle rum and brandy over – ignite. Spoon gently over a few times. Sprinkle cinnamon and quickly spoon over very hard frozen ice cream. Hard to beat!

When I Bake:
When I'm bad, I'm very bad!
I use all butter.
When I'm good, I'm pretty good.
I use half butter and half Fleischmann's Margarine.

## OLD FASHIONED POUND CAKE

1    **cup butter**
½   **cup Crisco**
3    **cups sugar**
5    **eggs**
3    **cups sifted flour**
½   **teaspoon baking**
      **powder**
½   **teaspoon salt**
1    **cup milk**
1    **Tablespoon vanilla**

**Sauce:**
1    **cup sugar**
½   **cup water**
1    **Tablespoon almond**
      **extract**

Cream together butter, Crisco and sugar, Add eggs one at a time. Sift together flour, baking powder, and salt. Add alternately with milk. Add vanilla. Pour into a greased and floured tube pan. Bake at 325 degrees for 80 minutes or until it tests done. This cake freezes well.

Bake according to directions. Cool 15 minutes and pour sauce over cake while still in pan.

In a small sauce pan, bring sugar, water and almond extract to a boil. Pour over cake while in pan. This will soak into cake. Let cool completely before removing from pan. This freezes beautifully!

Variations: Instead of vanilla use 1 teaspoon rum extract or 1 teaspoon coconut extract.

# ELLA MAE'S HOLIDAY FILLED POUND CAKE

*Absolutely fabulous and just delicious…just beautiful!*

**Filling:**
1   cup raisins puffed (steam in a colander about 30 minutes)
1   cup coconut (if not using fresh, I like the frozen the best)
1   cup chopped pecans
1   recipe <u>Lemon Curd</u>
1   recipe <u>Seven Minute Icing</u>

**Lemon Curd:**
1   stick of butter
1   cup sugar
2   lemons – juiced & the zest
2   eggs

Prepare one recipe of my <u>Old Fashioned Pound Cake</u>. Bake in three 9 inch greased cake pans at 35 degrees 30 to 40 minutes. Let cool. Put together as follows: Combine raisins, coconut and pecans. Between each layer spread lemon curd, then raisins, coconut and pecans. If you are ambitious, you can make an extra recipe of your icing and stir into your raisins, coconut, and pecans. Ice top and sides of cake with seven minute icing. If you have a little coconut left, sprinkle on the top of cake.

Lemon Curd: In a double boiler – melt butter, add sugar, lemon juice and zest. Add slightly beaten eggs, stirring constantly. Cook until thick. This keeps really well in the refrigerator.

<u>Variation</u>: Slice an angel food cake in half. Tunnel out bottom layer. Fill with lemon curd. Top and ice with seven minute icing. Wonderful and easy! This lemon curd is also perfect for your tarts. Very English!

*(Ella Mae's Holiday Filled Pound Cake, continued)*

**Seven Minute Icing:**

| | |
|---|---|
| 2 | **egg whites** |
| 1½ | **cups sugar** |
| 5 | **Tablespoons water** |
| ¼ | **teaspoon cream of tartar** |
| 1½ | **teaspoons light corn syrup** |
| 1 | **teaspoon vanilla** |

Place icing ingredients except vanilla in top of double boiler and beat until thoroughly blended. Place over rapidly boiling water. Beat constantly with rotary beater for 7 minutes. Remove from heat and add vanilla. Continue beating until mixture reaches spreading consistency.

# COLD OVEN POUND CAKE

| | |
|---|---|
| 3 | **cups sugar** |
| 2 | **sticks butter** |
| ½ | **cup Crisco** |
| 5 | **eggs** |
| 1 | **cup milk** |
| 3 | **cups flour** |
| ½ | **teaspoon salt** |
| ½ | **teaspoon baking powder** |
| ½ | **teaspoon vanilla** |
| ½ | **teaspoon lemon flavoring** |

Cream butter, Crisco and sugar; add eggs, then gradually add flour, salt and baking powder alternately with milk. Beat 12 minutes. Add vanilla and lemon flavoring. Pour into greased tube pan. Put cake in cold oven. Bake at 325 degrees for about 1½ hours. Do not preheat oven. Turn it on when you put the cake in. You cannot believe how good this makes your house smell in the morning or whenever.

# SPONGE CAKE

| | |
|---|---|
| 1 | cup cake flour – sifted |
| ¼ | teaspoon salt |
| 1½ | Tablespoons lemon juice |
| ½ | teaspoon grated lemon rind (The Zest) |
| 5 | large eggs, separated |
| 1 | cup sugar |

Sift the flour once. Measure again. Add the salt and sift 2 more times. Set aside. In your mixer, beat the egg yokes. Add the rind and juice and beat until very thick and light. In a separate bowl, beat egg whites until they are stiff enough to hold up in peaks. Slowly fold sugar into whites. Fold the egg yolk mixture, and slowly fold in the flour. Pour into an ungreased tube pan and bake in a 325 degree oven for 1 hour or more. Invert your pan for an hour before removing or until cold.

# CARROT CAKE

| | |
|---|---|
| 1½ | cups salad oil |
| 4 | eggs |
| 2 | cups sugar |
| 3 | cups grated carrots |
| 1 | cup nuts |
| 2 | cups flour |
| 1 | teaspoon cinnamon |
| 2 | teaspoons soda |
| ½ | teaspoon salt |

**Icing:**

| | |
|---|---|
| 1 | stick oleo or butter |
| 1 | (8–ounce) package cream cheese |
| 1 | box powdered sugar |
| 1 | teaspoon vanilla |

Beat eggs. Add oil. Add sugar gradually. Mix dry ingredients and chopped nuts. Add to oil mixture. Add carrots. Bake in three 9–inch greased cake pans at 350 degrees for 40 minutes. Let cool. Put together with following icing:

Cream butter and cream cheese. Add sugar gradually, keeping beater on medium speed. Cake must be cool before iced, or else this icing will melt.

# ITALIAN CREAM CAKE

1   stick butter
½   cup Wesson oil
2   cups sugar
5   eggs, separated
1   cup buttermilk
1   teaspoon baking soda
2   cups flour
1   teaspoon vanilla
1   cup shredded
      coconut
½   cup nuts, chopped

Icing:
1   8 ounce package
      cream cheese,
      softened
1   stick butter,
      softened
1   teaspoon vanilla
1   box powdered sugar
½   cup nuts, chopped

Cream butter, oil and sugar. Add egg yolks one at a time, beating after each addition. Stir baking soda into buttermilk. Add sifted flour into batter, alternately with buttermilk mixture. Add vanilla, coconut and chopped nuts. Beat egg whites and fold into mixture. Pour into a greased and floured 9 x 13 inch cake pan for a sheet cake and three 8 or 9 inch layer pans. Bake at 325 degrees for 45 minutes. Cool and ice.

Icing: Beat cream cheese and butter. Add vanilla, powdered sugar and nuts. Continue to beat until of spreading consistency.

## LEMON POPPY SEED CAKE

| | |
|---|---|
| 1 | **cup butter** |
| 1¾ | **cups granulated sugar, divided** |
| 1 | **package cream cheese, softened** |
| 5 | **eggs, separated** |
| ¾ | **cup lemon juice** |
| 2⅔ | **cups flour** |
| 1¼ | **teaspoons baking powder** |
| 1 | **teaspoon baking soda** |
| ⅓ | **cup poppy seeds** |

Heat oven to 350 degrees. Beat butter, 1½ cups sugar, and cream cheese in large bowl at medium speed with electric mixer until light and fluffy. Blend in egg yolks and lemon juice. Add combined flour, baking powder, and baking soda; mix well. Beat in poppy seed. Set aside. Beat egg whites until foamy. Gradually add reserved ¼ cup sugar, beating until soft peaks form. Fold in egg whites. Pour into greased 10 inch tube pan. Bake for 55 minutes.

## SPICE CAKE WITH OLD FASHION CARAMEL ICING

**Cake:**
| | |
|---|---|
| 1 | **box Spice Cake mix** |

**Icing:**
| | |
|---|---|
| 1 | **stick butter** |
| 1 | **cup brown sugar** |
| ¼ | **cup Pet milk** |
| 3 | **cups powdered sugar** |

Bake cake as directed in 2 round tins. Cool.

Melt butter in saucepan; add brown sugar and milk. Slowly add powdered sugar mixing until a good spreading consistency. Split cooled cake rounds in halves. Spread a little icing between each layer. Ice top with remaining icing.

## HERSHEY BAR CAKE

2    sticks butter
2    cups sugar
8    plain Hershey bars
     (small), melted over
     hot water (these
     may be added while
     warm)
4    eggs, one at a time,
     beat each
2½   cups flour
½    teaspoon salt
1    cup buttermilk with
     ¼ teaspoon soda
     added
2    teaspoons vanilla
2    cups chopped nuts

Cream together the butter and sugar. Add melted Hershey bars and beaten eggs. Mix the flour, salt and buttermilk with soda added. Add flour and milk mixture alternately to butter mixture. Add vanilla and nuts.

Bake in one 14 x 10 x 2-inch pan, well greased and floured at 325 degrees or bake in two 11 x 7 x 1¼-inch pans at 350 degrees. Bake for about 40 minutes or until a straw stuck in center of cake comes out clean.

## A CHOCOLATE DREAM CAKE

1    German chocolate
     cake mix (according
     to directions on
     box using a 9 x 13
     inch pan)
1    can Eagle Brand
     condensed milk
1    jar of caramel ice
     cream topping
3    or 4 Heath or Skor
     bars, which have
     been broken up in a
     processor – or
     whatever method

Prepare cake. While hot, punch lots of holes in the cake and pour condensed milk and ice cream topping over. Sprinkle broken up candy bars all over the top of the above. Save about ½ cup to top with. When cool, cover with Cool Whip and top with remaining Heath or Skor bars. When not in use, keep in refrigerator.

# FRESH APPLE CAKE

Yield: one 10– inch cake, 1½ cups glaze.

3　cups all–purpose flour
1¼　teaspoons baking soda
1　teaspoon salt
2　cups sugar
1½　cups vegetable oil
2　eggs, beaten
2　Tablespoons vanilla extract
½　teaspoon lemon juice
3　cups peeled, chopped cooking apples
1½　cups chopped pecans, toasted
　　Glaze (recipe follows)

Glaze:
1　cup sugar
1　cup firmly packed light brown sugar
¼　cup butter or margarine
1　teaspoon cream of tartar
1　teaspoon ground cinnamon
1　teaspoon ground nutmeg
½　cup milk

Combine flour, soda, and salt; mix well, and set aside. Combine sugar, oil, eggs, vanilla, and lemon juice; beat 2 minutes at medium speed of an electric mixer. Add flour mixture; beat at low speed just until blended. Fold in apples and pecans. Spoon batter into a greased and floured 10– inch tube pan. Bake at 325 degrees for 1 hour and 20 minutes or until a wooden pick inserted in center comes out clean. Cool in pan 10 minutes. Remove from pan; immediately drizzle glaze over warm cake.

Combine all glaze ingredients, except milk, in a heavy saucepan. Stir in milk. Bring mixture to a full boil, and cook 2 minutes, stirring constantly. Let cool to lukewarm.

# CHOCOLATE COOKIE SHEET

Makes 35 squares.

2   cups flour
2   cups sugar
½   teaspoon salt
1   stick oleo
1   cup water
½   cup shortening
3   Tablespoons cocoa
2   eggs, beaten
1   teaspoon soda
½   cup buttermilk
1   teaspoon vanilla

Icing:
1   stick oleo
3   Tablespoons cocoa
1   box powdered sugar
1   teaspoon vanilla
½   cup chopped nuts
6   Tablespoons milk
    Pinch of salt

Sift together flour, sugar and salt. In a saucepan put oleo, water, shortening and cocoa. Bring to boil and pour over flour mixture. Mix well. In another bowl beat eggs. Add soda, buttermilk and vanilla. Stir well and add to first mixture. Mix well. Bake in greased and floured cookie sheet (15½ x 10½ x 1 inch) at 350 degrees for 20–25 minutes. Start making icing during last 5 minutes of baking.

Icing: Using same saucepan as above, melt oleo and cocoa but do not boil. Take off heat and add powdered sugar, vanilla, nuts and milk. Ice cake.

# GERMAN SWEET CHOCOLATE CAKE

This recipe is on the Baker's German's Sweet Chocolate Box. The Best of All!

# CAPPUCCINO CHOCOLATE CAKE

Yield: 12 servings.

1     package devil's food
      cake mix
1     cup orange juice
⅓     cup cold coffee
⅓     cup cooking oil
1     Tablespoon brandy
1     teaspoon grated
      orange peel
3     eggs

<u>Frosting</u>:
1     can ready–to–spread
      fudge frosting
      supreme
1     teaspoon grated
      orange peel
½     teaspoon brandy
12    pecan halves or
      chopped pecans

Heat oven to 350 degrees. Grease and flour two 8 or 9–inch round cake pans. Blend cake ingredients; beat 2 minutes at highest speed. Pour into prepared pans.

Bake at 350 degrees. Bake 8–inch layers for 30 to 40 minutes; 9–inch layers for 25 to 30 minutes or until toothpick inserted in center comes out clean. Cool in pans 15 minutes; invert onto cooling racks to cool completely. By hand, mix frosting ingredients until well blended. Fill and frost cake, using ¼ cup of frosting between layers. Garnish with pecan halves.

Jackie Woods always baked this for our Birthday Group. Jackie, it's all yours!

# RUM CAKE

1   cup pecans, chopped
1   package yellow cake
      mix
1   package French
      vanilla instant
      pudding
½   cup water
½   cup Wesson oil
½   cup rum
4   eggs

Sauce:
1   stick butter
1   cup sugar
¼   cup water
2   ounces rum

Sprinkle chopped pecans on bottom of greased tub or bundt pan. Mix together cake mix, pudding, water, Wesson oil and rum. Beat in eggs one at a time. Pour batter into pan and bake 1 hour at 325 degrees. Let cool.

Sauce: Boil butter, sugar, water and rum together in saucepan. Pour over cake while in pan. This will soak into cake. Let cake completely cool before removing from pan. This freezes beautifully.

# BETTER THAN SEX CAKE

1   box yellow cake mix
1   20 ounce can
      crushed pineapple
1   cup sugar
1   3 ounce package
      instant vanilla
      pudding mix
1   cup coconut
1   8 ounce carton
      prepared whipped
      topping
1   cup chopped pecans

Bake cake mix as directed on box in 13 x 9 x 2–inch pan. Meanwhile, simmer pineapple and sugar. Remove cake from oven; punch holes in it, cover with pineapple, and chill. Mix instant pudding as directed on box. Add coconut; spread over pineapple. Cover with topping; sprinkle with nuts. Good! But, like Mama said, "don't believe everything you ever heard!"

# STRAWBERRY CAKE

| 1 | box white cake mix |
| 1 | cup Wesson oil |
| 1 | package strawberry jello |
| ½ | cup milk or ½ cup strawberry juice |
| 4 | eggs |
| 1 | cup crushed strawberries |
| 1 | cup chopped pecans |
| 1 | cup coconut |

**Icing:**

| ½ | cup crushed strawberries |
| 1 | box powdered sugar |
| 1 | stick butter |
| ½ | cup chopped pecans |
| ½ | cup coconut |
| ½ | teaspoon butter flavoring |
| ½ | teaspoon red food coloring |

Mix cake mix, oil, jello, and milk or strawberry juice. Add eggs one at a time (beat lightly after each egg). To mixture, add crushed strawberries, pecans and coconut. Blend thoroughly. Pour batter into greased and floured 10–inch cake pans. Bake 350 degrees for 30 minutes.

For icing, cream sugar with butter; add strawberries, pecans and coconut. Blend in butter, flavoring and food coloring. Ice cooled cake.

# SOUR CREAM COCONUT CAKE

*(Mrs. Preston Trousdale (Joy), of Florence, Alabama shared this cake and recipe with me years ago and it is a winner!)*

1   **Duncan Hines yellow cake mix**

**Frosting:**
1   **8 ounce container sour cream**
2   **cups sugar**
3   **packages frozen coconut**
1   **large container Cool Whip**

Bake cake according to directions in 2 round cake pans. Cool and split layers.

Combine sour cream, sugar and 2 packages of coconut. Stir every once in awhile when cake is baking.

Put smooth side of layer of cake on cake plate first. Ice the layer with the frosting, then spread a layer of Cool Whip on top. Continue to do this until you have frosted all layers. (Always place cut side of cake up so layers will absorb the frosting.) Then generously cover the whole cake with Cool Whip and sprinkle a package of coconut on top and sides. Refrigerate 24 hours.

# MINIATURE CHERRY CHEESECAKE TARTS

| | |
|---|---|
| 3 | 8–ounce packages cream cheese, softened |
| 5 | eggs |
| 1 | cup sugar |
| 1½ | teaspoons vanilla |
| 1 | teaspoon lemon juice |
| ½ | teaspoon finely grated lemon rind |
| 1 | can cherry pie filling |

**Icing**:

| | |
|---|---|
| 1 | cup sour cream |
| ½ | cup sugar |
| ½ | teaspoon sugar |

Preheat oven to 375 degrees. Beat cream cheese, eggs, sugar, vanilla, lemon juice and rind. Fill miniature cup cake papers, almost to the top. Bake 30 minutes; remove from oven and ice and top with a cherry...bake 5 more minutes.

# LOW FAT LEMONY CHEESECAKE WITH FRESH FRUIT

Vegetable cooking spray

¼ cup graham cracker crumbs

2 (8–ounce) packages fat free cream cheese

1 (14–ounce) can Eagle Brand Low Fat Sweetened Condensed Milk (NOT evaporated milk)

4 egg whites

1 egg

⅓ cup real lemon juice

1 teaspoon vanilla extract

⅓ cup unsifted flour

1 cup fresh assorted fruit

Preheat oven to 300 degrees. Spray bottom of 8–inch springform pan with cooking spray; sprinkle crumbs on bottom of pan. In mixer bowl, beat cheese until fluffy. Gradually beat in Eagle Brand milk until smooth. Add egg whites, egg, lemon juice, and vanilla; mix well. Stir in flour. Pour into prepared pan. Bake 50 to 55 minutes or until center is set. Cool. Chill. Serve with fruit.

# THE BEST LITTLE PECAN SQUARES

*Pretty to pass or a perfect dessert. Served warm with whipping cream!*

**Crust:**
- ⅔ **cup confectioners' sugar**
- 2 **cups all–purpose flour**
- 2 **sticks butter**

**Topping:**
- ⅔ **cup melted butter**
- ½ **cup honey**
- 3 **Tablespoons heavy cream**
- ½ **cup brown sugar**
- 3½ **cups pecans, coarsely chopped**

Preheat oven to 350 degrees. Grease a 9 x 12–inch baking pan. Sift sugar and flour together. Cut in butter and blend well. Pat crust into the pan. Bake about 20 minutes. Mix butter, honey, cream and brown sugar. Add pecans, mixing well. Spread over crust – careful not to spill over edges. Return to oven and bake about 25 minutes more. Cool before cutting.

# HELEN CORBITT'S SAND TARTS

*Everyone South of New York makes these Sand Tarts at Christmas time. They keep forever.*

Yield: 4 dozen.

- ½ **pound butter – room temperature**
- ½ **cup sifted confectioners' sugar**
- 2 **cups sifted cake flour**
- 1 **cup chopped pecans**
- 1 **teaspoon vanilla**

Cream butter; add sugar. Stir well and add flour, nuts, and vanilla. Shape into balls or crescents and bake on ungreased cookie sheet at 325 degrees for 20 minutes or until a light brown. Roll in powdered sugar while warm.

# RASPBERRY COCONUT SQUARES

1¼ cups all–purpose
 flour
1½ cups sugar, divided
¼ Tablespoon salt
½ cup butter or
 margarine
4 eggs
1 cup seedless red
 raspberry jam
¼ cup butter or
 margarine, softened
1½ cups shredded
 coconut

Put the flour, ½ cup sugar and the salt in a mixing bowl and blend well. With a pastry blender, cut in the ½ cup butter or margarine until particles are quite fine. Add one lightly beaten egg and toss to mix. Gather the mixture together, working quickly with your hands to form a dough. Press the mixture evenly on the bottom of a lightly buttered 10 x 15 inch pan. Spread the jam on top. Cream the softened butter or margarine with the remaining one cup sugar. Add the remaining 3 eggs, one at a time, beating after each addition. Beat until light and creamy. Add the coconut and mix well. Spread over the jam layer. Bake at 350 degrees for 20 to 25 minutes or until golden brown. Cool the pan on a rack. Cut in squares.

## LEMON CRISPS

*Better than Tea Cakes!*

½  **cup butter**
1½  **cups confectioners' sugar**
1  **egg yolk**
3  **Tablespoons lemon juice**
2  **cups flour**

Cream butter and sugar. Beat in egg yolk and lemon juice. Gradually add flour. Chill at least one hour. Lightly flour board and roll dough. Bake 10 to 12 minutes in a 350 degree oven. Watch them. Sift confectioners' sugar on top of warm cookies. When rolling cookies, be sure and use a heavyweight pastry cloth and rolling pin cover set on rolling pin, as this is a very short pastry.

I love to serve these with my Mint Sherbet...Perfect!

## CINNAMON STICKS

½  **pound butter**
¾  **cup sugar**
2  **cups flour**
1  **egg yolk**
4  **teaspoons ground cinnamon**
1  **teaspoon vanilla**
1  **cup chopped pecans**

Cream butter and sugar; gradually add flour, then egg yolk, cinnamon, and vanilla. Put on buttered cookie sheet and pat down until about ¼ inch thick. Put the unbeaten egg white on top, spread all over, then press chopped pecans down into all. Bake in 350 degree oven about 30 minutes. Cut in oblong pieces.

# OLD FASHION TEA CAKES

1   pound butter (you can use half butter and half Fleischmann's)
3   eggs
2   teaspoons baking powder
2   teaspoons vanilla
2   cups sugar
¼   teaspoon salt
1   teaspoon soda
1   Tablespoon vinegar
1   teaspoon nutmeg (optional)
6   to 8 cups flour

Frosting:
1½   cups sifted powdered sugar
½   stick butter
2   to 3 teaspoons lemon juice

Add enough flour to make dough the consistency to roll out paper thin cookies. I always divide my dough in 4 balls. Chill. Roll between 2 pieces of wax paper with a little flour and sugar. These are just perfect for your Holiday cookies, Valentines, Easter Rabbits, Christmas trees and Shamrocks and you can frost them too! I like them plain though!

To make frosting, cream powdered sugar with butter and enough lemon juice to make a spreading consistency. You can use food coloring.

## SNICKERDOODLES

Makes 5 to 6 dozen.

| | |
|---|---|
| 1 | **stick butter** |
| 1 | **stick oleo** |
| 1½ | **cups sugar** |
| 2 | **eggs, beaten well** |
| 2¾ | **cups sifted flour** |
| 2 | **teaspoons cream of tartar** |
| 1 | **teaspoon soda** |
| 1 | **teaspoon salt** |
| 2 | **Tablespoons sugar** |
| 2 | **Tablespoons cinnamon** |

Cream butter, oleo and sugar. Add eggs and beat well. Sift all dry ingredients, except cinnamon and sugar; add to egg mixture. Mix thoroughly and put in the refrigerator overnight. Roll into balls the size of a walnut; roll in cinnamon and sugar mixture. Bake on a greased cookie sheet at 375 degrees for 8 to 10 minutes. Let stand a minute before removing from cookie sheet.

## COWBOY COOKIES

*A favorite for children, young or old.*

Makes 8 to 9 dozen.

| | |
|---|---|
| 1 | **cup butter (can use half margarine)** |
| 1 | **cup brown sugar** |
| 1 | **cup white sugar** |
| 2 | **eggs** |
| 1 | **teaspoon vanilla** |
| 2 | **cups flour** |
| 1 | **teaspoon soda** |
| ½ | **teaspoon salt** |
| ½ | **teaspoon baking powder** |
| 2 | **cups rolled oats** |
| 1 | **small package semi-sweet chocolate chips** |
| ½ | **cup chopped nuts** |

Cream sugars, butter, eggs, and vanilla until fluffy. Sift dry ingredients and stir in. Add oatmeal, chocolate chips and nuts. Drop by a teaspoonful on cookie sheet. Bake at 350 degrees for 12 minutes.

## ICE BOX COOKIES

1    cup butter
2    cups sugar
½    cup brown sugar,
        firmly packed
2    eggs
4    cups sifted flour
3    teaspoons baking
        powder
¼    teaspoon salt
1    Tablespoon vanilla
2    cups finely chopped
        nuts

Cream butter and sugars. Mix in beaten eggs. Sift flour with baking powder and salt; add to egg mixture. Stir in vanilla and nuts. Make dough into rolls about the diameter of a fifty cent piece. Wrap in wax paper and refrigerate overnight. Slice thinly; bake on cookie sheet at 350 degrees until light brown. Remove from pan and cool. Keep in tightly closed container. This dough keeps up to 10 days in the refrigerator. It is nice to pull a roll out and bake fresh homemade cookies. Makes your house smell so good!

## A CHOCOLATE CHIP KISS

2    egg whites
⅔    cup sugar
1    teaspoon vanilla
      Pinch of salt
1    cup broken pecans
1    6 ounce package
        chocolate chips

Preheat oven 350 to 400 degrees. Beat egg whites until stiff. Blend in sugar; add vanilla and salt. Fold in pecans and chocolate chips. Drop on shiny side of foil on a cookie sheet. Put cookies in oven; turn heat off, and leave overnight. If too sticky, leave out in air to dry. Snow white and they melt in your mouth!

# HELLO DOLLIES

*Quick, easy and delicious.*

1¾  **cups graham cracker crumbs**
¾    **stick melted butter**
2    **Tablespoons sugar**
1    **cup chocolate chips**
1    **cup coconut**
1    **cup pecans, chopped**
1    **can condensed milk**

Mix graham cracker crumbs, sugar and butter until crumbly and press into the bottom of a 12 x 8 inch or a little smaller Pyrex dish or pan. Layer the chocolate chips, coconut and pecans. Pour condensed milk over top of layered ingredients. Bake at 350 degrees for 25 to 30 minutes. Cook and cut in squares. These are June Godfrey's and hers are the best!

If you're really in a hurry, use a ready made graham cracker pie crust.

# TEA TIME TASSIES

**Pastry:**
2    **3 ounce packages cream cheese**
1    **cup butter**
2    **cups flour**
**Filling:**
1½   **cups light brown sugar**
2    **Tablespoons melted butter**
2    **teaspoons vanilla**
     **Dash of salt**
2    **eggs, beaten**
1⅓   **cups chopped nuts**

Mix pastry dough with your hands. Roll into a big ball and chill 1 hour. Make into 1 inch balls and press to fit small ungreased muffin tins. Filling: Mix sugar, butter and vanilla. Add salt and beaten eggs. Fold in nuts and pour into uncooked pastry shells. Bake at 350 degrees until done, about 20 to 25 minutes. A perfect pick up dessert.

# COCONUT COOKIES

*When you taste this cookie, you will know the difference real butter makes! There is really no substitute!*

This makes about 4 dozen.

| | |
|---|---|
| 2 | **sticks butter** |
| ½ | **cup sugar** |
| 2 | **cups flour** |
| 1 | **teaspoon vanilla** |
| 1 | **3 ounce can Baker's Angel Flake coconut** |
| | **Confectioners' sugar** |

Cream butter and sugar thoroughly. Add flour, vanilla and coconut. Roll by hand into small balls. Put on a cookie sheet about an inch apart. Flatten these balls with a fork which has been dipped in cold water. Bake at 350 degrees for 20 to 25 minutes. Cool the cookies and dust with powdered sugar. These are very simple to make but very, very good and pretty on your cookie tray.

# BANBERRY TARTS

| | |
|---|---|
| 3 | **sticks butter** |
| 1 | **cup sugar** |
| 2 | **egg yolks** |
| 1 | **teaspoon vanilla** |
| 4 | **cups flour** |
| | **Jelly of your choice, preferably mayhaw** |

Cream butter and sugar. Mix in egg yolks, flour and vanilla. Roll balls the size of marbles. Indent with your thumb and fill with a dab of jelly. Bake at 350 degrees for 10 to 15 minutes. So pretty!

# PECAN DAINTIES

Yield: 3 dozen.

| 1 | egg white |
| 1 | cup light brown sugar |
| 1½ | cups pecan halves |

Beat egg white until stiff. Add brown sugar gradually, beating constantly. Work in the nuts and drop from a teaspoon onto a greased cookie sheet. Bake at 250 degrees for 30 minutes. Remove from cookie sheet immediately and cool.

# GINGERSNAPS

Yield: 4 dozen.

| 1 | cup sugar |
| 1 | cup shortening |
| 1 | cup dark molasses |
| 1 | Tablespoon ground allspice |
| 1 | Tablespoon ground ginger |
| 1 | Tablespoon soda in 4 Tablespoons boiling water |
| 2 | cups flour or more |

Mix sugar and shortening until light. Add the molasses, allspice, and ginger. Stir in the soda and water and flour. Roll as thin as possible and cut. Bake at 350 degrees for 10–12 minutes. They are crisp and wonderful.

## LACE COOKIES

½  **cup white corn syrup**
½  **cup brown sugar, packed**
½  **cup butter**
¼  **teaspoon almond extract**
¾  **cup instant type flour, Wondra**
½  **cup almonds, chopped fine**

Heat oven to 325 degrees. In a medium saucepan, heat corn syrup, brown sugar and butter. Stir in almond extract and flour; add nuts. Drop by level teaspoonsful, 4 inches apart, onto a greased cookie sheet. Bake 6 or 7 minutes. Remove from oven; let stand 1 minute. Remove, one at a time from the cookie sheet; quickly roll the cookie around the handle of a wooden spoon. If the cookies get too hard to roll, reheat in the oven a minute or two. Repeat with remaining dough. Cool. Store in a tightly closed cookie tin. These can be made a week in advance. Wonderful with ice cream or whipping cream.

# MAGIC PEANUT BUTTER CRISPS

Yield: About 4 dozen.

1    **cup peanut butter**
1    **cup sugar**
1    **egg, beaten**
1    **teaspoon vanilla**
      **extract**

Combine peanut butter and sugar; mix well. Stir in egg and vanilla. Roll dough into ¾–inch balls. Place balls on ungreased cookie sheets. Flatten with a floured fork. Bake cookies at 350 degrees for 10 minutes. Allow to cool before removing from cookie sheets.

# LEMON LOVES

1    **cup flour**
½    **cup butter**
2    **Tablespoons sugar**
1    **cup sugar**
5    **Tablespoons flour**
½    **teaspoon baking**
      **powder**
2    **eggs**
3    **Tablespoons lemon**
      **juice**

<u>Frosting</u>:
1½  **cups sifted powdered**
      **sugar**
½    **stick butter**
2    **to 3 teaspoons lemon**
      **juice**

Mix first three ingredients. Press into a 9 x 9 inch pan and bake at 350 degrees for 15 minutes. Sift sugar, flour and baking powder. Beat eggs with lemon juice. Mix with flour and pour in crust. Bake at 350 degrees for 25 minutes. Remove from oven and frost with powdered sugar creamed with butter and enough lemon juice to make a spreading consistency. These are so rich – sometimes I leave the frosting off and just sprinkle with powdered sugar.

# CARAMEL SQUARES

2  sticks butter (can
   use half margarine)
1  package dark brown
   sugar
2  eggs
2  cups sifted flour
2  teaspoons baking
   powder
2  cups chopped pecans
   Dash of salt
2  teaspoons vanilla
   Powdered sugar

Mix butter and brown sugar in a double boiler and melt. Cool the mixture and add eggs one at a time beating well after each. Add flour and baking powder. Mix well. Stir in pecans, salt and vanilla. Pour into a greased and floured 13 x 9 x 2 inch baking dish. Bake in a 350 degree oven for 25 to 30 minutes. Let cool, dust with powdered sugar and cut into squares.

# COCONUT SQUARES

*Like eating a piece of coconut custard pie. Carol LeDoux makes them best.*

4  eggs, beaten well
1¾  cups sugar
½  cup self–rising flour
½  cup oleo, melted
1  teaspoon vanilla
6  or 7 ounces coconut

Mix eggs, sugar and flour. Add oleo, vanilla and coconut. Pour into a well greased 8–inch square pan and bake at 325 degrees about 40 minutes or until lightly brown. Cool before cutting...gooey and good!

# BAKLAVA –
# A MIDDLE EASTERN FAVORITE!

Makes about 36 pieces.

1   **pound frozen filo dough**
2   **cups finely chopped pecans**
1   **cup clarified butter**
¼   **cup sugar**
1   **teaspoon cinnamon**
½   **teaspoon ground nutmeg**
    **Pinch ground cloves**
    **Honey syrup (see recipe on next page)**

Thaw filo dough to room temperature, about 2 hours. Cut filo dough in half crosswise. Cover with a slightly damp towel. Lightly butter the bottom of a 14 x 10 x 2–inch baking dish. Lay 10 of the half sheets of filo dough in the pan, brushing each sheet with the butter. Mix nuts, sugar and spices. Sprinkle half the nut mixture over filo in pan. Drizzle with some of the melted butter. Top with another 20 sheets of the half sheets of filo, brushing each piece with melted butter. Repeat with another layer of the nut mixture and the rest of the filo. With a sharp knife, cut into small diamond–shaped pieces – try not to cut all the way to the bottom. Bake in a pre-heated 350 degree oven for 50 – 55 minutes. Finish cutting and allow to cool thoroughly. Pour warm honey syrup over. Allow to stand several hours before serving. Can be frozen.

*(Continued on next page)*

*(Baklava – A Middle Eastern Favorite!, continued)*

**Clarified butter:**
1½  cups butter

**Honey syrup:**
1   cup sugar
1   cup water
1   Tablespoon orange
     flower water
½   lemon, sliced
3   Tablespoons honey

Clarified butter: melt butter over low heat. Remove from heat and let stand a few minutes. Skim foam off top and carefully pour off clear butter, leaving sediment in pan. Makes 1 cup.

Honey syrup: In a heavy saucepan, combine sugar, water, orange flower water, and sliced lemon. Boil gently 15 minutes. Remove lemon slices, and add honey. Stir until blended. Keep warm until ready to pour over baklava.

# NEIMAN MARCUS BROWNIES

*An easy and perfect pick up dessert!*

1   box Swiss Chocolate
     cake mix or a
     yellow cake mix
2   cups chopped nuts
1   egg
1   stick butter, melted

**Frosting:**
1   8–ounce package
     cream cheese, room
     temperature
3   eggs
1   box powdered sugar

Mix well the cake mix, nuts, egg and butter; dough will be very stiff. Press down in a 9 x 13 inch greased pan.

For frosting, mix together cream cheese, eggs, and powdered sugar. Spread on top. Bake at 350 degrees for 45 minutes.

# MELTING MOMENTS

Yield: 9 dozen.

1    cup butter, softened
⅓    cup powdered sugar
1¼   cups flour
½    cup cornstarch
     Lemon Frosting
     (Recipe follows)

Lemon Frosting:
¼    cup butter, softened
1½   cups sifted powdered
     sugar
2    Tablespoons lemon
     juice
1    Tablespoon lemon
     rind

Cream butter; add sugar, and beat. Gradually add flour and cornstarch beating until smooth. Drop by teaspoons onto ungreased cookie sheet. Bake at 350 for 10 – 12 minutes (cookies do not brown on top). Cool slightly on cookie sheets; then finish cooling on wire racks. Frost with lemon frosting.

Cream butter; gradually add powdered sugar and lemon juice, beating until smooth. Stir in lemon rind.

# MINI CHRISTMAS FRUIT CAKES

1    small can coconut
½    pound candied
     cherries
½    pound candied
     pineapple
2½   cups whole pecans
½    cup flour
1    can Eagle Brand
     condensed milk
     Miniature muffin
     pans

Mix all ingredients. Place pan of water under cakes. Bake at 300 degrees for 30 to 35 minutes, until brown. Makes 48 miniature fruit cakes. Do not overcook because they will get really dry. For a large cake, bake at 325 degrees for 1 hour. Note: This recipe works better if you mix the flour and condensed milk together first, then add rest of ingredients. So good and easy – perfect with eggnog!

# PIE

$\pi r^2$ – No pie are round – cornbread are square, according to Junior Samples of Hee Haw. See how my mind works and Mike Cage lets me take care of all his money...Hmmm.

Nothing is better than a beautiful baked pie. I am giving you my favorites and tips for flaky, tender pastry which is the secret of a good pie and tips for your meringue pies.

Soo good – pies are loaded with fat, so just remember – exercise, and count those fat grams on the day you are going to enjoy a piece of pie. Cut back on something else and treat "yo–self"!

Like Mama said, "Enjoy everything, just don't overindulge on anything!"

Don't forget! There are some delicious store bought pie crusts in the supermarket. A wonderful time saver.

## BUTTER PECAN CRUST

*Rich and wonderful for your ice box pies!*

1    **cup flour**
¼    **cup brown sugar**
½    **cup chopped pecans**
     **or walnuts**
½    **cup butter**

Cream together all ingredients. Press into the bottom of a 9 inch pie pan. Bake in a 350 degree oven for 20 minutes. Crumbs should be slightly brown.

# BASIC PASTRY RECIPE (WITH WATER)

Makes 2 crusts.

2½  cups flour
⅓  cup plus 1
    Tablespoon ice
    water
½  cup shortening

Sift flour and salt together in a bowl. Cut shortening until it is size of very small peas. Sprinkle ice water on mixture. Stir with fork. Press dough together. Divide in two parts. Shape each into a ball. Roll from center toward outside until large enough to fit a 9–inch pie plate. Use as little flour as possible. Place rolled dough in pie plate. Flute edges. Prick bottom and sides of dough if you're going to bake this without a filling in it.

# LOUISIANA FRESH STRAWBERRY PIE

1  quart fresh
    strawberries
¾  cup water
3  Tablespoons
    cornstarch
1  cup sugar
1  teaspoon lemon juice
1  cup cream, whipped
1  9 inch pastry crust

Line a baked pastry crust with fresh strawberries. Reserve about 1 cup of the berries for glaze. Simmer 1 cup of berries and ¾ cup water for 3 to 4 minutes. Combine cornstarch and sugar. Add this to berries along with lemon juice. Cook this mixture until thickened and clear. Pour over the berries in crust and chill in the refrigerator. Top with whipped cream.

# MILDRED'S HELPFUL TIPS FOR GOOD MERINGUE PIES

Fluffy, tender, meringue–topped pies rank near the top of the list of favorite desserts. To help you make meringue pies to be proud of, here are some helpful tips:

Much beating and slow baking are the keys to success. Start with fresh egg whites at room temperature. When separating the eggs, don't let a bit of yolk get in with the whites. Then beat the whites (sprinkled with a little salt or cream of tartar) until soft peaks form. Next sprinkle sugar, a tablespoon at a time, over the whites and continue to beat until they're definite peaks. Use 2 tablespoons of sugar for each egg white. The meringue should shine. If it's dull and dry, you've overbeaten it. Now, spread the meringue in swirls over the pie filling.

Spread the meringue clear to the edge of the pie so it touches the crust. This helps prevent shrinkage. If the filling is a cooked one, be sure it's thoroughly cooked. An undercooked filling may "water out" and you will blame the meringue while the filling is really at fault.

Then bake the pie in a moderate oven of 350 degrees for 12 to 15 minutes, or until delicately browned. Of course, if the meringue is a high one, 2 inches or more, reduce the heat to 325 degrees and bake about 20 minutes. Keep in mind that meringue pies do not keep well. They'll become tough if refrigerated, and they cannot be frozen successfully.

# CARAMEL–BANANA PIE

1   baked pie crust –
    deep dish
2   cups finely chopped
    pecans, toasted
    lightly
1   can sweetened
    condensed milk
2   or 3 sliced bananas
    Whipping cream or
    Cool Whip

Remove paper from condensed milk can, BUT DO NOT OPEN. Place unopened can in a deep pan and cover with water. Bring to a boil, then simmer (a slow boil) for 3 hours, to caramelize (make sure can is always covered with water). Cool completely before opening or it might EXPLODE. Please be careful.

Place ⅔ of pecans in bottom of crust. Pour cooled caramelized condensed milk over the pecans then the sliced bananas. Top with whipped cream or Cool Whip. Garnish with remaining pecans.

So easy and so wonderful!

# FRESH BERRY PIES

*(Blueberry, Dewberry, or Blackberry)*
*A summertime must!*

**My Pastry for double crust pie (page 298)**

4 **cups fresh berries of your choice**
1 **Tablespoon lemon juice**
1 **cup sugar**
¼ **cup water**
2½ **Tablespoons cornstarch, dissolved in ¼ cup water**
½ **teaspoon grated lemon peel**
½ **teaspoon cinnamon**
½ **teaspoon grated, fresh nutmeg**
⅓ **teaspoon salt**
2 **Tablespoons butter**

Prepare pastry. In a saucepan, add berries, lemon juice, sugar and water. Bring to a simmer. Add cornstarch, lemon peel, cinnamon, and nutmeg. Cook, stirring carefully, until slightly thick. Pour into unbaked pastry; dot with butter. Cover with top crust; seal and flute edges. Cut slits in top and sprinkle with about 2 tablespoons sugar and cinnamon, if desired. Bake 10 minutes in a 450 degree oven; reduce heat to 350 degrees and bake about 30 to 40 minutes longer or until crust is brown and juice bubbles through the slits. Serve warm. Delicious with vanilla ice cream!

# RHUBARB PIE

*Hazel and John Silkman are a perfect team and a delight to know. Her Rhubarb is the best!*

Serves 6; 610 calories per serving.

1⅓ to 1⅔ cups sugar
⅓ cup all–purpose flour
½ teaspoon grated orange peel
4 cups cut up rhubarb (½–inch pieces)
2 Tablespoons margarine or butter

Heat oven to 425 degrees. Prepare pastry. Mix sugar, flour and orange peel. Turn half of the rhubarb into pastry–lined pie plate; sprinkle with half of the sugar mixture. Repeat with remaining rhubarb and sugar mixture. Dot with margarine or butter. Cover with top crust that has slits cut in it; seal and flute. Sprinkle with sugar, if desired. Cover edge with 2 to 3 inch strip of aluminum foil to prevent excessive browning; remove foil during last 15 minutes of baking. Bake until crust is brown and juice begins to bubble through slits in crust (40 to 50 minutes).

*Rhubarb–Strawberry Pie: Substitute sliced strawberries for half of the rhubarb and use the lesser amount of sugar.

# APPLE BROWN BETTY

*(You can do this in the food processor.)*

*In 1952, United Gas had a children's cooking class. Mama enrolled me and this was one of the first things I learned to make – still is one of my favorites.*

| | |
|---|---|
| 3 | **cups coarse fresh white bread crumbs, including the crust** |
| ½ | **cup butter, melted** |
| 7 | **cups apples, peeled, cored and thinly sliced** |
| 2 | **Tablespoons lemon juice** |
| 1 | **cup sugar** |
| ½ | **teaspoon cinnamon** |
| ¼ | **teaspoon nutmeg** |
| ¼ | **teaspoon salt** |

Preheat oven to 400 degrees. In a medium bowl, toss bread crumbs with butter. Set aside. In a larger bowl, toss apples with lemon juice, sugar, cinnamon, nutmeg and salt. Spread ½ cup of crumbs over bottom of a 2–quart baking dish. Top with half the apples and sprinkle with another ½ cup crumbs. Spoon on remaining apples and juice – press down lightly. Top with remaining crumbs. Dot with a little extra butter. Cover with foil. Bake about 25 minutes. Remove foil; bake another 25 to 30 minutes. Serve warm with whipping cream or ice cream. A wonderful dessert or a really good breakfast dish!

## LEU WILDER'S APPLE PIE

| | |
|---|---|
| 6 | to 8 tart cooking apples, peeled and sliced |
| ¾ | cup brown sugar, packed |
| 1 | teaspoon grated lemon rind |
| ½ | teaspoon cinnamon |
| 2 | Tablespoons flour |
| 1 | to 2 Tablespoons butter or margarine |

Place sliced apples in an uncooked pastry–lined 9–inch pie pan. Mix sugar, cinnamon, flour and lemon rind. Sprinkle over apples. Dot with butter. Place top crust over filling. Seal edges and cut vents in top crust. Bake at 425 degrees for 10 minutes. Reduce heat to 350 degrees, and cook for 25–30 more minutes or until done. Cool before serving.

## THE BEST PECAN PIE

| | |
|---|---|
| 1 | stick butter |
| 1 | cup light Karo |
| 1 | cup sugar |
| 3 | large eggs, beaten |
| ½ | teaspoon lemon juice |
| 1 | teaspoon vanilla |
| 1 | dash of salt |
| 1 | cup chopped pecans |
| 1 | 8 or 9 inch unbaked pie crust |

Brown butter in saucepan until it is golden brown – do not burn; let cool. In separate bowl, add ingredients in order listed; stir. Blend in browned butter well. Pour in unbaked pie crust and bake at 425 degrees for 10 minutes; then lower to 325 degrees for 40 minutes.

# BEST EVER CHOCOLATE PIE

1   9–inch pie crust, baked, or <u>Butter Pecan Crust</u>
1½  cups sugar
3   Tablespoons flour
3   Tablespoons cocoa
    Pinch of salt
½   cup water
2   egg yolks, slightly beaten
1   small can evaporated milk
½   stick butter
1½  teaspoons vanilla

Mix dry ingredients, then add enough water to make a paste. Blend the egg yolks into the paste, then remaining water and milk. Stirring constantly, add butter as the mixture is cooking over low flame. When thick, add vanilla. Pour into baked pie crust. Top with whipping cream or Cool Whip. Mighty good!

This filling is the best for your Chocolate Tarts!

# CHESS PIE – JESS PIE OR CORNMEAL PIE

*This recipe is well over 150 years old. All ingredients were available on the plantation. As the story goes, Robert E. Lee's guests for dinner were Generals Jeb Stuart, James Longstreet, and Stonewall Jackson. Everybody loved the pie and wanted to know the name. Lee called in Mammy – "What is the name of this pie?" "Cooks" reply – "Jess Pie"*

1   (10 inch) pie crust, or individual tart crusts
¾   cup melted butter
2   cups sugar
1   cup milk
3   well–beaten eggs
½   cup yellow cornmeal
1   teaspoon vanilla

Heat oven to 325 degrees. Mix all ingredients well. Pour into unbaked pie crust. Bake 1 hour or until set in center.

# PUMPKIN PIE

Unbaked 8–inch pie
crust
3   eggs, slightly beaten
1   cup evaporated milk
1   cup sugar
1   cup pumpkin or
mashed sweet
potatoes
⅛   teaspoon salt
1   stick butter, melted
½   teaspoon cinnamon
½   teaspoon nutmeg
½   teaspoon allspice
½   pint heavy cream
Pecans

Streusel Topping:
½   cup brown sugar,
packed
¼   cup flour
¼   cup chopped pecans
¼   cup firm butter
½   teaspoon cinnamon

Cream eggs, milk and sugar. Add remaining ingredients, and mix in well. Pour into an unbaked 8 inch pie crust and bake at 400 degrees for 40 minutes or until a silver knife inserted in the center comes out clean. Cool. Have edge of crust crimped high, as this is a very generous filling. Whip cream and spread over the cooled pie. Shave pecans over top. This is a delicious pie. It is like a spicy custard pie. You can use a streusel topping, if you like.

# PEANUT BUTTER PIE

*So good and low fat!*

1   Graham Cracker
crust
1   half gallon vanilla ice
cream or ice milk
4   cups of light Cool
Whip
2   cups peanut butter
(plain or crunchy)

Soften ice cream and Cool Whip. Mix in peanut butter. Pour in Graham Cracker crust. Freeze. Take out of freezer 10 minutes before serving and top with Hot Fudge Sauce.

## OLD FASHION LEMON ICEBOX PIE

1   8 or 9 inch baked pie
    crust, graham
    cracker, or vanilla
    wafer crumb crust
3   egg yolks
1   can Eagle Brand
    Condensed Milk
    (can use low fat)
½   cup lemon juice
½   teaspoon lemon zest
3   egg whites, beaten to
    make a meringue

Preheat oven to 450 degrees. In medium bowl, beat egg yolks with condensed milk, lemon juice and zest. Pour into prepared crust. Top with meringue. Bake in a 400 degree oven for 5 to 10 minutes or until light brown.

## LEMON SOUFFLÉ ICEBOX PIE

Follow directions above on egg whites but, fold in meringue egg white mixture, with condensed milk, egg yolk, lemon juice mixture. Pour in prepared deep dish crust. Bake as above and freeze this. Remove from freezer about 10 minutes before serving. Top with a dollop of whipping cream and garnish with a sprig of mint. Outstanding – best lemon pie in town.

## PRALINES

*These are Marie Louise Snellings' and they are the very best!*

*Make these two or three times and you can whip them out in a New York second. You will be famous and when ever you take these to some event or serve them, there will not be one left!*

| | |
|---|---|
| 3 | **cups white sugar** |
| 1 | **cup milk – but no skimmed milk** |
| ½ | **cup sugar** |
| 4 | **cups pecans – lightly toasted** |
| 1 | **Tablespoon butter** |
| 1 | **teaspoon vanilla** |
| | **Newspaper and wax paper – spread out** |

Take the 3 cups sugar and milk and stir to a boil. Meanwhile in a small iron skillet, caramelize the ½ cup sugar. Be careful and don't burn it! Then add the caramelized sugar to the boiling mixture and cook it down to the soft ball on a candy thermometer. (I test mine in a cup of cold water). Add pecans, butter and vanilla. Cook back to soft ball stage. Remove from heat and beat until it looks like it is going to sugar. Spoon out small and thin. You have to work quickly – it's nice if you have someone to help you spoon out. If it gets too thick before you are through – add just a bit of milk – maybe a tablespoon ... be careful, not too much. Reheat. Spoon it up. Now, on spooning up this candy in order to pick it up easily, just take the whole newspaper; lay it out on the counter and cover with wax paper. Your pralines will lift right off. Keep in tins. Keeps very well for a week.

# BESS BURNS' HOLIDAY CANDY

*Bess Burns made this best!*

3    cups sugar
1½  cups heavy cream
1    cup white corn syrup
1½  teaspoons vanilla
1    pound Brazil nuts
1    pound English
        walnuts
½   pound each candied
        pineapple and
        cherries
½   pound pecans

Combine sugar, cream and corn syrup, and cook to soft ball stage. Remove from heat and begin beating immediately. Add vanilla and continue beating. Have fruit and nuts chopped finely and add to candy mixture, combining well. Mixture will be thick and sticky. Pack in pans lined with waxed paper, pressing with a wet spoon. After a few hours the syrup will become firm and almost white in color. Refrigerate. Slice after 24 hours into finger–length pieces. So pretty on your holiday candy tray!

# PEANUT BRITTLE ELLA MAE

*My Mama's is the best!*

1    cup sugar
⅔   cup white Karo
½   cup water
1    cup shelled raw
        peanuts
1    teaspoon soda
1    teaspoon vanilla
1    teaspoon butter

Cook sugar, Karo and water until it reaches the hard crack stage – about 20 minutes. Mixture will crack or pop when dropped in cold water. Add peanuts, stirring constantly. Cook until syrup is golden in color. Remove from heat; add soda, vanilla and butter. Pour on a greased flexible cookie sheet – spread out – thin as possible, when cool, break up and enjoy!

# OLD FASHION FUDGE

About 3 dozen candies.

3    cups sugar
⅔    cup Hershey's cocoa
⅛    teaspoon salt
1½   cups milk
2    cups chopped pecans
¼    cup butter or
     margarine
1    teaspoon vanilla
     extract

Butter an 8– or 9–inch square pan; set aside. In a heavy 4–quart saucepan, combine sugar, cocoa and salt; stir in milk. Cook over medium heat, stirring constantly until mixture comes to full rolling boil. Boil, without stirring, to 234 degrees (soft–ball stage). Remove from heat. Add butter and vanilla. Cool at room temperature to 110 degrees (lukewarm). Beat with wooden spoon until fudge thickens and loses some of its gloss. Quickly spread into prepared pan; cool. Cut into squares.

# CHRISTMAS CARAMELS

1   **pint cream**
1¾ **cups light corn syrup**
2   **cups sugar**
¾   **cup butter**
1   **cup chopped pecans**
½   **teaspoon vanilla**

Place ½ pint cream, syrup and sugar in deep iron skillet. Cook over low heat, stirring constantly. When mixture is boiling hard, add remaining cream and butter slowly so mixture does not stop boiling. Continue to cook slowly until mixture makes a firm ball when dropped in cold water (246 to 248 degrees). Sprinkle chopped nuts in well–buttered 8–inch baking dish. Add vanilla to mixture and pour over nuts. Let stand several hours.

These are sticky. You can wrap individually in Saran Wrap. Makes a pretty gift tin!

# TOFFEE–BUTTER CRUNCH

| | |
|---|---|
| 1 | stick butter |
| 1½ | cups sugar |
| 3 | Tablespoons water |
| 2 | Tablespoons light Karo syrup |
| | Pinch of soda |
| 2 | cups coarsely chopped pecans, toasted |
| ½ | teaspoon vanilla |
| 2 | or 3 Hershey bars – broken up |

In a large saucepan, melt butter. Add sugar, water and Karo syrup. Cook over medium heat, stirring occasionally to hard crack stage (300 degrees – needs to be turning a light caramel color). Quickly stir in soda, pecans and vanilla. Spread while hot onto a big, well greased flexible round metal pan. Quickly, while hot, spread on pan. Sprinkle broken Hershey bars over top. When it starts to melt, spread over roughly. Chill. Break into pieces. Store in air–tight container with plenty of wax paper. (Heath Bar – eat your heart out!)

# HOLIDAY DIVINITY

| | |
|---|---|
| 4 | **cups sugar** |
| 1 | **cup white Karo** |
| 1 | **cup water** |
| ⅛ | **teaspoon salt** |
| 4 | **egg whites** |
| ½ | **stick butter** |
| 1 | **teaspoon vanilla** |
| 2 | **cups pecans** |

In a heavy boiler, put sugar, Karo, water and salt. Cook to the hard ball stage using a candy thermometer. Turn fire off and let sit while you beat the egg whites very stiff and dry. Beat with mixer at medium speed while pouring the hot syrup into the egg whites. Mixture must be poured slowly in a very fine stream. Continue beating and add the soft butter and vanilla. Beat until the candy will hold its shape and then add the chopped, cold or frozen pecans. Spoon a little out on wax paper to see if it will hold its shape. If it does not, continue to beat by hand until it will drop by spoonfuls onto wax paper.

# DATE BALLS

| | |
|---|---|
| 1 | pound chopped dates |
| 1 | stick butter |
| 2 | egg yolks |
| ⅔ | cup sugar |
| 1 | teaspoon vanilla |
| 2 | cups Rice Krispies |
| 1 | cup chopped pecans |
| 1 | can coconut |

Using the chopped sugar rolled packaged dates really makes this quick and easy! Cook dates, butter, yolks, sugar and vanilla in a heavy iron skillet, stirring constantly until the mixture boils. Let boil, stirring, for 5 minutes. Add Rice Krispies and nuts. Shape into bite size balls, then roll in coconut. Just like the old fashioned Date Loaf – so much easier and just as good. Perfect for your holiday cookie tray!

# ORANGE PECANS

*(Nice for your Christmas tins!)*

| | |
|---|---|
| 2 | cups sugar |
| ¾ | cup milk |
| 3 | Tablespoons grated orange peel |
| 3 | Tablespoons orange juice |
| 2 | cups pecans |

Combine sugar, milk and orange peel in saucepan and cook to soft ball stage. Let cool a few seconds, then add orange juice. Beat this mixture until cloudy, then add pecans. Continue beating until mixture begins to turn to sugar. Pour into buttered pan. Let cool, then break nuts apart.

# Southern Gardening

My gardening tips and ideas are the things my husband, Mike Cage, and I enjoy and love in our beautiful garden with which God has blessed us!

There are so many wonderful gardening books and very knowledgeable gardeners and most love to give tips and ideas and share plants! Have fun!

If it has "Smith and Hawken" on it, I want it! My favorite garden shop!

**HAPPY GARDENING IN THE DEEP SOUTH!** We are in Zone 8. The zone map for the United States and Canada is based on the United States Department of Agriculture's Survey. I like to just look around, see what does well where you are – and go from there. This gives you a good guideline.

**January:**

Bring into your home blooming paper whites or amaryllis.

1.  Work on a landscape design. Remember, you can't have it all, but you can try! Be sure and plan for a fish pond, or bird bath; it will be one of your very favorite things. Helen Trousdale does the most beautiful designs of all. Try and plan for a splash of fall foliage in your yard. I love the Indian Sumac; its leaves turn a brilliant red in the Autumn and it has spikes of loose clusters of red berries that are nice for your Fall arrangements. Do not over look the Maples, Dogwoods, and Crepe Myrtles for pretty color in the Fall. Also, Virginia Creeper – I let mine run up my pecan tree – has dark green leaves that turn to bright Fall colors. Be sure to include a Sweet Olive Tree or several; you will love the fragrance in the Spring!

2.  Put up Wood Duck boxes.

3.  Always take care and feed God's birds, one of his many gifts to us. Locate the feeders in areas with a view.

4.  The Gold, Purple, and House Finches are on their way – get those thistle feeders out.

5.  Get your Martin houses cleaned out. The scouts are coming.

6.  Plan a little vegetable garden. Do not get it too big. If you have one already, till and turn soil.

7.  Make a list of seed purchases.

8.  Inventory garden supplies and tools; repair if needed.

9.  Plan an asparagus bed – like someone said, "an asparagus bed is like a good marriage, if you do it right the first time, you only have to do it once." I'm on my second one! Choose a sunny spot in your garden that won't be disturbed in coming years.

10. Get your compost pile going. Try to locate close to your storage or work area in a sunny to partial shady spot – out of view but convenient. We never cover ours and generally mix 3 parts brown material (old leaves, pine straw, etc.) to 1 part green material (grass clippings, vegetable scraps). Grind or chop if you can. Pile it up. Water it thoroughly and turn the pile every few days. You want it moist, but not soggy. Do not add animal scraps or fat; it smells and attracts pests. One day you will understand the meaning of black gold!

11. This is the month for moving or planting shrubs, trees and vines.

12. Plant a Persimmon tree. The orange color fruit is so beautiful for your Fall decorations at Halloween and Thanksgiving. The persimmon tree was one of Frances Montgomery's favorite things in her lovely garden.

13. Find a place for a French Mulberry or Beauty Bush. The Louisiana wild flower has 4 to 6 feet long stalks and in the Fall, it is loaded with clusters of the most beautiful light purple berries. If you can beat the birds to them, they are wonderful to cut and use in your Fall decorations. I mix mine with persimmons, pumpkins and gourds. If you are careful with them, they are just beautiful sprayed gold or silver to mix in with your

holiday and Christmas decorations. This bush dies down in the Winter. I love it!

14. Fertilize Camellias after blooming and for four to six weeks later.

15. Fertilize bulbs.

16. Seeds to plant:

| | |
|---|---|
| Sweet Alyssum | Larkspur |
| Chinese Forget me not | Lobelia |
| African Golden Daisy | Petunia |
| Hollyhock, Indian Summer | Phlox, Drummond |
| Pinks, Dianthus | Sweet William |
| Salvia (blue) | Candytuft |
| Snapdragon | Coreopsis |
| Sweet Pea | Cornflower |
| Verbena | Queen Anne's Lace |
| Shirley Poppy | |

17. Plants that can be placed in open ground in January:

| | |
|---|---|
| Sweet Alyssum | Pansy |
| Petunia | Bluebonnet |
| Phlox, Drummond | Calendula |
| Phlox, Louisiana | Candytuft |
| Pinks, Dianthus | Coreopsis |
| Queen Anne's Lace | Cornflower |
| Salvia | Daisy, English |
| Snapdragon | Daisy, Michaelmas |
| Stock | Daisy, Shasta |
| Sweet William | Delphinium |
| Verbena | Forget–me–not |
| Violet | Four O'Clock |
| Wallflowers | Hollyhock |
| Honeysuckle | Salvia (blue) |

18. Plant refrigerated Tulips.

**February:**

Check on St. Mary's Magnolia – a medium size, beautiful blooms and very fragrant.

Little Gem Magnolia – darling small leaves, little blooms. Wonderful in big pots and you can make a beautiful hedge out of them.

A Weeping Cherry Tree – just beautiful for your Spring flowering garden – you think Mary Poppins is going to float by with her parasol!

1. Feed and enjoy the birds and look for Martin scouts. Watch for Wood Ducks looking for a home!

2. Work on your landscape design. Look around...steal! steal! steal!, ideas from books, magazines and neighbors! You can be as bad as you want to – plan on putting big pots of Jasmine or anything sweet smelling, close to the main entrance of the house – smells so good! Be sure and include Nandina. Birds enjoy the red berries and I love the foliage to cut for your house, and it dries beautifully!

   Be sure and include a perennial bed in your landscape design, one of my favorite things!

3. Work on your compost pile.

4. You have to have a small herb garden. If you remember the Simon and Garfunkel song "Scarborough Fair", parsley, sage, rosemary and thyme. I add oregano, chives and basil for your pesto sauce. Aren't we having fun! O, the smell of basil in your garden after a Summer shower! Wonderful! Your pesto sauce freezes well. I love to put a big dollop on thick slices of fresh tomatoes and run under the broiler.

5. Fertilize Azaleas and prune long limbs. Fertilize again in about six weeks. If they have yellow leaves, may need some iron. Repeat application in about two weeks.

6.  Mulch beds with oak leaves, peat moss, pine straw, or cotton seed hulls.

7.  Prune evergreens and summer flowering shrubs.

8.  Transplant shrubs, trees and vines.

9.  Divide and re–set perennials which bloomed after June.

10. Plant Gladiolus bulbs every two weeks, all February & March.

11. Fertilize Spider Lilies.

12. Keep dead blooms cut from bulbs and don't cut the foliage (saps vitality of bulbs).

13. Plant roses.

14. Fertilize native Iris with complete fertilizer.

15. Fertilize all shrubs and trees and lawns.

16. Feed Pansies.

17. As bulbs cease blooming, fertilize with bone meal.

18. Seeds to plant. Nasturtium – one of my favorites! I plant some of mine in hanging baskets. So pretty and wonderful for salads and sandwiches.

| | |
|---|---|
| Sweet Alyssum | Larkspur |
| Chinese Forget–me–not | Lobelia |
| African Golden Daisy | Petunia |
| Hollyhock, Indian Summer | Phlox, Drummond |
| Arctotis | Salvia, Blue |
| Scabiosa | Snapdragon |
| Coreopsis | Sweet peas |
| Cornflower | Verbena |
| Salvia, Red | Gypsaphila |
| Early Cosmos | Queen Anne's Lace |
| Calliopsis | Nasturtium |

19. Plants to set out:

| | |
|---|---|
| Ajuga | Gerbera |
| Alyssum | Larkspur |
| Lobelia | Candytuft |
| Candytuft | Violets |
| Coreopsis | Petunia |
| Cornflower | Phlox |
| Daisies | Queen Anne's Lace |
| Dianthus | Salvia |
| Snapdragon | |

20. Plant your asparagus. In a permanent bed, dig a trench 18 inches deep and about 24 inches wide. Asparagus do not like wet feet. You need good drainage and rich, fertile soil. Time to plant potatoes and spinach.

## March:

Fig trees are as important to ole time families of the South as their bourbon is. Be sure to include one in your landscape plan. Mid July and August, you have to get up early to beat the birds and squirrels to get the figs. When gathering (or stealing) be careful; they are fragile. We eat them right off the tree, the very best! If you save some, try <u>Fig Preserves</u> or <u>Figs–N–Cream</u>!

Cut Yew, Ivy, Magnolia or any other greenery. Bring inside and arrange in glass vases or bowls!

1.  Feed the birds. Watch for the Martins – the scouts are here! Keep your bird books and a highlighter handy. In our bird book we date and highlight each new species as it appears. (Easter of 1995, a Summer Tanager appeared on our fountain! My favorite Easter present!)

2.  Work on landscape design. Find an out of view, convenient, sunny location for a small vegetable and cutting garden. We have ours close to the compost pile.

3.  Continue to plant Gladiolus and you can still set out Dahlias.

4.  Plant Hydrangea in partial shade – mostly shade. Fertilize and mulch with oak leaves or pine straw. Lime will keep them pink and sulphur will keep them a pretty blue. Don't forget the Oak–Leaf Hydrangea; it is the first to bloom in the Spring...big and pretty white blooms.

5.  Keep on spraying and fertilizing.

6.  Good time to put out patches of grass – Centipede or St. Augustine.

7.  Work lime around roots of Clematis.

8.  Fertilize your Sweet Peas.

9.  Divide and reset Cannas row. If you want quality blooms, thin out and share with your friends – makes you feel good!

10. Seeds to plant:

| | |
|---|---|
| Sweet Alyssum | Sunflower |
| Chinese Forget–me–not | Forget–me–not |
| African Golden Daisy | Four O'Clock |
| Gayfeather | Candytuft |
| Nasturtium | Ageratum |
| Petunia | Balsam |
| Zinnia | Marigold |
| Portulaca | Moonflower |
| Calliopsis | Phlox, Drummond |
| Salvia, Blue and Red | Periwinkle |
| Verbena | Early Cosmos |

11. Vegetables to set out:

| | |
|---|---|
| Potatoes | Lettuce |
| Cabbage | Spinach |

**April:**

One of my favorite places is my summer time cutting garden with Zinnias, Cosmos, Coreopsis, Phlox – the obedient plant, named so, for in flower arranging, the long beautiful stems of light purple flowers always obey, bend and stay. Cocks–Comb with the dark red velvet clusters, and ornamental peppers are wonderful. It is like being in the middle of a mid–summer circus with the butterflies and bees, bees, bees; they must come from miles and miles away. I wish I could stay all day.

You can be an artist with vines and wonderful perennials. Have fun and plan a masterpiece with a few of my favorites: Flowering vines on trellises, fences or poles, give instant effects for focal points or backgrounds. The Potato Vine, Moonvine, Coral Honeysuckle, Glorioso Climbing Lily, Cypress Vine, Luffa Gourd, Passion Flower, and the yellow and white Lady Banks are wonderful and fun to work with. I love to let the feathery Cypress Vine with its pretty little red flowers run and spread, the Hummingbirds have a ball!

Let your Moonvine run on a lamp post or gas light, it is pretty at night with the light shining through those sweet smelling giant white flowers.

My favorite perennials are Yarrow, Artemisia – pretty silver color and dries well for your arrangements, the Obedient plant, Cox's Comb, Phylox, perennial peppers, Four–O–Clocks, Daylilies, Daisies, Elephant ears, Banana plants – especially the red ones. These are just a few but enough to work with.

Whenever possible, open the doors and windows and give your house or apartment a good old–fashioned airing. Let the fresh air sweep through the rooms.

Don't forget to feed the birds. Enjoy your Wood Ducks and Martins.

Add to compost pile and water well.

1. Continue pruning Spring flowering shrubs that have finished blooming, such as Spirea, Forsythe, Quince and Weigela, Lady Banks, Climbing Roses that bloom once a year.

2. Spray roses. Keep new rose bushes set this Spring de-budded.

3. Divide and reset Chrysanthemums. New shoots make better plants than old crowns.

4. Divide Bearded Iris after blooming and fertilize each Rhizome with ¼ cup of bone meal as you plant it.

5. Can still put out patches of grass.

6. Plant Hibiscus and Caladiums. Put out bedding plants. I put about 1 teaspoon Osmocote under each new bedding plant. Try Penta; it comes in red, pink, and white. The Hummingbirds love the red.

7. Plant early blooming bulb foliage, but do not cut until nearly dead, I know it is ugly, but the bulb needs the nourishment.

8. Watch for ants in yard, in pots, and under plants. Sprinkle with Amdro.

9. Seeds to plant: Moonflower, one of my favorites when blooming, the Luna Moths which come visiting in the evening.

| | |
|---|---|
| Morning Glory | Sunflowers |
| Sweet Alyssum | Four O'Clock |
| Early Cosmos | Ageratum |
| Periwinkle | Balsam |
| Marigold | Moonflower |
| Zinnia | Portulaca |
| Chinese Forget–me–not | Ornamental Peppers |
| Gaillardia | Bells of Ireland |

For a night time showy garden – all white Impatiens, and Caladiums – just beautiful!

10. Bulbs, tubers, rhizomes to plant this month:

    Ginger                  Hosta
    Caladium                Tuberose
    Crinium                 Waterlily
    Dahlias                 Walking Iris
    Gladiolus               Liriope
    Daylilies               Calla
    Butterfly Lilies        Tritonia

11. Plants to set out: Anything else you see that looks interesting. I love a border of yellow Lantana and Pink Verbena and maybe Mandevilla – climbing on something.

    Begonia                 Ageratum
    Cosmos                  Aster
    Coleus

**May:**

Put sweet scented plants like Jasmine close to entrances of your house. You will enjoy and so will your family and friends.

Enjoy your Nasturtiums in salads and sandwiches. The fresh leaves contain Vitamin C and iron and they give a sharp, mustard–like flavor to salads. The flower can also be eaten. The flower buds can be preserved in vinegar and used as a substitute for capers...aren't we proud and aren't they good!

1.  If you have not pruned Spring flowering shrubs, such as Spirea and Flowering Almond, do so at once.

2.  Put out Plumbago, Impatiens, Begonia, Geranium, Hibiscus, and Caladium bulbs. It is just not summer time in the deep South without these annuals.

3.  Spray roses and watch for leaf spot.

4.  Keep beds mulched.

5.  Divide violets and fertilize.

6.  Stir compost pile as you are adding kitchen scraps and grass clippings.

7.  Spray Cape Jasmine, Camellias, and Ligustrum to control white fly and scale (oil emulsion or Malathion).

8.  Cut bloom stalks from Native Iris, unless you are saving seed.

9.  Keep blooms cut from Oleanders and Hydrangeas. This is all the pruning they need.

10. Fertilize Dogwoods with ½ bone meal and ½ cotton seed meal mixture – 1 handful per foot of height.

11. Water, water, water, but be careful and don't drown your periwinkle – they hate wet feet! Container plants need watering more often!

12. Spray St. Augustine lawns for Chinch bugs.

13. Time to plant bulbs, tubers, rhizomes, Iris, Hosta, Day-lilies.

14. Prune Confederate Jasmine (I like to plant a moon vine on my Jasmine to climb for the Summer and early Fall and oh the sweet smell – and you will have some surprise visitors...the Luna Moth and the Sphinx Moth, also known as the false Hummingbird).

15. Watch for mildew on Crepe Myrtle, Zinnias, Verbena. Dust with sulphur when foliage is dry.

16. When foliage of Spring flowering bulbs has turned brown, it may be cut off...thank goodness!

**June:**

Enjoy watching baby Martins learn to fly.

Take time to enjoy your beautiful yard; you have worked very hard!

If you get poison ivy, try 5–day deodorant pads – stops the itching!

1. Narcissus, all Jonquils and Daffodils, Snowdrops and similar bulbs, may be left in the ground year after year, until they become crowded.

2. Prune out all old wood and the dead canes from climbing roses which bloom only in Spring.

3. Fertilize Hibiscus, Impatiens, etc., every other week. I use Miracle Grow one time and Super Bloom the next.

4. Keep dead blooms cut from Hibiscus to promote new wood and more bloom.

5. You can root just about anything. This is a good time – Gardenias, Azaleas, Camellias, Boxwood – using this season's growth. Use a root stimulator.

6. Check for white fly, scale or red spider; use Malathion or Volck.

7. Save all vegetable and fruit scraps for compost pile. We put about 200 ears of creamed sweet corn up every year and always add the shucks and cobs to pile. Always cover with grass clippings or leaves.

### July: – It's hot – but the cotton is growing!

Put a whole sweet potato in half a glass of water, place in kitchen window, add and change water as needed. Watch it grow and enjoy!

Say goodbye to the Martins!

1. Fertilize shrubs and trees. Water well.

2. Check Chrysanthemums for plant lice. Spray every 10 days and Fertilize every two weeks.

3. Keep everything watered.

4. Add to compost pile and stir.

5. Find a cool shady spot and read a book!

6. Good time to plan for a Fall herb garden! There are so many wonderful books on herb gardening. Read up and enjoy! I love to plant creeping thyme on a stepping stone path, as you walk and crush some, what a wonderful fragrance!

7. Time to plant multiplying green onions or shallots and mustard and turnip greens.

**August:**

Mother Nature teases us with hints of Fall. I get a high on some of these cool mornings and breezy summer evenings!

1. Transplant Iris. Fertilize with bone meal.

2. Continue transplanting early Spring flowering bulbs.

3. Keep Azaleas and Camellias watered during dry spells. They are setting bulbs now.

4. Add grass clippings to compost pile and stir. Fall is on the way!

**September:**

Fall is on the way!

Aren't we glad we live in an area with seasonal changes?

The Red Spider Lilies are blooming. They always remind me of our sweet little children going back to school. "They are like children, they are everywhere". Be careful and watch out for them.

Dress your house for Fall! Buy Crotons in pots for partly shaded patio or entrance area. The brilliant reds, yellows and greens are so pretty for Fall. I love to mix them with pumpkins, hay, sugar cane, gourds, and peppers.

Time to cut fire wood. Confucius say, "man who cuts his own firewood, warms himself twice!" Mike Cage likes this one!

1.  Fertilize Chrysanthemums weekly until the flower buds show color. From then on, just water.

2.  After a good rain, dig up your Caladiums. I use a big yard fork. Spread out to dry. Store in airy baskets in a dry place...potting shed, storage room, etc., to protect from freeze. Always label color and variety – believe me, you will forget.

3.  As annuals fade, take up and prepare bed for Fall.

4.  Heap all leaves, grass clippings on your compost pile. Keep it moist! Remember, you are making "black gold"!

5.  Fertilize Wisteria and watch for fungus.

6.  If you are planning to plant Winter grass, fertilize the lawn and plant Winter rye grass seed two weeks after.

7.  Think about ordering your Paper Whites and Amaryllis for Christmas blooms.

**October:**

Good time to gather pine cones, cattails (to preserve, spray with hair spray) and Tallow Berries (cut just as they begin to open) for your Fall and holiday decorations.

1.  Cut back perennials like Banana plants and Elephant Ears. Divide and reset.

2.  Plant early blooming Sweet Peas and Forget–me–nots.

3.  Prune and take up Hibiscus plants before the frost gets them.

4.  Order Tulips and refrigerate 4 to 6 weeks before planting.

5.  Plant Anemone's ("eye up"). Ranunceulus ("feet down")

6.  Check your landscape design.

7.  Stir and water your compost pile.

**November:**

Good time to look in the woods for Smilax with most of the leaves off the trees! It is easy to spot. I love to use it for my Christmas greenery and Spring weddings. You cannot use the new foliage as it is too delicate.

1. For holiday blooms, plant in pots and keep in a place they will not freeze! – Amaryllis and Paper Whites. Plan on about 6 weeks until they bloom.

2. Clean beds up.

3. Prepare beds and pots for Pansies and Tulips.

4. Cut lower limbs on trees that make the house dark.

5. Prune shrubs that have grown over windows. Let light in.

6. Have your trees professionally pruned.

7. If you have not planned for an Asparagus bed – do so now! Choose a sunny spot in your garden that will not be disturbed in coming years – Asparagus is perennial!

**December:**

Merry Christmas!

<u>Desiderata</u>

Go placidly amid the noise and haste, and remember what peace there may be in silence. As far as possible without surrender be on good terms with all persons. Speak your truth quietly and clearly; and listen to others, even the dull and ignorant; they too have their story. Avoid loud and aggressive persons, they are vexations to the spirit. If you compare yourself with others, you may become vain and bitter; for always there will be greater and lesser persons than yourself. Enjoy your achievements as well as your plans. Keep interested in your own career, however humble; it is a real possession in the changing fortunes of time. Exercise caution in your business affairs; for the world is full of trickery. But let this not blind you to what virtue there is; many persons strive for high ideals; and everywhere life is full of heroism. Be yourself. Especially, do not feign affection. Neither be cynical about love; for in the face of all aridity and disenchantment it is perennial as the grass. Take kindly the counsel of the years, gracefully surrendering the things of youth. Nurture strength of spirit to shield you in sudden misfortune. But do not distress yourself with imaginings. Many fears are born of fatigue and loneliness. Beyond a wholesome discipline, be gentle with yourself. You are a child of the universe, no less than the trees and the stars; you have a right to be here. And whether or not it is clear to you, no doubt the universe is unfolding as it should. Therefore be at peace with God, whatever you conceive Him to be, and whatever your labors and aspirations, in the noisy confusion of life keep peace with your soul. With all its sham, drudgery and broken dreams, it is still a beautiful world. Be careful. Strive to be happy.

One of my favorites!

God Bless and Love!

# Lagniappe

# WAR ON CANCER
# AND
# ANTI AGING – PROLONGED YOUTH

You know this or have heard it a hundred times. This is just a reinforcement of what you know. Remember these two words: <u>Antioxidant</u> and <u>Phytochemicals</u> – they are not artificial additives, they are naturally occurring chemicals found in foods and are known to help protect cell damage from oxidation. They help prevent the decaying process of <u>tissue</u>, <u>such as skin</u>. Phytochemicals prevent cancer cells from multiplying the genetic material of the cells. What are the antioxidants and phytochemicals? All can be found in the food we eat. There is no way to get enough antioxidants in food alone – we must take supplements of vitamins and minerals.

1. Vitamin C – Antioxidant found in citrus fruits and juices. Other sources: tomatoes, potatoes, melons and berries.

2. Vitamin E – An antioxidant found in whole grain breads, cereals, and green leafy vegetables.

3. Beta Carotene – Antioxidant found in yellow/orange vegetables, fruit, and dark leafy vegetables such as carrots, sweet potatoes, pumpkins, cantaloupes, apricots, peaches, broccoli, kale, spinach, and romaine lettuce.

4. Phytochemical – is found in cruciferous vegetables like broccoli and cabbage, the garlic and onion family.

5. Fish oil deficiency is one of the leading causes of early aging.

6. Red grapes/red wine, and raisins – Help prevent artery damage and heart attacks and lower blood pressure and prolong a quality of life.

7.  The avocado is now extolled as a disease fighter. The fat is the good type that actually protects the arteries. It is rich in the important antioxidant, which zaps "free radicals" in the body. Free radicals promote aging and chronic diseases such as cancer.

8.  Excess alcohol ages you quickly!

9.  Eat a diet rich in fruits, vegetables, and fish, but low in meat, animal fat, and processed food.

10. Grains and Lentils – Fat–free protein and full of fiber. Lowers cholesterol and reduces heart disease risks.

11. Exercise regularly...Don't Stop!

12. Do not smoke and avoid smoke!

13. Remember – Moderation with the good life. I'm going to have a drink, a little wine, a good ice cold beer, eat a good steak, fried fish, fried chicken, cheese and sweets. Do not overindulge on a regular basis!

Mike Cage is a strong advocate of taking vitamin supplements – the scientific evidence is so strong and dramatic, it seems reckless not to do it.

Through eating fruits, vegetables, and fish and taking supplements of vitamins and minerals, we can cut down on the risk of cancer, heart disease, and drastically cut down on the aging process. You are not going to be immortal, but you have a better chance to live in good health to the end of your life and you may live longer.

## WHEN POSSIBLE

The Glenwood Wellness Center came up with this...it is good!

### Change a Little...Save A Lot!
### Ingredients Make A Difference

| ORIGINAL | SUBSTITUTE | FAT CALORIES SAVED |
|---|---|---|
| 1 cup whole milk | 1 cup non-fat milk | 70 |
| 1 cup heavy cream | 1 cup evaporated skim milk | 504 |
| 1 cup sour cream | 1 cup fat free sour cream or 1 cup fat free plain yogurt | 288 |
| 1 cup grated cheese | 1 cup fat free grated cheese or 1 cup lowfat grated cheese | 720 120 |
| 8 ounces cream cheese | 8 ounces fat free cream cheese or 8 ounces light cream cheese | 720 200 |
| ½ cup oil | ½ cup applesauce or ½ cup liquid butter buds or ½ cup fat free plain yogurt | 907 |
| 1 stick butter or 1 stick margarine | ½ cup applesauce or ½ cup diet margarine | 747 400 |
| 2 tablespoons oil | 2 tablespoons wine or broth | 240 |
| 1 cup cream soup | 1 cup broth | 150 |
| 1 cup walnuts | ½ cup walnuts | 427 |
| 1 cup chocolate chips | ½ cup chocolate chips | 456 |
| 1 cup coconut | ½ cup coconut (baking) | 233 |
| 1 pound ground beef | 1 pound ground white meat turkey (skinless) or 1 pound diced chicken breast | 1,037 585 |
| 2 whole eggs | 4 egg whites | 94 |
| 1 cup cottage cheese | 1 cup fat free cottage cheese | 90 |
| ¼ cup brown gravy | ¼ cup broth | 160 |
| 1 cup mayonnaise | 1 cup fat free mayonnaise | 1,580 |

## What Mama Said!

1.  In the evening and on dark cold days, Mama always turned our front lights on, and a light in the front window. It is a warm and welcomed feeling. Martha Jane Upshaw always has her front room lights on in her charming home and it is lovely!

2.  Growing up my mama always told me, "Honey, you are smart, darling, and charming, but remember, you are mostly charming". I believed every word!

3.  Mama always stressed: "Do unto others as you would have them do unto you". If you stick to this, you will have lots of friends.

4.  "The friendship that comes to an end, never really began."

5.  Think about this – "If you are really a Christian, then you can do anything you please."

6.  Remember, be the master of your ship. If you do not take care of your business, no one else will, or it most likely will not be what you intended.

7.  "Do not judge, or you too will be judged. For in the same way you judge others, you will be judged, and with the measure you use, it will be measured to you" (Matthew 7:12). When we judge others, we place ourselves at risk of harsh judgment. Mama said, "always be sweet to others, no matter what."

8.  Too many things complicate your life – remember possessions are to a man what a saddle is to a horse. If you aren't using or wearing something, get rid of it. You will not miss it. There are exceptions to every rule, but if you buy it on sale you really did not need it! I think that is why people like to go to the camp or Florida or a condo somewhere – 1 pair of jeans, 2 pairs of shorts, 3 T–shirts, 1 pair tennis shoes, 1 windbreaker, 1 pot holder and a skillet. Very simple, uncomplicated and very relaxing. (O yes, I forgot, ½ gallon of Jack Daniels!)

9.  Mama did not say this, but if she had read it, she would have. "Man is admonished to praise God from whom all blessings flow." The important thing is not the effect our praise has on God, but the effect it has on us! We cannot praise God (or man) without becoming better persons. True praise involves a sense of personal discovery – of genuine gratefulness." Author Unknown.

10. When someone gives you a compliment, say "Thank you". For some reason we all have tendencies to have ungracious and self–depreciating responses. The proper response to a compliment is a courteous "Thank You".

11. Learn how to cook and master one certain thing, from <u>Cowboy Cookies</u> to <u>Cheese Straws</u> to <u>Pralines</u> to <u>Red Beans and Rice</u>. When you are asked to bring something or you need to take something, it will not be a big ordeal and you will be known for the very best and people will look forward to your contribution.

## TABLE SETTINGS GUIDELINES FOR
## FORMAL DINING AND ENTERTAINING

Use the following rules as a guideline for setting your table:

**The Dishes:** When choosing the dishes that will be set, try to choose a neutral pattern and color in order to emphasize the presentation of the food. If serving soup, salad or an appetizer before the main course, make serving easier by presetting the dinner dishes and place the pre–dinner plate on top of it. Always remember when serving a sit–down dinner, serve from the left and remove from the right.

**The Flatware:** Flatware is placed in the order in which it will be used during the meal beginning from the outside and working toward the plate. For example, if a salad is being served first, as it is in American tradition, place the salad fork to the far left and then the dinner fork to the right toward the plate. Always place the knife with the blade facing the plate. Although flatware can be placed in an incremental fashion, the basic and formal rule is to place all flatware even with the plate about an inch from the edge of the table.

**The Glasses:** For convenience, it is best to preset all glassware before the meal. If you need to place coffee cups, place them. I like to serve my coffee in the living room after dinner. Never keep your guests at the dinner table too long – I mean 2 or 3 hours. I knew someone who made a dinner party a Triathalon. You had to take a tranquilizer or drink too much to stand it! One hour for cocktails is enough for dinner. If someone is late, let them have one quick cocktail and serve! Place glasses just above and to the right of the knife with the handle turned to the right. Set glasses on a diagonal from the tip of the knife to the top to the dinner plate in the order in which they will be poured. Begin by setting the water goblet at the top of the plate followed by the wine glass. Pour water in goblets just before dinner so ice cubes will not melt before the guests are seated.

**Table decoration, Linens and Napkins:** Depending on the theme of the party, this is an area that can set the tone and

formality of the occasion. If the dinner is formal, then stick with white or solid colored linens and napkins. If the dinner is for a special occasion or festive event, use your imagination to come up with unique and innovative table settings. Gail Bullock's Collectique on DeSiard Street, in Monroe, is a great place to start looking for some creative entertainment ideas.

### On Entertaining

1.  No one anywhere has more beautiful weddings, finer parties, fantastic food, beautiful flowers, the best dancers and the most beautiful people than Monroyans.

    The following story illustrates something that has not yet been done in Monroe, Louisiana, but I am waiting.

    In 1820, Charles J. Durande, an enormously wealthy man, came to Louisiana from France, to an area around St. Martinville. For the wedding of two of his daughters, he had large spiders brought from China and set them free in the large oak alley of trees leading to his plantation home. Great webs had been spun. On the morning of the wedding, the slaves were given bellows and gold and silver dust, and with these the webs were coated. Beneath this utterly fantastic, sparkling gold and silver canopy, that billowed in the soft Summer breeze, that quivered and glinted in the touch of light when the sun descended, the bridal party and guests were led down this pathway. Upon leaving in the evening, guests were treated to a shimmering array of moonbeams, shining through the golden–silvery webs. Wish I could have been there!

2.  People love to pick up something easy, like our pretty tea time sandwiches. At one of the most elegant receptions I have enjoyed, the waiters passed warm mini muffalettas, tiny ham and biscuits with a mayonnaise–mustard spread, and small slices of Reuben sandwiches. A real crowd pleaser because they are delicious and easy to manage.

3.  Make sure your guests are served a drink as soon as possible, when they arrive at big receptions and parties. Once you get something in your hand, you can relax. Try and locate spaced out stations of drinks close to the entrance.

4.  On entertaining, be prepared; plan ahead; so you can relax and enjoy your guests – you have worked very hard and it ain't cheap! Always serve your family favorites, from hamburgers, hot tamales, to roast leg of lamb. Let your guests help if they offer – makes them feel at home and useful.

5.  Every town has a Coney Island. Their hot dogs and hot tamales are the best! For my big parties, no matter how fancy, I serve them in a casual room and maybe in the carport or utility room. Be sure to have a big bottle of Tabasco handy. You always find the cutest men there. Come to think of it, I believe that is where I met Mike Cage!

6.  What is one of the most important tips on entertaining? People like to be together – don't you just hate to go to a restaurant and be the only one there? When we are out, we like people around us. Do not spread your party entertaining space out too far or in too many locations. Keep a good flow and space guests comfortably, but cozy. Same for your dance area – you would rather be crowded than feel alone. We like to be together, which reminds me of "The Goose Story".

## The Goose Story

Next fall when you see geese heading south for the winter flying along in a "V" formation, you might be interested in knowing what science has discovered about why they fly that way. It has been learned that as each bird flaps its wings, it creates an uplift for the bird immediately following. By flying in a "V" formation, the whole flock adds at least 71% greater flying range than if each bird flew on its own. *People who share common direction and sense of community can get where they are going quicker and easier, because they are traveling on the trust of one another.*

Whenever a goose falls out of formation, it suddenly feels the drag and resistance of trying to go it alone, and quickly gets into formation to take advantage of the lifting power of the bird immediately in front. *If we have as much sense as a goose, we will stay in formation with those who are headed the same way we are going.*

When the leader goose gets tired, he rotates back in the wing and another goose flies point. *It pays to take turns doing hard jobs.*

The geese honk from behind to encourage those up front to keep up their speed. *An encouraging word goes a long way.*

Finally, when a goose gets sick, or is wounded by a gun shot and falls out, two geese fall out of formation and follow him down to help and protect him. They stay with him until he is either able to fly or until he is dead, and they launch out on their own or with another formation to catch up with the group. *If we have the sense of a goose, we will stand by each other like that.*

AUTHOR UNKNOWN

# NOTES

# INDEX

# Garden District Books
119 Glenmar Avenue
Monroe, Louisiana 71201
(888) 203-5888
Fax: (318) 323-8216

Please send _____ copy(ies) of
*Cooking and Gardening with Dianne* @ $17.95 each _____
Postage and handling @   3.00 each _____
Louisiana residents add sales tax @   1.55 each _____
TOTAL _____

Name _____

Address _____

City _____ State _____ Zip _____

*Please make checks payable to Garden District Books.*

---

# Garden District Books
119 Glenmar Avenue
Monroe, Louisiana 71201
(888) 203-5888
Fax: (318) 323-8216

Please send _____ copy(ies) of
*Cooking and Gardening with Dianne* @ $17.95 each _____
Postage and handling @   3.00 each _____
Louisiana residents add sales tax @   1.55 each _____
TOTAL _____

Name _____

Address _____

City _____ State _____ Zip _____

*Please make checks payable to Garden District Books.*

---

# Garden District Books
119 Glenmar Avenue
Monroe, Louisiana 71201
(888) 203-5888
Fax: (318) 323-8216

Please send _____ copy(ies) of
*Cooking and Gardening with Dianne* @ $17.95 each _____
Postage and handling @   3.00 each _____
Louisiana residents add sales tax @   1.55 each _____
TOTAL _____

Name _____

Address _____

City _____ State _____ Zip _____

*Please make checks payable to Garden District Books.*